John Watson

The Theory and Practice of the Art of Weaving by Hand and Power

With Calculations and Tables

John Watson

The Theory and Practice of the Art of Weaving by Hand and Power
With Calculations and Tables

ISBN/EAN: 9783337813253

Printed in Europe, USA, Canada, Australia, Japan

Cover: Foto ©Thomas Meinert / pixelio.de

More available books at **www.hansebooks.com**

THE THEORY AND PRACTICE

OF THE

ART OF WEAVING

BY HAND AND POWER;

WITH

CALCULATIONS AND TABLES,

FOR THE USE OF THOSE CONNECTED WITH THE TRADE.

BY

JOHN WATSON,

MANUFACTURER AND PRACTICAL MACHINE MAKER, AND PATENTEE OF THE
DAMASK POWER-LOOM.

ILLUSTRATED BY DRAWINGS OF THE BEST POWER-LOOMS.

PHILADELPHIA:
HENRY CAREY BAIRD,
INDUSTRIAL PUBLISHER,
406 Walnut Street.
1869.

PREFACE.

To acquire a competent knowledge of any Art it must be learned, either by reading, verbal teaching, observation and reflection, or actual practice; and as it is of the utmost importance to the apprentice in any branch of business to be told the theory of it, and shown how to use the tools connected with that particular branch, it must be of use to the apprentice or young beginner in the Weaving Trade also. Believing this, I have written this volume on the theory and practice of Weaving, and have through its pages given instructions how any one with ordinary capacity and perseverance may learn the theory of the Art. The Writer, when a beginner in the trade, had often felt the want of such a book, and considering that others would be similarly situated, was induced to undertake to write this work; for at the time he began his apprenticeship in the Power-Loom Trade, it was more the rule to keep the apprentice in ignorance, than teach him the theory of the Art; however, that narrow-minded selfishness is, happily, now the exception. This volume is written more especially for Power-Loom Weaving, but it may prove of equal use to the Hand-Loom manufacturer, as the principles in both are the same.

CONTENTS.

INTRODUCTORY REMARKS.

The Antiquity of Weaving—The Indian Mode of Weaving—An old Tradition—Weaving introduced into Great Britain—The Progress of Weaving, found from the Consumption of Cotton—Prices of Cotton in different years—The probable increase of the Consumption of Cotton.

CHAPTER I.

Gristing Yarn—Diameter of Reel—Hanks and Yards in one Spyndle—Yarn in Cope—Yarn on Beam—Yarn in Chain—How Spinners make an Average Number—Linen Yarn—Wool Yarn—The Scotch and English Reed—The Fineness of Cloth by Porters—A Uniform Standard—Calculation of Warps—Number of ends in a Web—Warp in a Web—Short Method—The Shrinkage in Cloth—Calculation of Wefts—Short Method for finding the Quantity of Weft.

CHAPTER II.

Ancient Mode of Weaving, &c.—Winding Machine—Winding from Bobbins, Copes, and Hanks—Pirn Winding Machine—Warping Mill—Warping by Power—Warping Striped Work—How to make the Patterns—Beaming Yarn, Dyed in Chain—Sizing—Dressing—Crank-Dressing Machines—Cylinder Machine—Setting the Reeds—How to make Dressing—Tape-Leg Dressing Machine—Drawing or Entering the Web—Twisting—Draughts or Treading—Plain Cloth—Tweeling—Three Leaf Tweel—Herring Bone Tweel—Four Leaf Tweel—Sheeting Tweel—A Seven, Eight, and Nine Leaf Tweel—Blanket Tweel—Five Leaf Tweel for Damasks—Ten Leaf

Fancy Tweel—Twelve Leaf Fancy Tweel—Sixteen Leaf Satin Tweel—Diapers for Three, Four, Five, Six, Seven, and Eight Leaves—Eight Leaf Diaper, with Fourteen Treads—Ten Leaf Diaper, with Thirty-six Treads.

CHAPTER III.

Starting Power Looms—How to arrange and place the Looms—How to Level the Looms—How to find the Length of the Belt—Selecting the Shuttles—How to Pitch the Loom—Putting the Web in the Loom—How to find the proper Pinion for a given number of Shots.

CHAPTER IV.

On Power-Looms—The old Power-Loom at Pollockshaws—The advantage of its Uptaking Motion, and its Moveable Reed—An old Method for driving Power-Looms—Double Looms, Vertical and Horizontal—Their Advantages and Disadvantages for two Webs—Two Webs in the Hand Loom—Air Pump Pick—Common Power-Loom—Weft Stopper—Fly Reed—Bullough's Specification—Remarks on Bullough's Improvement—Todd's Loom—Float or Scob Preventer—Shuttles with Hooks or Cutters—A Contrivance for Changing the Shuttle—Articles about a Loom.

CHAPTER V.

Check and Damask Power-Loom—Description of the Drawings—How the Jacquard gets its motion—Form of Cam—Disengaging Apparatus—Mode of Working the Heddles—The Stenting Rollers—Selvage Protector—Shifting of the Shuttle Boxes—Taking back the Driver—Box Protector—Double Weft Stopper—Mounting a Harness Loom—Mails, Leads, Harness Twine—Slabstock—Harness or Hole Board—Standers—How to prepare the Harness—Tying up the Harness—Position of the Jacquard Machine—Adjusting the Jacquard Machine—Making Cloth—Pressure Harness Looms—How the figure is formed—How to find the Threads for each Mail—Drawing the Web—Mounting the Heddles—How to regulate the number of Shots for each Card—The use of the Stenting Rollers for Flax Yarn—Shedding a Pressure Harness—Power-Loom, with six Shuttles—Making Cloth Patterns—Hints for making Check Looms—Putting on the Check Pattern.

CONTENTS.

CHAPTER VI.

Lappet Weaving, &c.—Imitation of Sewing—Ground of Lappet Cloth—Different kinds of Whip—How Whip should be made—Lappet Loom—Lappet Wheel—New kind of Lappet Wheel—Lappet Needles and Pins—Lappet Lay—Arranging the Frames and Needles—Best kinds of Lappet Looms—Starting a Lappet Web—Drop Lappets—Gauze Stripes—Plain Gauze—Gauze made without Heddles—Jacquard Machine for working Gauze and Lappets—Sewing Frames for Looms—The Principle of Sewing Frames—Mode of working the Frames—Rack and Circle Frames—Tube or Bottle Sewing Frames—The Difficulties of applying the Sewing Frames to the Power-Loom.

CHAPTER VII.

Mounting for Tweels, Diapers, &c.—How the Tweeling Shafts are Driven—Top Mounting for Three Leaves—Four Leaf Mounting—Double Barrel—Mounting for Five Leaf Tweel—Traverse of Treadle—Diameter of Barrel—Tweeling Treadles—Mounting for a Six Leaf Tweel—Mounting for a Seven Leaf Tweel—Mounting for an Eight Leaf Tweel—Four Shots of Tweel and Plain alternately—Plain and Tweel Stripes in the Warp—Diaper and Plain Cloth—Mounting for a Ten Leaf Tweel—Mounting for a Twelve Leaf Tweel—Mounting for large Tweels—Mounting for a Sixteen Leaf Tweel—Mounting for Diapers—Mounting for Three Leaf Diapers—Mounting for Four Leaf Diapers—Mounting for Five, Six, Seven, and Eight Leaf Diapers—Mounting for Ten Leaf Diapers, with Thirty-six Treads—Diced Work—Double Cloth Mounting—Tube Weaving—Bags woven without a Seam—Bed and Toilet Covers—To make Broad Cloth in a narrow Loom—Crumb-Cloths—Carpets Plain and Tweel, with Weft Cords—Tape Checks made with one Shuttle.

CHAPTER VIII.

Calculations, Tables, &c.—Costing Goods—Rating for Shirting—Rating for a Tape Check—Rating for a Blue and White Check—Form of Rating Book—Oncost Expenses—Statement for Expenses for One Year—Charges for One Loom per Day—The Advantage of a Large Production—Manufacturers', Warpers', and Beamers' Tables.

CHAPTER IX.

Miscellaneous Remarks connected with Power-Loom Weaving—Erecting a New Factory—Situation—Size of the Mill—Arrangement—Steam Boilers—How to Keep the Boilers Clean—Management of Furnaces—Smoke Burning—New Patent Furnace—Steam Engines—Speed Indicator—Gearing—New Mode of Driving Looms without Belting—Calculations of Speeds—Speed of Engine—Speed of Shafts—Examples—Safety Valves—Quadrant—New Mode of Picking (W. & J. Todd's.)

INTRODUCTORY REMARKS.

To discover the origin of Weaving would be rather a difficult task, and one that does not form part of our plan in this work; our purpose being more to show its present state, and give a description of the latest improvements that have been made in the power-loom, than to go into a long history of its origin, although we believe that it would be both interesting and amusing if such a history had been kept, there being scarcely anything of more importance to the human family than the records of the arts of the preceding generations. However, we will give some of the remarks that can be found. It will be seen that the art of weaving is very ancient from the following passages taken from the sacred volume: —Exodus xxxv. 25, "And all the women that were wise-hearted did spin with their hands, and brought that which they had spun, both of blue, and of purple, and of scarlet, and of fine linen." 35, "Them hath he filled with wisdom of heart, to work all manner of work, of the engraver, and of the workman, and of the embroiderer, in blue, and in purple, in scarlet, and in fine linen, and of the weaver, even of them that do work, and of those that devise cunning work." 1 Chronicles ii. 23, "And he slew an Egyptian, a man of great stature, five cubits high; and in the Egyptian's hand was a spear like a weaver's beam, and he went down to him with a staff, and plucked the spear out of the Egyptian's hand, and slew him with his own spear." Job vii. 6, "My days are swifter than a weaver's shuttle, and are spent without hope." Many more passages from the sacred volume might be taken to show that the ancients were very well up to the art of weaving, although we do not understand the mode they had of doing it. It is evident they were able to make a great many kinds of figured work. It is frequently stated by writer's that weaving is one of the arts which furnishes one of the main distinctions between savage and civilized life. One says—"For though we find finery and external adornment common to every people, yet comfortable clothing is almost exclusively confined to the inhabitants of those portions of the globe which are far advanced in civilization."

The Hindoos and Egyptians have been acquainted with weaving for thousands of years, and it is well-known, that the fabrics made in India were much valued, and yet they have made little or no improvement in their looms, although it appears that looms were originally invented in the East. One writer says, when speaking of the common forms of the loom, "that simple as they are, they can yet be favourably contrasted with the rude contrivances still pursued in India, where the wretched weaver performs his labours in the open air, choosing his station under trees whose shade may protect him from the scorching rays of the sun. Here extending the threads which compose the warp of his intended cloth lengthways, between two bamboo rollers, which are fastened to the turf by wooden pins, he digs a hole in the earth large enough to contain his legs when in a sitting posture, then, suspending to a branch of a tree the cords which are intended to cause the reciprocal raising and depressing of the alternate threads of his warp, he fixes underneath and connected with the cords two loops, into which inserting the great toe of either foot, he is ready to commence his operations. The shuttle with which he causes the cross-threads or woof to interlace the warp is in form like the netting needle, and, being somewhat longer than the breadth of the warp, is made to perform the office of a baton, by striking the threads of the woof close up to each other."

With this rude apparatus the patient Hindoo succeeds in weaving fabrics which, for delicacy of texture, cannot be surpassed, and can scarcely be rivalled by the

European weaver, even when his labours are aided by the most elaborate machinery. But it is only in climates where the absolute natural wants of men are few, and under systems of government, where the oppressions of the dominant caste deprive the unhappy bulk of the people of all means for obtaining more than suffices for the barest supply of those wants, that such labour can be performed.

An American writer gives the following on the antiquity of weaving; and we leave the reader to form his own opinion of it:—

"'It appears,' says His Holiness, Pope Alexander VI., 'that the world was first indebted to one Arkite Ghiden Ghelen, an extremely ingenious artisan of Nodville, for the first regularly manufactured piece of cloth ever produced on the surface of this terrestrial globe;' and, although it was akin to what we at this day and generation call matting, and produced by twisting and interlacing leaf stems and fibres together, yet the workmanship cannot be surpassed by the best manufacturers of Bolton cloths of the present day. From this it would appear that His Holiness had a sample of the cloth actually in his possession. Perhaps, sewing the fig leaves, as mentioned in the Book of Genesis, has reference to the same process.

"'An obvious improvement on the garment of leaves,' proceeds His Holiness. 'which was suggested by twisting the peel of rushes into fine strings, by which means superior textures were produced; but this improvement was not adopted generally, in the part of the country of which we speak, till after the death of Methuselah.' 'It did not escape the notice of the mat weavers, that their work was rendered more flexible and agreeable to the wearer (particularly for undergarments), by the use of a finer fibre, and accordingly we find that numerous trials were actually made with the fibres of various kinds of plants, such as those of the hemp and flax species.'

"It is curious how the descendants of our first parents obtained the knowledge of spinning flax into thread. We are credibly informed that it was by supernatural agency. We are indeed told by C. G. G., a learned metaphysician of Oxford, that a tradition exists in England which goes far to prove that spinning was first effectually practised in that country; but we disregard such testimony, as we have found the true and original story from which C. G. G.'s one is evidently copied. This discovery we have made in the collection of Sir Henry Hunlock, and we think it right to give his version, which is as follows:—

"'There was once an old woman and her daughter who lived at the side of a hill (not under a hill as the Oxonian would fain have it), in the midst of a forest, near Nodville. They were very poor, and their only support was obtained from selling the thread which the daughter spun with her spindle and distaff.

During the long winter, when the roads were so bad that merchants of the surrounding nations could not come to purchase the thread, the daughter, who was one of the most lovely creatures on earth, worked without cessation, in order that she might have enough of thread when the spring market came, to enable her to purchase a cloak for her mother, and a scarlet shawl for herself, in order that they might be properly attired while attending their devotions. (Where these shawls and cloaks were manufactured, is a question for hierologists to solve.)

" 'It so happened that the king of that country, whose name was Zannkul K. Euzen, had an only son, who, while out one day deer-hunting, went astray in the forest of Akiel, and called at the widow's cottage to inquire the way. He was greatly struck with the girl's beauty, and not less with the numerous hanks of yarn which lay upon the floor of the cottage, and equally attested her skill and industry. He asked how it happened, that she had collected such an immense pile, and the old woman, whose name was Zabozok, replied that her daughter had spun the whole in a week. 'In a week!' exclaimed the astonished prince; 'if this be true, I have found a ' gal ' more worthy of my attachment than any other in the whole country. I will send you a load of flax, and if she has it done by the end of a week, I will, without any other proof of her merit, choose her as my bride; but, if not, I will have you both cut in pieces and thrown to the cormorants and loons, for deceiving the son of your sovereign.'

"' On the very next day, a long train of camels, laden with flax, stood before the door of the cottage, and the drivers, having unloaded them, told the girl that she must spin this quantity in a week, or prepare for death. When they departed, her poor heart was crushed with despair. She, however, was unwilling to reproach her mother, even by a look, but she went into the forest, and sitting down under a tree began bitterly to bewail her sad fate. While she was thus weeping and lamenting, a decrepit old man came up, and enquired the cause of her tears, and in reply she told him the whole story. 'Do not weep, daughter,' he said, ' I will execute every one of the tasks imposed upon you by the prince, provided you will either give me your eldest son when he is twelve months and a day old, or that you shall, in the intervening time, find out my name.' She agreed at once to the terms. The old man, by some mysterious agency conveyed away the flax, and about an hour before the time appointed for the prince's arrival (which was half-past five o'clock in the morning) returned with the finest and best twisted thread that had ever been seen in Nodville. The prince, according to his promise, married the girl, and conveyed her with her mother to the palace, which stood upon a beautiful rising piece of ground about a quarter of a mile from the city, and overlooking it. (This palace must have been a very magnificent building, as it cost rather more than eleven and a quarter talents of gold.)

" 'Every Monday morning, before sunrise, the prince gave out to his beloved the quantity of flax which he expected to be spun during the week, and every Saturday night the yarn was made ready for him by the mysterious old man. At length the princess became the mother of a beautiful boy, and the thoughts of the bargain she had made almost drove her to distraction. Every effort she made to discover the name of the wonderful spinner utterly failed, and he, at every visit, reminded her that the time was near when he would have the right to claim her child.

" 'One evening, as she sat oppressed with melancholy, her husband, who had just returned from hunting, enquired the cause of her sadness, but she was unable to answer him a word. 'Come, my love,' said he, 'do not be cast down, and I will entertain you with an account of a very surprising incident which occurred to me this very day. I lost my way while pursuing a fine stag, which ran towards the great rocks beyond the forest. While searching for his lurking place, I thought I heard a human voice, and following the direction of the sound, came to a cave, where I saw an old man, who did not notice my approach, so deeply was he engaged in a strange sort of labour; he was spinning, not as you do with the distaff, but with wheels which flew round as rapidly as lightning, and gave out thread like water falling from a mountain torrent, and all the while he never ceased singing :—

> ' My mistress, little she knows my name,
> Which shan't be forgot, which shan't be forgot,
> When a prince as heir to the fortune I claim,
> Of Wallotty Trot, Wallotty Trot.
> I come, at the end of a year and a day,
> And take the young prince, my heir, away.
> With my whack ! she goes !
> While nobody knows,
> My trusty machine,
> In this cave unseen,
> Here is the spot
> For Wallotty Trot.

"'The princess made her husband repeat the rhymes several times, until she was sure that she could remember them perfectly, and waited with confidence for the return of the old man. He came at the appointed time, and claimed the child. 'Stop, neighbour,' said she, 'there goes another word to that bargain. I have found out your name; it is Wallotty Trot.' 'You have, indeed, detected my name,' said he, ' and my business on earth is well nigh finished ; but before I depart I am bound to tell you the secrets of my art.' So saying, he went into the forest, and in a few seconds returned with his wheels. He then taught the lady their use, showing her that she could spin sixty-six times more with them than she could accomplish by means of the distaff, and then vanished, after which he was never again seen in that part of the world.

"'The prince and princess taught this new branch of industry to their subjects, which so enriched them that all the surrounding nations regarded them with envy and admiration.'

"These wheels are of similar construction to those introduced into Great Britain by Samuel Crompton, which are known by the appellation of the "hall-in-the-wood" machine. It is unnecessary for us to give drawings and descriptions of them; Mr. Baines of Leeds, and Dr. Ure of London, in their histories of the progress of the cotton manufacture in Great Britain, having already done so.

"After the death of Methuselah, the art of weaving appears to have made considerable advances in many parts of the East, and particularly in China, India, and Persia. The first loom of which there is any authentic record still in existence is that invented by Arkite Ghiden Ghelen, when a lad of about seventy years of age; and after having been at great trouble and expense, we have succeeded in procuring a drawing of it, copied from an ancient parchment scroll, found among the curiosities of Sesac, founder of the Egyptian dynasty, (who reigned thirty-four years;) but from the dilapidated state of the document, and the draughtsman (Alexis Kersivenus of Alexandria) not being a weaver himself, we fear it is not in every particular like the original. This scroll appears (from indorsements on its back) to have been once in the possession of the Emperor of China, Teling Ching Ouang, from whom it descended to Chao Kong-hi-hi, his successor.

" From this representation the loom was of a vertical construction, and seems to have been chiefly applied to the manufacture of plaids and chequers, the patterns of which were most probably suggested by the interlacing of bark or stripes of broad-leaved plants. Indeed, the modern plaids so obviously represent this origin of their patterns, that no one, except the most sceptical, can for a moment doubt the correctness of this opinion.

" The process of weaving in this loom must have been very tedious, and, of course, the fabrics produced would be expensive in the same proportion. The inventor does not appear to have been acquainted with any instrument analogous to the shuttle, for we find from the perusal of accidental records (imperfect as they certainly are), that some weavers drew the weft through the web with their fingers, and others used an implement somewhat like a knitting needle, but having a hook at one end, similar to the crook of a shepherd's staff, which doubtless insinuated the first idea of that most useful instrument."

There is no very reliable authority to tell us of the different kinds of implements (mountings) used by the ancients in weaving the different kinds of figured cloth, the only description being that of the Indian loom; and we shall now proceed to show the progress it has made in our own country.

When weaving was first introduced into Great Britain the exact date is not known, but it appears, from what we can gather from history, that there was a considerable number of weavers in London in the year 1351. Twelve years previous to the above date, in the city of Bristol, which is 118 miles west of London, we find looms started for weaving woollen cloth; very likely these looms were put up by foreigners, as England was frequently invaded previous to this period.

It will be seen from early history, that the inhabitants, who had settled near the sea-coast, possessed some property, and were therefore more easily intimidated than those tribes that were dispersed through the forest. None of them cultivated the ground; they all lived by raising cattle and hunting. Their dress consisted of skins; their habitations were huts made of wicker-work and coarse rushes; their priests, the Druids, together with the sacred women, exercised a kind of authority over them.

We find the following letter, which was written by one of the kings about the year 1030, from which will be seen that many foreigners must have been in England. In it mention is made of rich mantles and garments being given as presents.

Part of this letter is given, not for anything it contains concerning weaving, but to show the strong probability that this country was first indebted to foreigners for this art; as we see from the letter, that the king himself was on friendly terms with them.

"Canute, King of all Denmark, England, and Norway, and part of Sweden, to Egelnoth, the Metropolitan, to Archbishop Alfric, to all the Bishops and Chiefs, and to all the nation of the English, both Nobles and Commoners, greeting. I write to inform you that I have lately been at Rome, to pray for the remission of my sins, and for the safety of my kingdoms, and of the nations that are subject to my sceptre. It is long since I bound myself by vow to make this pilgrimage, but I have been hitherto prevented by affairs of state, and other impediments. Now, however, I return humble thanks to the Almighty God, that he has allowed me to visit the tombs of the blessed Apostles, Peter and Paul, and every holy place within and without the city of Rome, and to honour and venerate them in person. And this I have done, because I had learned from my teachers, that the Apostle St. Peter received from the Lord the great power of binding and loosing, with the keys of the kingdom of heaven; on this account I thought it highly useful to solicit his patronage with God.

"Be it moreover known to you, that there was at the festival of Easter a great assemblage of noble personages, with the Pope John, and the Emperor Conrad, namely, all the chiefs of the nations, from Mount Gargano to the nearest sea, who all received me honourably, and made me valuable presents; but particularly the emperor, who gave me many gold and silver vases, with rich mantles and garments. I therefore took the opportunity to treat with the pope, the emperor, and the prince, on the grievances of my people, both English and Danes, that they might enjoy more equal law, and more secure safeguard in their way to Rome, nor be detained at so many barriers, nor harassed by unjust exactions. My demands were granted both by the Emperor and by King Rodulf, to whom the greater part of the barriers belongs, and it was enacted by all the princes, that my men, whether pilgrims or merchants, should, for the future, go to Rome and return in full security, without detention at the barriers, or the payment of unlawful tolls."

At the time the above letter was written, the inhabitants of Britain who wore woven clothing must have got it from the East, or the Continental nations; but when we pass on to the year 1376, we find woollen cloth made in Ireland, and a company of linen weavers established in London ten years afterwards. North-west from London 262 miles, stands

Kendal, a borough town, which has long been celebrated for its woollen manufacture, and mention is made of its coarse cloth as far back as the year 1390, and from the spirit and industry of its inhabitants, they have continued to flourish ever since; they have now mills established for both spinning and weaving. We now pass on to Manchester, the great centre of the cotton manufacture, and we find in the year 1641, the merchants of that place buying linen yarn from the Irish in great quantities, and getting it woven into cloth, and then returning the cloth to Ireland to be sold.

In the year 1685, Louis the XIV. revoked an edict which was issued by Henry the IV., in the year 1598, the effect of which was that many foreign weavers came to Great Britain at this time, all adding to the industry of the country. Many other incidents might be taken notice of, but we will pass on to the factory period, and we preface our remarks with a quotation from Dr. Ure :—

"How different is the spirit of modern philosophy since it was first directed into the path of utility by Galileo, Bacon, Pascal, and Newton. It places its chief delight and honour in investigating the relations of number, figure, and all material substances, in order to apply the resulting discoveries, to assuage the evils and to multiply the enjoyments of social life. In its modern familiarity with the sublimest of speculations, that of the equilibrium and movements of the celestial bodies, mechanical science does not, however, disdain to study the most humble machine of manufacturing industry, and, indeed, may hold many of them up to the admiration of the transcendentalist, as the happiest achievements of the human mind. Should any one ask where, let him enter a cotton factory and look around."

" 'We enter the factory and look around, and we first make enquiries as to age, and obtain answers which satisfy us that the factory system is little more than eighty years old; then we observe the fine arrangement of the different machines connected with power-loom weaving, the mode of working them, the regularity of their management, &c, which things constitute the principal theme of this volume; we allow the mind to contemplate the great number of different tradesmen that are required, and the amount of labour that is spent before these machines can be made. It gives a kind of pleasure in making a contrast between our loom of the present day and that of the Hindoos, which has been explained. Before one of these factories, with a thousand looms, can be put into operation, it will have given employment to more than one thousand individuals for more than six months, at the rate of three shillings per day for each individual. The parties who receive this employment are coal, iron, lead, and copper miners; labourers, brickmakers, bricklayers, plasterers, slaters, sawyers, joiners, glaziers, glassmakers, nailers, millwrights, engineers, boilermakers, machine-makers, gasfitters, tinsmiths, and a whole host of others; indeed, it would be difficult to mention any kind of employment that does not get part of the money put out on the erection of a factory.

Before the power-loom was brought into operation, the weaving power of this country was a mere drop in the bucket compared to what it is at the present day; indeed, it is within the last forty years that power-loom weaving has been brought to that extent that it could be called a trade, and now it is one of the most important in the kingdom. What has brought the power-loom trade to its present extent, must be attributed to a number of circumstances; for the power-loom would have been of little use, had not the invention of the spinning jenny taken place, which was about 85 years ago; and neither the spinning nor the weaving machinery would have arrived at their present magnitude, had not the steam-engine been brought to their aid; while many other improvements in the other arts have contributed to advance the power-loom trade. It may also be stated, that had it not been for the industry of the people, and the security that capital has in this country, the power-loom trade could never have arrived at its present greatness. For unless capital is protected in such a manner that

d

there is a fair chance of it being made profitable, by it being invested in business, it will not be employed where the chance does not exist; and the work-people should consider this subject more than they have done in many cases, before they make a turn out, leaving the whole machinery standing idle; for what is the interest of the employer, is also the interest of the employed. We have felt a degree of diffidence in making this statement, knowing well the opinion that once existed among some workmen; but when a good feeling exists between the employer and his workers, both parties are benefited by it. The reason is obvious without explanation.

The weaving of cotton goods being the most extensive in this country, a very good idea may be formed of the progress of the power-loom from the quantity of cotton consumed at different periods.

The time was when there was only a few bags of cotton consumed in Great Britain, but we will not go further back than the year 1822. The quantities will be given in bales, considering each bale to average 440 lbs., which is about the average weight at the present time; although the average weight was little more than the half of this in the year 1822; however this is taken into consideration in our calculations; and it appears that in 1822, the number of bales (at an average of 440 lbs.) were 330,564. The next year we take is 1825, and the increase over 1822 is

48,256 bales, which gives for that year 378,820 bales. The year 1826 was a very bad year for the cotton workers, as a great many of them were out of employment, and consequently for that year the consumption is considerably less than the four years previously; but in 1827 trade revives, and the consumption increases. As prices may have had something to do with the increase we will give the extreme prices for the year 1825, 1826, and 1827, of the three principal kinds of cotton, namely:—Surat, Uplands, and New Orleans, which are as follows:—

Price of	Surat	Cotton	for 1825, ...	$5\frac{1}{4}$d.	to 16d.	per lb.
—	Uplands	—	—	6d.	— $19\frac{1}{2}$d.	—
—	New Orleans	—	—	8d.	— 22d.	—
—	Surat	—	for 1826, ...	$4\frac{1}{2}$d.	— 7d.	—
—	Uplands,	—	—	$5\frac{1}{4}$d.	— $8\frac{3}{4}$d.	—
—	New Orleans,	—	—	$5\frac{1}{4}$d.	— $11\frac{1}{2}$d.	—
—	Surat	—	for 1827, ...	$3\frac{7}{8}$d.	— $6\frac{1}{2}$d.	—
—	Uplands,	—	—	$4\frac{7}{8}$d.	— $7\frac{1}{4}$d.	—
—	New Orleans,	—	—	$5\frac{1}{2}$d.	— $9\frac{1}{2}$d.	—

It will be observed that the prices for 1825 are high and very irregular, and that in 1826 and 1827 the prices are lower and more regular. The increase of consumption in 1827 over 1825 is 80,652 bales, the whole number of bales consumed being 459,472 bales. In 1829, the consumption is 508,040 bales, and the prices are as follows:—

Price of	Surat	Cotton	in 1829, ...	$2\frac{7}{8}$d.	to $5\frac{1}{2}$d.	per lb.
—	Uplands	—	—	$4\frac{5}{8}$d.	— 7d.	—
—	New Orleans	—	—	$4\frac{3}{4}$d.	— 9d.	—

We now pass on to 1832, and find the consumption to be 629,928 bales, which is nearly double the quantity that was required for the year 1822. The year 1833, the quantity consumed is rather less; but it comes up again in 1834. The following are the lowest prices for 1822 and 1832:—

Lowest Price of Surat Cotton in 1822,...... $5\frac{1}{2}$d. per lb.
— — Uplands — — ...... $5\frac{3}{4}$d. —
— — New Orleans — — ...... 6d. —
— — Surat — in 1832,...... $3\frac{1}{2}$d. —
— — Uplands — — ...... 5d. —
— — New Orleans — — ...... $5\frac{1}{2}$d. —

The price of cotton is higher in the year 1835, yet the consumption is greater than any year previous, it being 715,520 bales. The following are the extreme prices for the year 1835:—

Price of Surat Cotton, for 1835, ... 6d. to 9d. per lb.
— Uplands — — ...... $6\frac{7}{8}$d. — $13\frac{1}{4}$d. —
— New Orleans — — ...... $6\frac{3}{4}$d. — $14\frac{1}{2}$d. —

About this period many thought that cotton goods were being produced in too great quantities, and that ere long there must be a reaction; but instead of this their production is still more and more. About ten years after this period we find the consumption of cotton, instead of 715,520 bales, to be about 1,664,000 bales per annum, showing the consumption to be more than double what it was in 1835, and it still goes on increasing, for we find at the present time, if the mills were all on (but unfortunately the greater portion are stopped, by over-production and the American War), that the consumption would be 2,596,000 bales per year, nearly eight times what it was in 1822, forty years since.

When the American crop of cotton alone is seen to be upwards of 4,000,000 bales, independent of all the other places that send us cotton, the quantity used in Great Britain, at first sight, does not seem very large, until we calculate the quantity of cloth the 2,596,000 bales of cotton will make, then it appears very different.

Suppose the yarn spun to average No. 40s, and the cloth to average 10^{00}, with 10 shots 36 inches wide, and allowing 20 per cent. for waste on the cotton, and 4 per cent. on the yarn, the cloth woven from the 2,596,000 bales of cotton would be 8,122,595,554 yards, or about 270 yards of cotton cloth per annum for each individual in Great Britain and Ireland, or about ten yards for each person in the world. Although this quantity of yarn is spun in Great Britain, it is not to be understood that it is all made into cloth by the looms in this country, for rather more than one-sixth part of it is exported. But to counterbalance this exportation of cotton yarns, there are thousands of looms, both hand and power, that are employed weaving linen, woollen, silk, and jute yarns.

How long the weaving trade in this country will continue increasing as it has done, is a question no one can answer, as it is liable to be affected by so many unforeseen circumstances, that it is almost impossible to predict, with anything like certainty, what may be the condition of it a few years hence; but supposing there are no national struggles or commotions, and still heavier taxation, things which cannot be forseen nor calculated upon, we do not think that there is anything in our condition, or in that of any of the manufacturing countries of the world, that should lead us to anticipate a reaction in the weaving trade for a long time. The natural capabilities possessed by this country for carrying on the business (all things considered) are decidedly superior to those of any other people. And the superiority to which we have already arrived is perhaps the greatest advantage in our favour, and so long as this superiority can be kept up to that degree as will enable this country to make goods cheaper than any other, the probability is, that in other ten years after this the consumption of cotton will be at least 800,000 bales more per annum than what it is at present, which will then make the consumption to be about 3,500,000 bales. However, we will state what has been written by another bearing on this subject.

At the time when our consumption of cotton was about 600,000 bales, the following remarks regarding the cotton trade were made by Dr. Ure. At this time there was a duty on cotton of 5-16th of a penny per lb. We state this so as the remarks will be better understood.

"The superior skill and dexterity of British operatives have been assumed as constituting one of our chief advantages. Their experience must no doubt be more extended, in proportion as the range and variety of British fabrics are greater than those of any other country; but in such goods as the foreigners carry into neutral markets the superiority of the British operatives is a point by no means decided. Manufacturers of the United States, and of some parts of the Continent, claim for those employed by them at least an equality within the sphere of their own productions, and to which their competition with the fabrics of Great Britain is necessarily limited. The late remarkable ingenuity of the American artisans, in their mechanical improvements, gives no countenance to the notion of their inferiority,

"The impolicy of the import tax on cotton wool is so glaring as hardly to require illustration. A tax on the raw materials of such manufactures as are principally consumed within the United Kingdom, would be comparatively harmless; but since two-thirds at least of British cotton goods are exported, a tax upon their raw material operates as a bounty upon the cotton manufactures of other nations. Where duties have been imposed on importation, as in the case of sugars, wines, spirits, &c., a corresponding drawback on their exportation has been always allowed; yet cotton, as if undeserving of fiscal justice, has been ever since the year 1798 persecuted with a series of imposts, in twelve successive rates, all tending to turn the balance in favour of our foreign rivals in that trade. No government, except our own, possessing any pretensions to the title of enlightened, lays a tax upon the import of cotton wool, which is not countervailed by an equivalent drawback on exportation. The peculiar pressure of the competition in America is upon those coarse yarns and heavy cloths, for the production of which it possesses the advantages of an indigenous raw material, unencumbered with taxation, and procured at the minimum cost of carriage. The spinning also of the Continent of Europe has been hitherto directed principally to the coarse numbers of yarn, which are worked up into heavy fabrics, and with the effect of depriving this country of almost all European customers whom she not long ago supplied.

"The very existence of this country depends on retaining an ascendancy in the cotton manufacture, as the principal means of enabling her to sustain the enormous burden of taxation accumulated by the warfunding system. Were Great Britain as free from taxes as the States of America, or the Continent of Europe, she might surrender to them a share of her cotton trade without suffering any national misfortune; but she has nothing to spare without involving her people in distress, and her public credit in jeopardy."

THE
THEORY AND PRACTICE

OF THE

Art of Weaving.

CHAPTER I.
GRISTING YARN.

This chapter will be found to contain a number of calculations and observations that are necessary for Manufacturers and Managers in the Weaving Trade.

In commencing it may be remarked, that almost every substance that can be made to answer for warp or weft is now woven for some purpose or other; but as cotton yarn is the most common material now used in this country, we will begin with it.

To find the Grist or fineness of Yarn, it was necessary to have some rule or standard to go by; and for cotton yarn it has been adopted in Great Britain and other countries where it is bought and sold, to have 15,120 yards in the spyndle, the yard being 36 inches; and cotton spinners in this country all keep to the same measurement for the size of the reel, it being 54 inches in circumference, and eighty turns of the reel make one skein—this is the first shift made on the reel, and seven of these shifts make a number or hank. It is from the quantity of numbers contained in 1 lb. avoirdupois that the size of the yarn is determined; so that, when the yarn is said to be No. 50's, there are 50 numbers or hanks in 1 lb.; when No. 60's, there are 60 hanks; when 70's, 70 hanks, and so on.

The common way yarn is reeled is as follows:

    120 yards 1 skein.
    840 " 7 " 1 No. or hank.
  15,120 " 126 " 18 ,, 1 spyndle,

and put up in 10 or 5 lb. bundles to be sold. It will easily be seen then, by counting the No.'s in the bundle, whether the proper sizes of yarn are given or not, by multiplying the weight of the bundle by its numbers.

For example, a 10 lb. bundle of 36's should have 360 hanks or numbers, because

$$36 \times 10 = 360.$$

A 5 lb. bundle of 60's should have 300 No.'s as

$$60 \times 5 = 300.$$

Cotton yarn is also sold in large quantities in cope, and on beams, and also in chains. The way to find the size of the yarn in copes, is to take 7 of them, and reel 1 skein off each, which will make 1 number, and weigh it, either on a quadrant, or small beam and scale for the purpose, and from this, the size of the yarn will be found.

YARN ON BEAM.

To find the size of yarn when on beam, take off 80 ends 54 inches long—this will make 1 skein; but it will be more exact to take 560 ends, 54 inches, and this will make 1 No., then weigh it to find the size.

YARN IN CHAIN.

To find the size of the yarn in a chain, take the whole chain and weigh it, ascertain the number of ends that are in the chain, also the length of it, and the hanks will be found from the length and number of ends; then divide the hanks by the lbs., and the answer will be the size of the yarn. Suppose a chain is 8 lbs., and has 846 ends, and is 284 yards long: then 846 × 284 is 240,264; divide by 840, and the answer is 286, the Numbers in the chain: this divided by 8, the weight of the chain in lbs., is $35\frac{3}{4}$, being the size of the yarn.

EXAMPLE.

```
846 Ends.
284
-------
3384
6768
1692
-------
240264
```

```
              8
840)240264(286·02
    1680
    ————      35¾
     7226
     6720
     ————
      5064
      5040
      ————
       2400
       1680
       ————
        720
        840
```

It may be remarked here that the yarn bought in cope, chain, or beam, is in general from 3 to 6 per cent. coarser than the size ordered; this should not be, but still it is the case. Some spinners are more in the habit of spinning coarse than others, but it would be better to keep to the average size, and charge a little more per lb. for the yarn. It is well-known that it is almost impossible to keep the proper size in spinning, as there are so many things to contend with that alters the sizes; but suppose that 60's is the number wanted, it might range from 57's to 63's, and the average would be 60's; and to keep any of the yarn from being too soft spun, a twist pinion for 63's should be put on, for if the twist was for 60's, then the yarn that sized 63's would be too soft. When yarn is bought in bundle, the proper length is given, and no more than the weight in lbs., this is managed by spinning average No.'s, in the following manner :—

Suppose a spinner is selling 40's in bundle; as observed before; the proper length must be in every bundle, as the buyer will not pay for more than 10 lbs., and must have both the weight and the length. When the party who has the charge of the sizes, sees only 38's, then he has to get as much spun of No. 42's, and mix the two sizes in equal quantities to make them average 40's. If this was attended to by the spinners, the weavers would have less difficulty in keeping the cloth to the proper weight, and the calculations for it would be more correct.

The same principle of calculations apply to all the other kinds of yarn; the main thing to know is, the number of yards contained in a given weight, and how the particular kind of yarn is sized.

LINEN YARN.

This yarn is spun from flax, and should be reeled (according to an act of Parliament) on a reel 90 inches in circumference1—20 turns of the reel will make 1 cut, and 48 cuts 1 spyndle. As 90 inches is $2\frac{1}{2}$ yards, multiply the 120 by $2\frac{1}{2}$, and the product by 48, which will give the yards in a spindle.

EXAMPLE.

$$120 \times 2\frac{1}{2}$$
$$2\frac{1}{2}$$

$$240$$
$$60$$

$$300 \times 48$$
$$48$$

$$2400$$
$$1200$$

$$14400 \text{ yards in a spyndle.}$$

But the spyndle is divided into other parts besides the above, as will be seen from the following table :—

	Cut.	Heer.	Hesp.	Spyndle.		
	1	0	0	0	300	yards.
	2	1	0	0	600	"
	24	12	1	0	7200	"
	48	24	2	1	14400	"

		Cut.	Heer.	Hesp.	Spyndle.
or	300 yards	1	0	0	0
	600 "	2	1	0	0
	7200 "	24	12	1	0
	14400 "	48	24	2	1

The fineness of linen yarn should be found from the number of cuts in the lb. avoirdupois. If there be 25 cuts in 1 lb., that is No. 25's; if 50 cuts, No. 50's, and so on for every cut more in the lb., one number finer; but the fineness is expressed in different places by different terms; however, it would be better to have one common scale, and the number of cuts in 1 lb. of 16 oz. is considered the best; and it will also be observed that

No. 48 linen yarn is equal in weight to No. 18 cotton, because, there is 48 cuts of No. 48's in 1 lb. of linen yarn, and 18 hanks in 1 lb. of No. 18 cotton yarn, and 1 spyndle in both : the cotton spyndle has 15,120 yards, and the linen has 14,400, making a difference of 720 yards ; but as linen yarn has less elasticity than cotton, 1 spyndle of linen will make as many inches of cloth as 1 spyndle of cotton yarn, unless it be woven tighter than what is commonly the case in weaving cotton.

WOOL YARN.

Wool yarn is spun from the short fibres of the fleece that is taken from the animal, and Worsted yarn from the long staple. They are reeled on different sizes of reels; the Wool is in general reeled on the 54 inch reel, and has 18 hanks to the spyndle, but is one-third heavier than cotton yarn :—For example, 1 lb. of 18's wool yarn has only 12 hanks, 840 yards long ; and 1 lb. 18's cotton has 18 hanks.

Worsted yarn is sometimes reeled on the short reel, and sometimes on the long one, and is sold by the gross, a gross being 144 hanks.

THE REED.

The Reed is a very important article in weaving, it divides the warp threads, and may also determine the fineness of the cloth, but a coarse web may be made in a fine reed, and a fine web may be made in a coarse reed, consequently, it is really the number of warp threads contained in a given space, that determines the fineness of the cloth or web. For example, a 6^{00} web can be made in a 12^{00} reed, by putting only 1 thread in the split; and a 24^{00} can be made in the same reed, by putting 4 threads in the split; or an 18^{00}, by putting 3 in the split. However, the common practice is to put 2 threads in the split, and when speaking about the fineness of a web, it is always understood that 2 threads are in the split; but in other localities there are different scales or rules by which they name the fineness of the web.

In Scotland, the reeds are almost all made on the 37 inch scale, which usually was called the Scotch Ell. What is meant by the 37 inch scale is, the number of splits contained in 37 inches; if there are 300 splits contained in 37 inches, that reed is called a three hundred (marked 3^{00}); if 600, it is called 6^{00}; or if 1200 are in the 37 inches, it is called a 12^{00}, and so on; for every 100 splits more, it is 1 set finer. By the common web glass used in Scotland, the fineness of the reed may be ascertained by counting the number of splits that are seen through the aperture in it, when placed upon the reed: if 5 splits are seen, it is a 10^{00}; if 6 splits, a 12^{00}, and so on; the measurement of the aperture is contained 200 times in 37 inches, so by multiplying the number of splits seen through the glass, by 200, the fineness of the reed will be found.

EXAMPLE.

7 splits multiplied by 200 is a 1400 reed. But when the glass is placed upon cloth, and 7 threads of the warp are seen, it is a 7^{00}, or if 12 threads are seen, it is a 12^{00}, and so on, for every thread more, 100 finer. In England, the splits are called dents, and many of the reeds are rated by the number of splits contained in 1 inch, which is more simple than the Scotch scale for calculating warps, and their glasses are made with two spaces, of half, and quarter of an inch. If the half-inch glass is used, and 25 threads are seen, it is called a 50, or if 36 threads are seen it is called a 72, and so on. In some places the fineness of the web is named by porters, as a 25 porter, a 30 porter, and so on; the meaning of this is, that 20 splits or 40 threads are called a porter (and some keep to this yet), so that a 25 porter is equal to a 5^{00}, because

$$25 \times 40 = 1000 \text{ ends.}$$

Threads in a Splits 2)1000
$\phantom{\text{Threads in a Splits 2)}}$500 Web.

A 30 porter is equal to a 6^{00}, and every 5 porters 100 finer on the 37 inch scale. It is hoped that enough has been said to make the principle understood, how the fineness of a web is to be found, as it would be too tedious to give all the rules used in the different localities where weaving is carried on; it would however be better, if one scale for the reed was adopted by all the Manufacturers throughout the country, and as an inch is a measurement of very general use, it might be made the standard, and the inch scale would answer for all the variety likely to be required. The old reeds could be wrought out in course of time, without any extra expense to the Manufacturer. If all new reeds required were made on the 1 inch scale, it would be no inconvenience to the trade in general; for reeds could be made within a very small fraction on the 1 inch scale to the other scales now in use. Take a 12^{00} Jaconet for example, it measures 33 inches of cloth, and has in it 2264 threads just now, and it fills $34\frac{9}{10}$ inches in the reed; if 2264 is divided by $34\frac{9}{10}$, it will give the number of threads in 1 inch, which is nearly 65; the difference is so small between a 12^{00} and a 65, that no Merchant would complain of the alteration.

As most other trades are endeavouring to get a common measure established for the different articles they make, the weaving trade, which is of great importance, should have one common measure also. Some people may object to this, and think it against their interest, but what is to be a benefit for the country at large, is in general good for every individual, when taken in a proper view; this hint is merely made for others to consider, as it does not answer to discuss it here.

CALCULATION OF WARPS.

Having explained the principle of gristing yarn, and how to find its Nos., also the measure for the reed, it may now be shown how to calculate the warp of a web.

The first thing to be ascertained is, the number of ends, or runners, that will be required to make the proper breadth for the cloth wanted. The old method of calculation for warps, was to do it by ells, splits, porters, and spyndles, and that may have been the best at one time; but as all cloth is now sold by the yard, and as a warp is just so many threads, so many yards long, it has been thought better just to keep by the threads, yards, and hanks, this plan being more simple.

When the number of threads are found, it is a simple matter to get the porters or spyndles, if they are required.—For porters, divide the number of ends in the web by 40, and for spyndles, divide the hanks in the web by 18.

To find the number of ends in a web, ascertain the number of ends in an inch, multiply the number of ends in 1 inch by the given quantity of inches that are to be in the breadth of the web, and the answer is the number of ends required. EXAMPLE.

Breadth of web 34 inches.
Threads in 1 inch   54
———
136
170
———
1836 ends in the web.

In the Scotch scale of reeds there is always a fraction in every breadth, except 37, 74, and 111 inches; but the general way to find the number of ends is by simple proportion, taking 37 for the first term, the number of ends in 37 inches of the given set for the second term, and inches required in the breadth of the web for the third.

*** EXAMPLE.**

Say a 12^{00} reed, 33 inches wide. If 37 inches give 2400 ends, what will 33 inches give?—

```
    37    :    2400    ::    33
                33
              ─────
              7200
              7200
              ─────
          37)79200(2140 Ends for 33 inches.
              74
              ──
              52
              37
              ──
              150
              148
              ───
               20
              ──
               37
```

° Any one who wishes to save time in calculating for the Ends in a Web, should procure one of the Tables that are published, showing the number of Ends or Splits in any given number of inches. These Tables may be had from the Publisher of this Work.

WARP IN A WEB.

To find the quantity of Warp that is required for a Web, say 265 yards long, with 2400 ends, multiply the ends by the yards, and divide them by 840 for the hanks.

EXAMPLE.

```
      2400 Ends.
       265 Yards.
      ─────────
     12000
     14400
      4800
     ─────────
840)636000(757 Hanks 1 Skein.
    5880
    ─────
     4800
     4200
     ────
      6000
      5880
      ────
       120
```

The above example gives 757 hanks, 1 skein, and suppose the warp to be No. 50's, divide the 757½ by 50 for lbs.

```
50)757½(15·2¼ ounce full.
   50
   ───
   257
   250
   ───
    7½
```

If the spyndles are required to be known, divide the 757¼ by 18, and the answer is the spyndles.

EXAMPLE.

18)757¼(42 Sp. 1 Hk. 1 Sk.
   72
   ──
   37
   36
   ──
    1
    7
   ──
7)8(1 Hank.
  7
  ──
  1 Skein.

In calculating warps, it has been a common rule to add 5 per cent. for waste and shrinking, but there can be no fixed standard for it; the manager or manufacturer must find this out by practice, on the different fabrics they make, as it entirely depends on the kind of cloth, and quality of the stuff that the web is made of. Therefore, all the examples given in this work are made out nett (except where stated), with the percentage added, that has been found in practice to be correct, and even in the examples given it will not be always the same, as a great deal depends on the quality of the yarn.

A short method to find the hanks in the warp of a web:—

Always take 80 yards for the length, and divide

the number of ends or runners that is required to make the warp by 10, and the answer is the number of hanks, with an allowance of 5 per cent: and as 80 is a number very easily divided, it can be reduced, or added to, with very little trouble in calculation. If the manufacturer is wishing to rate his goods by 5, 10, 30, or 40 yards, instead of 80, then for

$$
\begin{array}{rl}
5 \text{ take a} & \frac{1}{16} \\
10 \text{ ,,} & \frac{1}{8} \\
20 \text{ ,,} & \frac{1}{4} \\
40 \text{ ,,} & \frac{1}{2}
\end{array}
$$

When the number of threads has been found that will make the warp of a web, for example, say, 1920 ends.

EXAMPLE.

To divide by 10, throw off the figure to the right hand, and the remainder is the answer.

1920 Ends in the web, that is

$$
\begin{array}{rlrl}
192 & \text{Hanks for} & 80 & \text{Yards.} \\
96 & \text{,,} & 40 & \text{,,} \\
48 & \text{,,} & 20 & \text{,,} \\
24 & \text{,,} & 10 & \text{,,} \\
12 & \text{,,} & 5 & \text{,,}
\end{array}
$$

In the example given (page 45), the warp has 2400 ends, and is 265 yards long: these numbers are given to the warper with the number of pieces that are to be in the web: and suppose it is a plain white web, the warper has to know how many numbers are on each bobbin, and divide the hanks in the web by the hanks on the bobbin, and the answer is the number of bobbins that will be required for the web.

EXAMPLE.

Say 8 Numbers on each bobbin, then 8 in 757—

```
8)757(94 keeping out the fraction.
  72
  ──
  37
  32
  ──
   5
   8
```

This shows that 95 bobbins will be required to make the warp of the web. It is generally left to the warper's own judgment how to arrange the bobbins in the bank. The process is explained under warping.

To find the quantity of cloth that a given quantity of yarn will make, find the number of hanks in the given quantity of yarn, which will be found from a rule already stated; then fix upon the number of ends that will make the breadth of the cloth wanted.

Suppose 220 hanks is the quantity of yarn, and the number of ends to make the breadth of the cloth to be 1800, multiply by 840, and divide by 1800, and the answer is the length of the web.

EXAMPLE.

$$
\begin{array}{r}
220 \text{ Hanks.} \\
840 \\
\hline
8800 \\
1760 \\
\hline
\end{array}
$$

$$
\begin{array}{r}
1800)184800(102\tfrac{2}{3} \\
1800 \\
\hline
4800 \\
3600 \\
\hline
1200 \quad 2 \\
\overline{} = \overline{} \\
1800 \quad 3
\end{array}
$$

And suppose that 5 per cent. is the proper allowance for waste, &c., then the quantity of cloth would be 97 yards.

The following are a few different fabrics with the kind and quantity of yarn that was required to make them; and it will be seen from each, the shrinkage both in length and breadth, which may be of some advantage in rateing fabrics of a similar nature:—

A 10^{00} 33 inch Shirting, 11 shots, No. 18's warp, 20's weft, required 1876 runners, which is 35·07 inches in the reed; and to make 60 yards of cloth, it required 64 yards of yarn, which is nearly 7 per cent. for shrinkage in length, and about 6 per cent. for the breadth.

A 34 inch 10^{00} 11 shots Window Holland, No. 18's warp, and No. 18's weft, required 2024 runners, which gives in the reed, 37·44, or nearly $37\tfrac{1}{2}$ inches, this web also required 64 yards of yarn to make 60 yards of cloth, but in the finishing, it gained about 3 yards.

A 54 inch 10^{00} 11 shots Window Holland, 18's warp, 18's weft, required 3168 ends, the breadth in the reed was 58·60, or nearly $58\frac{5}{8}$ inches, and 64 yards of yarn for 60 yards of cloth.

A 9^{00} $11\frac{1}{2}$ shots Cross-over, 24's warp, 12's white weft, and No. 14's blue weft, required 1848 ends, and 65 yards of yarn to make 60 yards of cloth.

A 38 inch 9^{00} $11\frac{1}{2}$ shots Cross-over, required 1904 ends. The white weft No. 12's, and the blue No. 14's, required 65 yards of yarn to give 60 yards of Cloth.

A 33 inch 12^{00} 11 shots Jaconet, with 60's warp and 80's weft, required 2264 ends, which fills $34\frac{8}{10}$ inches in the reed; and to make 25 yards of cloth, it required 26 yards of yarn.

CALCULATION OF WEFTS.

To find the quantity of weft for a given piece of Cloth, first find the quantity of shots in one yard, and multiply them by the number of yards in the given piece of cloth, and the product by the breadth of the web in inches; then divide by 36 for yards, and the product by 840 for hanks.

EXAMPLE.

25 yards, with 11 shots on the glass, 35 inches wide. As there is 200 shots on the yard for every shot seen in the glass, a web with 11 shots will have 2200 shots on the yard; so multiply 2200 shots by 25, for the quantity in 25 yards, and by 35 for inches, and divide by 36 for yards.

$$
\begin{array}{r}
2200 \times 25 \\
25 \\
\hline
11000 \\
4400 \\
\hline
55000 \\
35 \\
\hline
275000 \\
165000 \\
\hline
\end{array}
$$

$$36)1925000(53472\tfrac{2}{9} \text{ Yards.}$$

$$
\begin{array}{r}
180 \\
\hline
125 \\
108 \\
\hline
170 \\
144 \\
\hline
260 \\
252 \\
\hline
80 \\
72 \\
\hline
\tfrac{8}{36} = \tfrac{2}{9}
\end{array}
$$

$$840) 53472 (63\tfrac{2\,2}{3\,5} \text{ or about } \tfrac{2}{3}.$$

```
      5040
      ----
      3072
      2520
      ----
       552   23
       ---=---  or about 2/3
       840   35
```

There are shorter methods, however, than the one given, for finding the quantity of weft for a piece of cloth, but the preceding one shows the principle clearer than any other. The quantity of weft may be got from the quantity of warp that is in the web or piece of cloth, in the following manner:—

Suppose a 12^{00} 33 inch Jaconet, it will be seen that there is 2264 ends, and from the 25 yards of cloth, there is 70·07 hanks; if 12 gives 70 (keeping out the fraction), what will 11 give?—$\tfrac{1}{12}$ less, or in proportion to whatever the shots may be.

EXAMPLE.

```
   12 : 70 :: 11
           11
           --
   12)770
```

In proportion $64\tfrac{1}{6}$

always taking the hanks found in the warp of the web for the second term, and the sit of the reed for the first, or divisor; or in other words, multiply the hanks by shots, and divide by the sit of the reed, thus

$$\begin{array}{r}70\\11\\\hline 12)770\\\hline 64\tfrac{1}{8}\end{array}$$

The foregoing is sufficiently correct for any practical purpose.

Another mode of finding the quantity of weft that is required—make 50 yards the standard, or fixed number of yards to calculate by, multiply the breadth of the web in inches by the shots on the glass, and the product by 33, and the answer will be the number of hanks, after taking off the two figures at the right hand.

Suppose the Web is 35 inches broad, and 11 shots to be on the glass; then $35 \times 11 = 385 \times 33 = 127\cdot 05$.

$$\begin{array}{r}35\text{ Inch.}\\11\text{ Shots.}\\\hline 385\\33\\\hline 1155\\1155\\\hline\end{array}$$

127.05 = 127 Hanks of Weft.

If the foregoing length do not suit, it will be an easy matter to find a number to multiply by for any other length that the Manufacturer or Manager wishes to rate by.

CHAPTER II.

WEAVING.

WEAVING is the making of cloth from yarn or threads; this is the most simple explanation of the word. Like all other arts that are carried on to any extent, the division of labour is found to be advantageous in weaving also. The first process is winding, and it may be mentioned here, that the ancient mode of winding, warping, and weaving, was as follows :—winding they had none, as they spun the yarn on a spool or bobbin or into balls; and when a web was to be made, only one bobbin was taken at a time. The whole warping and weaving apparatus that was required was two sticks, like walking canes, a little longer than the breadth of the intended piece of cloth: these sticks were placed in the ground at two or three yards apart, the length of the web; then taking the bobbin in hand, the person ran round the two sticks, making the warp of the web. After the proper quantity of yarn was fixed on the two sticks, the web was made, and the weft put in, much in the same manner as darning a hole in a stocking, so that the primitive weaver required neither heddles, treadles, reeds, nor shuttles. But now in our days, winding machines, warping machines, dressing machines, twisting frames, and weaving machinery, are all required to bring out the cloth at a cheap rate. The yarn as it comes from the spinning factories, is either in cope or hank, except when in some instances the spinners have both winding and warping, and sell their yarn warped on beams, ready to be put into the dressing machine; but when it is silk, worsted, or linen, it is generally got in hank. Then the power-loom weaver requires winding and warping machines, which will now be explained.

WINDING.

There are many varieties of Winding Machines, but they are all made to perform the same thing, although some do it better than others. The best winding machines for winding water twist yarn, or the yarn from small bobbins on to larger ones, are those that have the following improvements applied to them: the small bobbins as they come from the throstle frames to the winder are full of yarn (the yarn being spun on them). The small bobbins are put on a verticle spindle, running in a step and collar, tapered like a cone. When the throstle bobbin is put on, the bobbin being on a tapered part of the spindle, its own weight is sufficient to keep it tight on the spindle, that when the yarn is winding, the small spindle turns with the bobbin.

This is a great improvement over the old mode, when the throstle bobbins had to run on a rod of iron or wood, causing the bushes in the bobbin to be more worn in the winding than they were in the spinning; and those who are acquainted with the throstle spinning, will know the bad effect that this produces. Another improvement is a thin plate of iron put along the machine with small slits in it, one for each thread, and the yarn, when in the process of winding, passing through this slit, it takes off all the loose pieces of cotton seed or what is called gins, or any other loose substance that may be sticking to the yarn. It also serves to catch bad piecings, when the winder ought to take them off and knot the ends anew. After this, the thread passes through a brush, or over a woollen cloth, put on the machine in order to keep the yarn clean. In many of the machines yet in use, there is just one rod of iron for the ends to run under for building or guiding the yarn on to the large bobbins, but it is better to have a small piece of wire for each thread or spindle, with the one end of it screwed, so as it can be set up or down when required, and this will save all the washers or pieces of leather or cloth that is put underneath the bobbins to make them build properly. But even with all these improvements, if the winder is not careful, bad piecing and lumps on the yarn will be passed.

The winding of cope (or mule) yarn is done in the same kind of machine, with this exception, that the copes are put on to skewers, and winded from the cope standing upright. But if the cope does not run till it is finished, which frequently happens, the skewer is put in a horizontal position and allowed to run free in centres, and at the same time steady: this is accomplished by having the centres made moveable, and held up to the end of the skewer with a small spring. In winding warp from the hank, swifts or whisks are used, and as it is more difficult to do, the winder is not able to keep so many spindles employed as with the former. Sometimes a different kind of machine is used for this kind of winding, as the hank yarn takes up more room than the cope or bobbin. This machine has no cylinder nor spindles, and of course requires no banding for driving the spindles. It has one shaft the whole length of the frame, with small drums on it, one for each bobbin. The drums are made to fit the size of the bobbin between its ends. This machine has the advantage over the spindle kind, as the yarn always runs at the same speed; whereas, in the spindle machine, the speed of the yarn increases as the bobbin fills.

The next machine we will notice is for winding weft, or what is called a Pirn Winding Machine; but to describe all the different kinds that have been made during the last thirty years, would take up too much time. The best that have yet been made are those that have the mechanism or contrivance for accomplishing the following things:—A separate building apparatus for each spindle; also one to stop the spindle when the thread breaks; also the plan to prevent doubles (that is, two ends going on the pirn at the same time), and the mechanism to make the yarn run at the same speed at the thick part of the pirn as at the small. When the machine wants this apparatus, the quantity winded is much smaller than with it. Also the apparatus for stopping the spindle when the pirn has received its proper quantity of weft.—A machine made with all these appliances will make a pirn much superior to the pirns wound by the hand.

WARPING.

Having explained winding and the winding machine, the next process in the art of weaving is warping, and it is done both by hand and power.

Warping by hand requires a person with some knowledge of arithmetic, where complicated patterns are to be made in the warp, but this is treated on in another place. The common warping mills are constructed of different circumferences and heights, but those most in use are the five-ell mills; it is a reel with 3 rows of arms, and 20 arms in each row: on the end of the arms are fixed 20 spokes, and these spokes are divided into 20 equal parts

$11\frac{1}{4}$ inches, which is $\frac{1}{4}$ of an ell to each; so $20 \times 11\frac{1}{4} = 225$ inches $\div 5$, is equal to 5 ells. The arms are mortised into three centres, and these centres are put on a piece of wood with iron pivots at each end for the mill to run upon: the mill is placed perpendicular, and the web is warped on to it from the bobbins in the bank in a spiral form. The length of the web is regulated by the number of turns the warper gives the mill before reversing its motion, and the breadth of the web is according to the quantity of bobbins in the bank, and the number of bouts the warper gives the mill. After the proper quantity of yarn is on the mill to form the web, it is taken off by the warper in links and put up into a chain; but before taking it off, a lease must be taken with the heck for the drawer or twister's guidance.

Warping by power is far more simple than by hand, and is done cheaper. In general, the fourth part of the web is warped at once, by putting into the bank a sufficient number of bobbins to make up the fourth part, and putting all the ends through two reeds, with one thread in the split, the reeds being of the proper sit to keep the warp on the beam the same breadth as the intended web; the reed nearest the bank is made in the common way, but the other which is to conduct the yarn on to the beam, has every alternate split filled with solder, about an inch from its rim, for the purpose of taking the lease.

There are many different kinds of warping machines

in use—the make most approved of is what is called the Cylinder Warping Machine, with its latest improvements, which are explained in another place, our object here being to show how the warping is done in these Machines.

Suppose a 12^{00} with 1160 splits or 2320 ends, is to be warped, then the fourth of 2320 is 580 bobbins, which will require to be put into the bank, each space in the bank holding 20 bobbins, leaving 29 spaces to be filled up to make the number 580, or $14\frac{1}{2}$ spaces on each side of the bank. Care should always be taken to have an equal quantity on each side of the bank, so that there may be an equal quantity of yarn on each side of the beam, from its centre, otherwise the yarn will be badly warped. After all the bobbins are in the bank, and the yarn taken through the two reeds, a rod of wood is cut the exact length of the space of the reed which is filled with the yarn, and the cylinder is made up to the same length as the rod, then the beam is flanged to answer the cylinder; when this is done, and the measuring apparatus set at its proper place, the Warping commences. After a little yarn is on the beam, it is common to hang a weight at each end of it, so as to make the yarn build harder on the beam, but it will be obvious, that unless the beam be of equal weight at both ends, it will have what is called a slack side, which is very annoying to the dresser, and makes the yarn after it is dressed, break more when it is being woven in the loom. The machine, and all the other things being adjusted, the warper's duty is to watch when any of the threads break, stop the machine, and take the ends in (although some machines have an apparatus that when a thread is broken it stops itself.) With the old Warping Machines, a long practice was required before the worker was able to stop it properly, as they had no fly-wheels; but with the new machines, nothing more is required than to shift the belt from the fast pulley to the loose one, as the fly-wheel does the rest. The use of the fly-wheel on a Warping Machine is to allow the bobbins to stop gradually, for if the machine was stopped instantly, they would over-run, and break the threads. There is also a small roller, made of wood, used for this purpose, which floats upon the yarn, and if the beam is instantly stopped, the weight of the roller keeps the yarn from being slack, by it descending a little towards the floor.

Suppose the length that is wanted is 6000 yards, the warper must watch when that quantity is indicated on the measuring apparatus, and take out the full beam, and put in an empty one, then go on as before, till he has four beams filled, which makes the set for the web.

TO WARP STRIPPED WORK.

If the pattern is to be 2 of blue (or any other colour), and 2 of white; or 4 of blue, and 4 of white; or 6 of blue, and 6 of white, or any other pattern that is half-and-half, up to 40 ends of the one, and 40 of the other, it may be warped 2 beams of blue, and 2 beams of white, and the exact pattern is made by the twister when twisting the web; or if the pattern is $\frac{1}{4}$ of one colour, and $\frac{3}{4}$ of another, then warp 3 beams of the one and 1 beam of the other, and the drawer or twister makes the pattern. But if a pattern similar to the following is wanted :—

        24 of Brown.
         4 " White.
         4 " Red.
        14 " White.
         2 " Red.

which is 48 ends in all, in 1 repeat of the pattern, and say the pattern is repeated 42 times, then 48 × 42 = 2016 ÷ 4, is 504 ends on each beam, which may be warped as follows :—

2 beams with 6 Brown and 2 beams 6 Brown.
        1 White,   1 White.
        1 Red,   1 Red.
        3 White,   4 White.
        1 Red.
         12   12

Another example of this kind will show how the most difficult pattern can be warped on beams :—

      60 ends of Brown.
       2 " Red.
       2 " Orange.
       2 " Yellow.

THE ART OF WEAVING.

8	"	Green.
2	"	Brown.
20	"	Slate.
2	"	Brown.
8	"	Green.
2	"	Yellow.
2	"	Orange.
2	"	Red.
10	"	White.
10	"	Brown.
10	"	White.
4	"	Red.
14	"	White.
14	"	Brown.
4	"	Green.
2	"	Orange.
20	"	Brown.
20	"	Slate.

9 times over.

2 Beams with 15 Brown, and 2 Beams 15 Brown.

1 Red,	1 Orange.
1 Yellow,	2 Green.
2 Green,	1 Brown.
5 Slate,	5 Slate.
1 Brown,	2 Green.
2 Green,	1 Yellow.
1 Orange,	1 Red.
2 White,	3 White.
3 Brown,	2 Brown.
2 White,	3 White.
1 Red,	1 Red.
4 White,	3 White.
4 Brown,	3 Brown.
1 Green,	1 Green.
	1 Orange.
5 Brown,	5 Brown.
5 Slate,	5 Slate.

The following will show how the pattern should be on paper, and that paper is to be given to the warper, then the dresser, and after the Web is dressed, the drawer gets it for his guidance:

		2 Beams.	2 Beams.
60	Brown,	15	15
2	Red,	1	0
2	Orange,	0	1
2	Yellow,	1	0
8	Green,	2	2
2	Brown,	0	1
20	Slate,	5	5
2	Brown,	1	0
8	Green,	2	2
2	Yellow,	0	1
2	Orange,	1	0
2	Red,	0	1
10	White,	2	3
10	Brown,	3	2
10	White,	2	3
4	Red,	1	1
14	White,	4	3
14	Brown,	4	3
4	Green,	1	1
2	Orange,	0	1
20	Brown,	5	5
20	Slate,	5	5
220		55	55

9 times over.

9 times over means that the pattern is repeated 9 times in the breadth of the Web, which in this pattern makes 1980 ends, and say 8 threads for the selvage, gives 1988 in all, and this divided by 4, makes 497 ends for each beam.

To warp patterns with fine and coarse yarn, the best method is to put the coarse on one beam, and the fine on another, and make the pattern in the dressing machine, or, by the drawer, when drawing the web into the heddles, whatever way the pattern answers best; but if both the coarse and fine are put on one beam, it will then be necessary to bank for the pattern, and in taking the yarn through the warper's reed, it must be observed that splits will require to be left empty in proportion to the coarse yarn; for example, if the fine yarn is No. 60's, and the coarse No. 20's, then one thread of 20's must have the space of 3 splits to keep it from forming a larger diameter on the beam than the fine. Suppose the pattern to be 80 threads of No. 60's, and 10 threads of No. 20's, then the 10 threads of 20's would require to be drawn through the warper's reed, 1 split full, and 2 splits empty alternately, and the 60's will have 1 thread in each split as usual.

In power-loom warping it is a common practice for the warper to take out the bobbins before they are run near empty. Sometimes a considerable quantity of yarn is left on them, and to avoid this as much as possible, the barrel of the bobbins should be at least $1\frac{1}{4}$ inch in diameter, for if they be less the bobbins will not run until they are empty, without the risk of the yarn breaking frequently. Another advantage is gained by having the barrel of the bobbins large, namely, that less yarn is allowed to go to waste, the bobbins are stronger, and less liable to be broken.

Some Manufacturers have their bobbins painted different colours, a colour for each size; when this is done, the warper can see at once when the yarn is mixed.

BEAMING.

After the process of warping next comes beaming (if the web is to be dressed in the loom), which is to put the warp on the weaver's beam in a proper manner. The first thing is to ascertain the number of half-gangs, and the breadth of the web, then pass two rods through the half-gang lease, which is made by the warper for the purpose of getting the Web put into the ravel. After this is done, the ravel must be set to answer the breadth of the web, then fix the end of the chain to the beam, and commence winding it on. Ravels are now made to answer any set, the old kinds were made like reeds, and marked 5, 6, 7, or 8 score, according to the fineness of the ravel.

The beamer must be particular to tie all the broken threads, and in doing so, not to cross them, or the weaver will have a deal of unnecessary trouble in making his Web, by being obliged to stop frequently to take out the crossed yarn and put it in its proper place. Many of the beams yet used by the hand-loom weavers have no flanges on them to support the selvage of the Web; and it is necessary to have the ravel coarser than the

Web, to form the headings in the process of beaming; this is done by holding the ravel oblique, as the beaming proceeds.

In beaming for the power-loom, the Web, or Chain must be starched or sized before commencing to beam.

Generally the machine is driven by power. Sometimes a reed is used instead of a ravel, and two threads put into one split of the reed, with a rod between them, so that when the yarn is wound on the beam, every thread takes its own place. This sort of beaming does much better for power-loom weavers in general, than having the Web beamed in half-gangs. When the chain or Web is to be beamed in this manner, the warper of the chain will require to take a thread lease at both ends of the chain: it is obvious that the yarn will have less chance of being crossed on the beam when it is beamed in this way.

When the yarn is dyed in the chain and is to be dressed in the dressing machine afterwards, the reed should be used instead of the ravel, as it is more convenient for the dresser, and for making patterns in the warp.

For large quantities of one pattern, a considerable saving is made by having the yarn dyed in the chain, and the white bleached, as it does not require to be reeled into hank first, and then winded after having been dyed. The same principle as stated under warping for making patterns, will answer for making the pattern in the beaming machine. For example: the pattern to be made has in it white, green, blue, orange, and black. The pattern being drawn out on paper in the usual way, it can be ascertained how many ends of each colour will be required to make the Web, then dye a chain for each colour, and indent them at the beaming machine according to pattern. When a number of chains are required for one Web, the beamer must be very careful to have them all kept the same tightness; otherwise, some parts of the yarn will be overstrained.

SIZING AND DRESSING.

SIZING

Is to put the yarn that forms the warp of the Web through a process whereby the fibres of the thread are all laid or glued together. There have been many different ways of accomplishing this.

The method used by the hand-loom weaver is to put the dressing on with two hand brushes, but before beginning to put the paste on, the lease rods will require to be taken back from their working place, to the yarn beam, and that part of the yarn that is to be dressed, should be cleared of all lumps, and the long ends of knots that would damage the cloth, or retard the progress of the weaving; when this is done, the dressing should be brushed on tenderly and regular, so as not to have one part of the Web with too much, and the other part with too little of the size. The weaver then separates the threads of the Warp with the lease rod, by turning it on its edge; he then uses a fan for the purpose of drying the Warp, at the same time, using one of the brushes to keep the threads from sticking together. After the Warp is dried, sometimes a little soap or tallow is brushed over it, to make the Web smoother. It is a very important part of the hand-loom weaver's work, to be able to dress his Web well; and it may be stated here, that when dressed yarn is allowed to stand (with the common dressing generally used), for any considerable time before being woven into cloth, the air has a tendency to make it hard and brittle, and the yarn then has little or no elasticity, which makes it very difficult for the weaver to work; besides, the cloth is not so smooth and even, and the drier the weather is, the effect will be the worse.

Another mode of sizing warps, although it cannot be called dressing, is to put the whole chain or chains as the case may be, through a starching machine. This machine has the starch boiling in a large cistern, and the chain is conducted (in the shape of a rope) through this cistern by means of rollers working inside of it; and after it has traversed for a sufficient length of time in the starch, it moves out at the opposite side of the cistern from where it entered, and passes through between two rollers which presses the superflous starch out of the chain; it then passes round a number of steam cans for the purpose of being dried. The number of cans in this machine are various, the more cans the greater the power of drying; and it is the drying power of the machine that regulates its speed.

After the chain has passed over all the cans, it is rolled up into a ball, and if required, put through the machine again. (This is called double starching.) When a chain is put through the second time, the weaver does not require to dress his Web. A great many chains now are done in this manner, as it requires less labour from the weaver, and consequently the cloth is woven cheaper. However, this will only do for certain kinds of work; where the yarn or reed is very fine, it still requires to be dressed in the loom or dressing machine.

To prevent the yarn of the chain being torn or cut in the process of starching, (which frequently happens), the rollers should be kept very smooth, and the starch put through a sieve, to take out any impurities that may be mixed with the flour. The chains that are starched in this kind of machine, should be allowed to lie in some damp place for at least twenty-four hours' before being beamed, otherwise the yarn will be brittle. Also care must be taken to put them in a place that is free from rats and mice.

DRESSING.

The Old Crank Dressing Machine is the best yet out for making good work when the yarn is fine. It is also well adapted for coloured yarns; but the drawback with it in common work, is the small quantity that can be produced, although it may yet be improved in this respect. (See crank dressing machine).

The yarn is first warped on four beams, and two beams put at each end of the machine. It is then drawn through the back reed, two threads in each split; from this reed it is drawn into the copper (or hole board), with one thread in each hole, this keeps every thread perfectly distinct, and from the copper into the fore-reed, with one in each split. The fore-reed is made so as a lease can be taken with it; but in putting the Web at first into the machine, it is better to draw dressed yarn into the coppers and reeds, and then twist the beams to the yarn in them. This is in general done by the person that draws the Webs for the looms.

To work the Crank Machine properly the following observations will be found useful to the new beginner: The machine should stand perfectly level on the floor; this can be ascertained by putting a straight edge along the machine, and applying a spirit level on the straight edge, and then putting it across the rolls. When it is made level and fixed down to the floor, set the yarn so that when the yarn is stretched in the machine it will be level also. Then pitch the machine for the brushing. This is done by taking the wheels out of gear that drives the wyper shafts, and placing the one shaft with the full part of its wypers exactly up, and the other with its wypers exactly the reverse. The crank shaft is then turned with its crank fair up or down as the case may be, so as to make the brushes take hold of the yarn when they are in the act of moving from the copper. The wheels should all be put into gear again when the three shafts are in the position above described, and the machine will then be pitched. A piece of cloth or leather of an equal thickness, the size of the friction wheel, should be put in between it and the plate. Some oil and a little black lead should be used to make the friction work regularly. If the machine is new it should be allowed to run for a short time without the yarn for the purpose of seeing that all the working parts are correct.—It is essential that all the dressing rolls be of the same diameter, otherwise the yarn will be strained in some parts more than it should be. The belts for the fans and brushes being on and other little things in their places, the machine is ready for dressing, the workman must temper the dressing to answer the fabric of the cloth. This can only be known by experience, but the first Web after it is in the loom will give an idea what is required. The yarn after passing through between the dressing rolls should continue in a moist state until it passes through the copper, but never allowed to go on to the weaver's beam before it is properly dried. Many a web has been spoiled by allowing the yarn to go on damp. The brushes must be kept clean by being washed regularly. Some workmen wash them every hour, some every two hours, and so on; but it altogether depends on the kind of work and the quality of the yarn, as foul yarn will require that they be oftener washed than clean yarn. When all things are nicely set about the machine, the workman has just to move about and watch that the yarn is properly dried, and be very expert to mend any broken thread before it is out of his reach, and then he will have no complaints about bad work.

CYLINDER MACHINE.

This is another Machine for Dressing Warps, and does its work very well with coarse yarns, but it is not so well adapted for fine as the crank machine. The observations made for working the Crank will also apply to the Cylinder Machine:—the difference is, that it has no hole board. It has the back reed, the brush reed, the fore reed, and a set of heddles for taking the lease. It derives its name (cylinder) from the brushes, as they are made cylindrical, and brush the yarn as they revolve. To have the reed at the brush properly set is very important, and the proper way is to have it so as the brush may just touch the yarn with the points of the hair. This is regulated by thumb screws, with their points resting on the side framing of the machine.

The dressing used in these machines is in general made from American sour flour, and is prepared in the following manner:—the flour is steeped in the proportion of 5 pounds of flour to 3 gallons of water, for two or three days. It is then put into the boiler and boiled for about two hours. When it is sufficiently boiled the dressing is drawn off, and put into tubs, and allowed to stand for two or three days more, before it is used, for, when it is used too new, the yarn is not well dressed.

TAPE LEG DRESSING MACHINE.

A machine has been in use for twelve or fifteen years, which is known by the name tape leg dressing machine (see tape leg dressing machine), it combines both the starching and dressing, and the yarn is put on the weaver's beam, at the same time. There are different kinds of these machines, which will be explained under the head sizing and dressing machines, it will be sufficient to notice here the working of it, which is very simple. The yarn for this machine should be warped as wide on the beams as the machine will take in, so as to give it the greatest power of drying. The warpers' beams are placed in such a manner as to allow the yarn on the beam, next to the machine, to unwind from the top, and the second from the bottom, the third from the top, the fourth from the bottom, and so on alternately, from top and bottom. The yarn is then taken and tied to cords, or pieces of an old chain, previously placed in the machine, round the cylinder, and over and under the different rollers that the warp has to pass in the process of dressing. The steam should now be put on, and after the dressing is brought to the boiling point, the yarn is submerged into it, and the machine put on till the dressed yarn reaches the weaver's beam. Then the yarn is put into the ravel, to answer the breadth of the intended web. The workman requires to calculate the number of threads that are to be put into each pin to bring out the proper width, and it is requisite, before stopping the machine (when it is to stand for more than five minutes), to take the yarn out of the boiling dressing. This is done by winding up the copper rolls that keep it submerged. If this is not attended to, the threads get all fixed one to another. To keep each thread distinct on the weaver's beam, a lease cord is put between each of the warper's beams, and run through the machine, until they come within a few inches of the ravel; and then round iron rods are put into the place where the lease cords are, and these rods remain in their place till all the yarn is dressed that is on the warper's beams. This machine should have the elastic ravel, and the new improved keeling motion to make it complete.

DRAWING OR ENTERING.

When the Web is beamed, either by a beaming machine, or in the dressing machine, it is ready for the drawer. The beam is then hung up with two ropes or iron hoops about six feet from the floor, and a sufficient length of yarn turned off, so as to allow the end of it to come down to the drawer, who sits on a stool, with the heddles before him. Two rods are inserted into where the lease cords are, these lease cords are put into the Web either at the warping mill, or dressing machine. The ends of the rods are then fixed together, and the warp spread out to its proper breadth. The ingiver takes thread by thread, and hands it to the drawer, to take through the heddles with a hook, and the drawer takes the heddles in regular succession according to the draught of the Web. When the Web is drawn into the heddles, it next requires to be put into the reed, which is in general done by the same person, who has a sley hook for the purpose. He commences at the right hand side of the Web, and takes out the number of threads from the heddles that are intended to go into one split.

This operation being done, the Web is ready to be put into the loom, which is explained under weaving.

TWISTING.

As drawing and reeding a Web is more expensive

than twisting one, they are always twisted, except when new heddles are required. This operation is performed by boys.

The heddles and reed, as they come from the loom with the yarn in them, are hung up in the twisting frame, opposite the Web. The twister puts a piece of rope round the pulley, on the end of the beam, or round the beam itself, and hangs a weight to the end of it. He then takes a portion of the yarn, and fixes it between his knees, till once the rods are put into the lease of the Web. After the rods are in, and the yarn all made straight, he begins to twist the ends of the Web, to the ends that are in the heddles. He picks out the yarn from the rods in the Web, with his right hand, and twists with his left.

In drawing or twisting Webs that have difficult draughts, or patterns, the worker should get his instructions given him on a piece of paper, and this should be kept before him, until he can do without it.

DRAUGHTS AND TREADING.

After the Web is put into the heddles and reed, it it ready for the loom; but before beginning to explain the operation of making it into cloth, it has been deemed proper to give the draught and treading of a few different kinds of fabrics, and the description given here, will answer for both the hand and power-loom. The explanations for mounting the different tweels will be given under another head.

PLAIN CLOTH.

Is made by causing every thread of the warp and weft to cross each other at right angles, and tacked together alternately. This is done, by drawing the Web into two leaves of heddles with equal quantities on each leaf. But a plain Web is in general drawn on four leaves, to keep the heddles from being too crowded on their shafts, and the two fore leaves are fixed together as one, and the two back ones, as another, and mounted in the loom, as if they were just two leaves. The figures as shown at No. 1, is the draught of a plain Web with four leaves.

No. 1

	4		
2		6	R.
	3		
1		5	S.

The figures 1, 2, 3, 4, 5, and 6, show how the yarn is drawn through the headles, and R S are the shafts.

They are sunk and raised alternately, to form plain texture. The term plain cloth as applied here, must be understood as the kind of weaving, as there are many fabrics made by plain weaving, that are not commonly called plain cloth, such as the great variety of ginghams, fancy dresses, blue and white checks, &c.; but only to distinguish it from that class of goods where the yarn is flushed, and it is this flushing that forms all the variety of tweels, and figures, that are made in the loom by the warp and weft, being produced by the order and succession in which the weft is interwoven with the warp.

TWEELING.

Tweeled cloth is made for many different purposes. But before proceeding further, it may be remarked, that so far as its strength depends on the mode of weaving, it is rather diminished than increased, when compared with plain cloth, containing an equal quantity of warp and weft; for, in making plain cloth, as stated before, every thread is alternately interwoven, while in that of tweels, they are only interwoven at intervals, according to the kind of tweel. Now in the latter case, the threads can have no support from each other, except at the intervals where they are caught by the weft, and that part of them which is flushed, must depend on the strength of the individual threads, those of the warp being flushed upon one side, and those of the weft upon the other.

For illustration, take the following:—Let two Webs be made of equal length, breadth, quantity, and fineness of yarn; let the one be plain, and the other tweeled, and their strength as far as material is concerned, ought to be the same. But if the strength is to be understood by the durability of its wear, the tweeled cloth, will be worn out, long before the plain cloth is much injured.

Tweeling is adopted for the purpose of getting a greater quantity of yarn put in the same space, which this mode of weaving affords, and the larger the tweel is, the heavier the cloth can be made; this will be easily illustrated: When the shed of any Web is opened, every thread of warp, either above or below the thread of weft, will oppose a certain resistance to the operation of weaving. Now in plain cloth, every thread is alternately interwoven, and therefore, opposes its portion of resistance, whereas, in a six leaf tweel, every sixth thread is only intersected, and it will easily be seen, that less resistance will be given to get the weft on.

A THREE LEAF TWEEL.

Three leaves are the smallest quantity that can make a tweel, and its fabric comes nearest to the fabric of plain cloth. There are a great many different kinds of cloth made by the three leaf tweel, such as jane stripes for shirting, ticking for beds, and pillows, furniture stripes, &c. &c. From Figure No. 2, it will be seen, that two-thirds of the warp, is on one side of the cloth, and two thirds of the weft upon the other; this is accomplished by sinking two leaves, and raising one every shot.

No. 2

		3
	2	
1		

No. 3

3		6	1	4	
	2	5		2	5
1	4			3	6

It will also be observed, that the yarn is drawn through the headles, as follows—one thread on the first, or front leaf, one thread on the second leaf, and one on the third, or back leaf; and the first shed is to sink the first and second leaves, and raise the third; the second shed is to sink the first and third leaves, and raise the second; the third shed is to sink the second and third, and raise the first, and repeat.

To make what is called a herring bone tweel, with three leaves, the same treading as above will do, but the draught will be as follows:—Suppose the cloth is for bed tick, and the pattern 12 of blue, and 12 of white—Then the Web will require to be drawn as shown in No. 3, which is 6 threads of blue drawn through the headles, beginning with the first leaf, and 6 threads beginning with the third, and the white drawn in the same manner. It will be observed that the tweel turns upon two threads, which does not make the herring bone so neat; but if it be drawn, as shown in No. 4, with 10

No. 4

	3		6		9		13		16		19	
2		5		7		10	12	15		17		20
1		4			8	11	14			18		

threads of blue, and 10 threads of white, then the tweel will turn on one thread, which is the proper way.

A FOUR LEAF TWEEL

Can either be drawn straight over, or a headle on each leaf alternately; when it is drawn straight over as shown in No. 5, the first shed is

No. 5

E				4	D	4 fourth.
			3		C	3 third.
		2			B	2 second.
	1				A	1 first.

the back leaf up and the other three down; the second is the third leaf up and the other three down; the third is the second up and the other three down; and the fourth shed is the first (or front) leaf up and the other three down. Let the beginner understand this figure No. 5 thoroughly, and there will be no difficulty with the other tweels that follow. That part of the figure at E, is a representation of design paper, or the cloth with a four leaf tweel, and the dark squares are the warp threads that are above the weft, and the white squares are those that are below it. The spaces that are marked A B C D, represent the leaves of the headles, and A is the leaf next to the lay, or what is called the front leap; the figures 1, 2, 3, 4, are the draught in the headles once over,

If a four leaf tweel be drawn as shown in No. 6, which is the common way for the power loom, it being more convenient where both plain and tweel cloth are working in the same factory; because by this draught, plain cloth is made by fixing the two front leaves together as one, and the two back ones as another, and fewer spare thrums will be required, as they will do for either tweel or plain.

No. 6

				4	D	4
				2	C	3
				3	B	2
				1	A	1

In this plan the treading will be different; the fourth leaf will be raised first; the second, second; the third, third; and the first fourth.

A very large quantity of cloth is made by a four leaf tweel, where the warp and weft are equal on both sides of the cloth, this is managed by sinking two leaves, and raising two alternately.

Take No. 6 for an example—

    1st sink A and C
    2nd   "   B " C
    3rd   "   B " D
    4th   "   A " D

This tweel answers better for sheeting and skirt lining than the common four leaf tweel. The appearance it has on the cloth is shown by figure No. 7, the sheding being repeated two times over.

No. 7

A FIVE LEAF TWEEL.

Figure 8 is a regular Five Leaf Tweel, and figure 9 is what is called a broken one. And in these two

THE ART OF WEAVING.

No. 8

				▨	5
			▨		4
		▨			3
	▨				2
▨					1

No. 9

	▨			5
		▨		4
▨				3
		▨		2
▨				1

figures, as in the other plans that follow, the black squares are the leaves that are raised, and the white ones those that are sunk, and the numbers 1, 2, 3, 4, 5, are the draught.

SIX LEAF TWEEL.

No. 10 is a Six Leaf Tweel, and No. 11 is the same broken.

No. 10

				▨		6
			▨			5
		▨				4
	▨					3
▨						2
▨						1

THEORY AND PRACTICE OF

No. 11

No. 12 IS A REGULAR SEVEN LEAF TWEEL.

No. 13 Broken.

No. 14 IS A REGULAR EIGHT LEAF TWEEL.

No. 15 Broken.

No. 16 IS A REGULAR NINE LEAF TWEEL.

No. 17 Broken.

The examples given will be sufficient to show how regular tweeling is done. It is seldom that more than nine leaves are used for a regular tweel, for when the tweel is large and regular, the cloth has the appearance of small diagonal stripes, but when the draught or treading is changed, so as to raise the warp threads at intervals, of one, two, three or more from each other, the tweel will be broken, and the cloth will not have the corded appearance.

The following plans are all Broken or Fancy Tweels, and they may be varied according to taste. But when it is possible, the intervals should be regular, as it makes the tweel more perfect; and the tweel is said to be imperfect when the number of leaves will not admit of this.

It will be observed in the foregoing examples of tweels, that one leaf is raised, and the others sunk; but in what follows, they are sunk and raised in all varieties to make the pattern wanted. No. 18 is the tweel generally called the blanket tweel; it is also used for making sheeting, and a number of other fabrics.

No. 18 BLANKET TWEEL.

			4
			3
			2
			1

No. 19 is a five leaf tweel, very much used for making table-cloths; and No. 20 is an eight leaf damask tweel, also much used in making table-linens. We will have more to write about this tweel under damask weaving.

THE ART OF WEAVING.

No. 19 A FIVE LEAF TWEEL FOR TABLE-CLOTHS, AND No. 20 IS AN EIGHT LEAF DAMASK TWEEL.

No. 19.

No. 20.

No. 21 A TEN LEAF FANCY TWEEL.

No. 22 A TWELVE LEAF FANCY TWEEL.

No. 23 A SIXTEEN LEAF TWEEL, WHICH IS CALLED THE FULL SATIN TWEEL.

		▨														16
				▨												15
						▨										14
								▨								13
										▨						12
		▨														11
				▨												10
						▨										9
								▨								8
										▨						7
▨																6
		▨														5
				▨												4
						▨										3
								▨								2
▨																1

DIAPER.

Having given the draught and treading of a number of tweels, it is presumed that the examples given will be sufficient to make the principles of common tweeling understood; and if so, the method of drawing Diapers, and the treading of the same will be readily comprehended. The few following patterns given here, have not been published before, so far as known to the writer: they were brought out about ten or twelve years ago, for dresses and other fancy goods, and at that time had a very good run, and I see that a number of them are still made, and sold at the present time.

Diaper weaving was at one time chiefly confined to the manufacture of towelling and table-cloths, but it is now applied to a great many different kinds of goods. At the present day, hundreds of power-looms are making nothing else but diaper cloth, which is sent to the Indian market, under the name of figured long cloths, figured shirtings, &c. &c. The diaper is also used for pinafores, cloutings, neck-ties, ribbons, and dresses of all kinds, and they are all woven on the same principle, viz:—reversing the tweel, and altering the draught. It will be obvious, that the more leaves that are used, the greater will be the scope for making a large variety of patterns; the mounting of them in the loom will be explained under the head, diaper weaving.

No. 24 A THREE LEAF DIAPER,
A IS THE DRAUGHT, & B IS THE TREADING.

No. 24 B.

		1
		2
		3
		4
		5
		6

No. 24 A.

	3	6
2		4
1	5	

This Diaper is called the Irish eye, and is the best of all for Nursery Diapers, Cloutings, and such like cloth.

No. 25 IS A FOUR LEAF DIAPER, A IS THE DRAUGHT, & B IS THE TREADING.

No. 25 B.

No. 25 A.

It will be seen on examination, that the three leaf Diaper has two-thirds of the weft thrown to the one side of the cloth, and two-thirds of the warp to the other; but the four leaf Diaper has the warp and weft equal on both sides, which makes by for the best bird-eye diaper, although the three leaved one looks much finer, if they are both woven in the same set of reeds, and both have the same quantity of shots on the glass. But suppose the warp of the three leaf tweel to be white, and the weft brown, or some other dark colour, then the one side of the cloth would be much darker than the other; this answers very well for some kinds of goods.

No. 26 A FIVE LEAF DIAPER WITH EIGHT TREADS.

No. 27.

Drawn as shown at No. 27, which is called the diamond draught, and it has eight different treads to complete the pattern.

No. 28 is also a Five Leaf Diaper with Eight Treads, and the Nos. 1, 2, 3, 4, 5, 6, 7, 8, on the right hand side of the pattern show how the treading proceeds, and all the other patterns are treaded on the same plan.

No. 28.

				1
				2
				3
				4
				5
				6
				7
				8

No. 29 is a Five Leaf Diaper. This pattern when woven, has the appearance of being striped, and makes a neat little pattern for a cravat or neck-tie, when made in silk or worsted.

No. 29.

				1
				2
				3
				4
				5
				6
				7
				8

No. 30 is a Five Leaf Diaper, with Ten Treads, and answers for the same kind of cloth as No. 29; it has a bolder appearance when the warp and weft are different colours.

No. 30.

▨	▨			1
	▨	▨		2
	▨	▨		3
		▨		4
	▨	▨		5
▨			▨	6
	▨		▨	7
		▨		8
▨	▨			9
	▨	▨		10

No 31 is a Five Leaf Diaper, with Eight Treads; the figure in this one appears smaller than in No's. 29 and 30.

No. 31.

▨		▨		1
▨				2
	▨			3
		▨		4
▨		▨		5
		▨		6
	▨			7
▨				8

No. 32 is also a Five Leaf Diaper, and is the last one with five leaves that will be given in this place;

the cloth of it is firmer than the preceding ones, and will be better adapted for bleached cloth than for coloured goods.—It has only Eight Treads too.

No. 32.

No. 33 is a Diaper with Six Leaves, and has Ten Treads to complete the pattern; and although it has six leaves and ten treads, it makes as firm a piece of cloth as four leaves and six treads can do.

No. 33.

No 34 is another Six Leaf Diaper with Ten Treads upon it; also No. 35.

No. 34.   No. 35.

No. 36 is a Six Leaf Diaper with Ten Treads; it is very much flushed, and is a pattern that will answer well for a heavy piece of cloth.

No. 36.

No. 37 and No. 38 are both Six Leaved Diapers with Ten Treads; they are good patterns for dresses, as the figure is well brought out, and a good fabric of cloth kept up.

No. 37

No. 38

No. 39 is a Seven Leaf Diaper with Twelve Treads, which does very well for towelling, in linen, when large diaper pattrens are wanted for a fine class of goods; it also suits for figured long cloths and shirtings.

No. 39

No. 40 is an Eight Leaf Diaper with 14 Treads, and has a fine bold appearance, and will answer for the same description of goods as No. 39.

No. 40

No. 41 is another Eight Leaf Diaper with 14 Treads, from the manner of its flushing, it is well adapted for making a heavy fabric; suitable for vest pieces, or any other kind of stout cloth.

No. 41

No. 42 is an Eight Leaf Diaper with 14 Treads; it is a sort of double figure, and looks very neat in fine cloth.

No. 42

No. 43 is an Eight Leaf Diaper with 14 Treads; this one makes a kind of star.

No. 43

No 44 is a Ten Leaf Diaper with 36 Treads; it makes a very good fancy diaper figure.

No. 44

It is given in this place, merely to show that almost any range can be taken, by increasing the number of movements in the round of the barrel so as to get more treads, and by putting on more flanges to increase the headle leaves, if the loom will admit of the mounting. From No. 26 to No. 44 inclusive, are all drawn the diamond draught, which is shown at No. 27.

CHAPTER III.

ON STARTING POWER-LOOMS.

In the preceding pages we have given a general outline of how a Web should be prepared, and brought it forward till it is ready for the loom ; also a number of draughts, and how the headles should be treaded. We will now endeavour to show how the yarn is to be made into cloth ; and as it is the loom that makes the cloth, an explanation of how it should be worked is deemed necessary.

Manufacturers, Managers, and Tentors, or those who have the charge of setting Power-looms agoing, should have a complete knowledge of the whole Theory ; and as this is intended alike for beginners, as well as for those who have got a little practice, no excuse will be made for placing before the reader, in the plainest language possible, the whole system of starting powerlooms. In another part of this work it will be taken notice of how a power-loom should be made.

The reader is now to suppose himself in a factory where the Gearing is already up, all right and ready for motion. Well, the first thing to be done is to get a plummet; take the line that is attached to the plummet, and hang it from the end of the first shaft that is to drive the looms, and where the point of the plummet touches the floor, make a mark with the point of it, and put a chalk mark round the plummet mark, then go to the other end of the shaft and plum it in the same manner. After this is done, take a cord and rub it all over with chalk, then fix it on the floor, being careful to have it passing right over the two plummet marks; then take hold of the cord with the points of the finger and thumb, near the centre, and lift it up a few inches from the floor, and then let go; this will leave the mark of the line on the floor. This line should also be drawn with a sharp point, to leave a permanent mark on the floor, so as it may be referred to at any time when required; and in some mills it is required pretty often when shifting looms, or taking down shafts and hangers. If the gearing is properly put up, all the shafts will be parallel with each other, and also with the line on the floor, so that there is no necessity for plumming all the shafts, if care be taken in the measurements.

Now, that the first line has been got across the flat of the mill or shed, as the case may be, draw a line at right angles with the first line, along the whole length of the flat, as the walls of the mill are not in general straight, it is not the proper way to take measurements from them; the proper way to get this line is off the first: take a rod of wood or a cord about ten feet long, and fix a nail or draw-point at each end, then put one point into the plummed mark which is on the first line, and draw part of a circle with the other point; then take the rod and go to the other plummet mark, and describe another part of a circle, till it intersects or crosses the other line drawn as part of a circle; when this is done, find the centre between the two plummlet marks on the first line, then stretch a cord the whole length of the flat, causing it to pass over the marks in the centre of the first line, and over that part where the circle lines cross each other. Having got both the lines drawn to take the measurements from, for placing the looms, care must be taken to have them all set parallel with the shafts, or the belts which drive the looms will not work well. At the same time that they are set with the cross line, they must be kept at the proper distance from the line that is drawn along the flat, and that distance will depend upon the space that is to be allowed for the passages. If the looms are made with the driving pulleys to suit, then they are all set at the same distance from the long line; but if the looms are made with the driving pulleys all at the same distance from the ends of the looms, then they must be set to answer the belts, by keeping the one out from the long line one inch and the breadth of the pulleys farther than the other, and so on alternately; this is done for the purpose of giving the belts room to work. When the looms are all set in their places, the next thing to be done is to get them made level: a straight edge and spirit level is required for this work. Place the straight edge along the loom, and put the level on it; if the loom is not standing fair, put a piece of wood under the foot at the low side, to bring it up to the level.—If the looms are to be placed down on stones, the stones should be made level before placing the looms upon them.

When the looms have been all set fair and square and bolted down to the floor, the next thing to be done is to look if all the wheels are properly pitched; and the workman should not mind who is the maker of them, for the very best machine makers have sometimes careless workmen, and a bad job may escape the eye of the manager at times; it is therefore better to look and see that all is right about the working parts himself, and to put a little oil on each journal before putting the driving belts on. To ascertain the length of the belt, the usual way is to take a cord and pass it round the drum and loom pulley, and measure the belt from it; but if the looms are to be driven from the flat below them, this will not be so easily done; and the method for finding the length of the belt in this case, is as follows:—Take the distance from the loom pulley to the floor, and from the floor to the shaft below; and find out the distance from the loom to the shaft, by boring a small hole in the floor, and putting down a plum-line right below the loom shaft; then measure from the cord to the shaft, and draw the drum and loom pulley on the floor, at the distance found by the measurement; also draw a line to represent the floor, and the exact place will be seen where the floor should be cut for the belt, the length of the belt can be taken from this drawing.

When putting the belt on to drive the loom, care must be taken to have all the joinings of the belt running in the same direction, and they should also run with the pulley or drum. The writer has seen workmen that had been years at the trade, who did not know, or if they did, they paid no attention to this simple rule, although it is a very important one. After fixing up the protector, and taking off the weft stopper fork, the belt should be put on and the loom allowed to run for a few hours without the shuttles; then put a reed into its place in the lay. A pair of shuttles should now be selected, and to ascertain if they are a pair, try them with callipers to see that they are both the same breadth, and place them on the race of the lay, or some other plain surface, to see if their tips are all the same distance from the bottom of the shuttle; this can be done by bringing the tips of each shuttle in contact with the tips of its neighbour; if the shuttles are not properly matched, the workmen need not expect to have a good working loom; for if the shuttle box is made to fit the one it cannot fit the other, and the shed may answer for one of the shuttles and the other dip below some of the yarn, which will spoil the cloth.

HOW TO PITCH THE LOOM.

The common meaning in the Trade as applied to Pitching a Loom, is to set the Shedding and Pitching Motion in the proper relation to each other; but the correct definition of pitching the loom extends to the fixing and setting of all its working parts; and the first thing to fix is the shuttle boxes, and the front box side should be set parallel with the back one, (not wider at the one end than it is at the other, as is very commonly done by some workmen who do not understand their business). The shuttles should go into the boxes quite easy, but not to have too much play; the boxes should be about the tenth-part of an inch wider than the shuttle is broad. After the shuttles are fitted into their boxes, the next thing is to put on the drivers, and if the lay has spindles, the drivers should be made to slide along on them quite free, and not to touch the race of the lay; when the drivers are got on, then put on the shuttle cords, keeping them both the same length, and when the lay is half way back, the drivers should come within one inch of the end of the lay. If the drivers are allowed to strike against the end of the lay, the weft copes will be in danger of being torn, and also the drivers themselves will have a tendency to be split.

The loom will now require to be what is (commonly) called pitched; that is, setting the shedding and picking motion in their proper positions in relation to the other working parts of the loom. If it is for heavy work, the shed must be full open when the lay is just at the turn to go back; if it is for muslins, then the shed should be close when the lay begins to go back. This is in general done by taking the main wheel out of gear, and turning the wyper shaft round until it comes to the proper place for the shedding. After this is accomplished, the picking pulley (or cone, or whatever other article the loom has got for giving motion to the shuttle) is next set in its proper place, and as a general rule, the lay should be nearly half way back when the shuttle begins to move. To ascertain that the picking is properly set, the workman takes hold of the lay with the one hand, and the driver with the other, and turns the loom until he feels the driver begin to move; he can then see if the lay is at its proper position, and if it is not, he alters the picking pulley to suit; if the loom is made on the right principle, the driver should come within two inches of the spindle head when the shuttle is full picked; if the driver comes up tight to the spindle head, the form of the picking apparatus has not been made right, which will cause a loss of power.

The protector or mechanism that stops the loom when any accident occurs, can now be arranged and put in right working order, so that when the shuttle is out of its place, the loom will be stopped in a proper manner; this should be attended to very carefully, as carelessness in setting this motion causes many smashes in the warp. If it is a loom with the old knock off (or chap off as it is called in Scotland) motion, with the spike and frog, the spike should be allowed to touch the frog, when the shuttle is out of the box, and be of sufficient length to have the loom stopped when the lay wants at least two-and-a-half inches from being full forward; and when the shuttle is in the box, it should clear the frog about a quarter of an inch. But if the loom be made with the fly reed motion, then the spike for stopping the loom does not act, except when the shuttle stops in the shed, and the reed is thrown back. The spike in this loom should be set so as just to touch the small nob on the handle of the loom, and the weight or spring which keeps the reed in its place when the shuttle is running must be so set as to allow it to go back at the instant the cloth begins to press upon the shuttle.

The loom should now be put on to work for a short time with the shuttles, before the Web is put into it; this is the best time to examine all the working parts again, to see if they are all in good working trim; it is also the best time to see how the shuttle runs along the lay. If it runs straight and enters the box without any stammering, it is all right; but if it has a quaver when it runs across the lay, and does not go easily into the box, then there is something wrong, and that something must be made right. The following is a few of the things that occur to cause the shuttle to run uneven:—The shuttle itself may be round on its back, which will cause it; the reed may not be fair with the back of the shuttle box; the race of the lay may not be straight; the spindle for the driver, or the grove for the tongue of the driver may be wrong; the box sides may be so placed as to cause it, or the picking itself may be too strong; and many a time it is caused by obstructions which occurs for want of cleanliness, by allowing oil and dust to cluster in small pieces about the box.

After all has been ascertained to be right, the Web can be placed in the loom; the cords are now put into the heddle shafts at the places where they will suit for the roller above, and the marches or treadles below; the heddles are then hung to the small straps for supporting them, and the reed is fixed in the lay. The eyes of the heddles should now be made to hang opposite the centre of the reed, and parallel with the race of the lay; the pace cord is next put on, and then the yarn of the Web is tied to a rod which is fixed with cords to the cloth beam; this is knotting up the Web, (as it is termed in the Trade). While knotting up the Web, the workman uses a brush to bring forward all the slack ends before he ties them; after all is tied, the heddles are moved a little backwards, and as much yarn unwound from the beam as will allow the rod to pass over the breast-beam. The heddles are next attached to the treadles, and are adjusted with the cords, straps, or screws, in such a manner as both the heddles and treadles will be even at the same time when the treadles are in contact with the wypers. By moving the loom now, it will be seen how the warps are shedded; if the sheds do not please, the heddles can be taken up or down by means of the cords, or straps, till once a proper shed is made; when the shed is full open, the warp threads should not be rubbing on the race of the lay, but as far down as just to clear it, nor touching the top rim of the reed; indeed, for light work the smaller the shed is the better, if the shuttle has sufficient room to pass freely through it; but in heavy work the sheds are made larger, for the purpose of putting a proper finish on the cloth, by spreading the warp threads, &c.

The Loom and the Web is now ready for making cloth, which can be done by putting the shuttle in with weft in it, and setting the loom in motion, either with the hand for a few shots at first, or putting on the belt. It is the workman's duty who starts the loom, to see that the proper quantity of shots are on the cloth, and that all other things are right about the loom and Web before it is left to the superintendence of the weaver; it is very annoying to the weaver to have occasion to call him back frequently to adjust some trifling thing which might have been done at first.

If the loom has a regular uptaking motion for the cloth, which requires the pinion to be changed to alter the quantity of shots, the pinion required is in general found by simple proportion; but when the loom is new, as the reader may suppose the one under explanation, the rule is very different, which will now be explained. The first thing is to ascertain the number of shots that are to be on the cloth; then find the circumference of the beam that winds up the cloth, (commonly called the card or immery beam), also the number of shots contained in the cloth, the length of which will be equal to the circumference of the beam; also count the teeth of the wheel on the end of the beam, and the number of teeth in the ratchet wheel, and from these the proper pinion will be found.

EXAMPLES.

Suppose the cloth is to have 10 shots on the glass, (Scotch glass), or 54 shots on the inch, which is nearly the same; and suppose the circumference of the beam to be 13 inches, and the wheel on the end of the beam to have 140 teeth, and the ratchet wheel 120; multiply the shots on one inch by the circumference of the beam, and divide by the number of teeth in the ratchet wheel, and the answer will be the divisor for the beam wheel, and when divided, the quotient will be the number of teeth for the pinion.

Shots on one inch,   54
Circumference of Beam,   13 Inch.
                          ―――
                           162
                            54
                          ―――
Teeth in Ratchet Wheel 120)702(5·85
                           600
                          ―――
                           102·0
                            96·0
                          ―――
                             600
                             600
                          ═══

The teeth in the wheel on the end of the beam is divided by this number, 5·85, as under:—

5·85)140·0(23·93, nearly 24 Teeth.
     1170
    ―――――
     2300
     1755
    ―――――
     5450
     5265
    ―――――
     1850
     1755
    ―――――

It will be seen from the above calculation, that the pinion required has 24 teeth, and for any other number of shots more or less, the pinion can be found by simple proportion. For example, if 10 shots require 24 teeth, what will 8 require; 8 will require more; thus,

M

```
      24
      10
     ───
  8)240
     ───
     30 Teeth for 8 Shots.
```

The principle upon which looms are made at present, a proper pinion cannot at all times be found to answer the exact number of shots; but if they were made with the shifting pinion to be the driven instead of the driver, then the proper number of teeth could be got for any given quantity of shots, and this would only require a little alteration in the construction of the loom for the uptaking motion.

Suppose the loom is all in good working order for making cloth, the weaver's principal work is to fill and shift the shuttles, and tie and take in through the heddles and reed, all the broken ends. The weft stopper will stop the loom when the weft is exhausted in the shuttle; and when a warp thread breaks in the shed in a position to make a scob or float, the scob preventor will also stop the loom, and an apparatus may also be applied to change the shuttle without stopping the loom; but those things will be explained in the next chapter, along with a number of other things that are now attached to the power-loom.

CHAPTER IV.

ON POWER-LOOMS.

The construction of Power-Looms as they were made some sixty years ago, will still be remembered by many people yet living, as it is only a comparatively short time since they were working in Messrs. John & Robert Cogans' Mill at Pollockshaws. They were at first started by Mr. John Monteith, at that village, and they are taken notice of here for the purpose of showing the young reader how the power-loom has progressed, and it may be mentioned that the principle of some of the movements about this loom has formed subjects for patents within the last twenty-five years.

The framing of the loom was made of wood, much in the same manner as the common hand-looom, and the lay swung from the top, and was made on the same plan as a hand-loom weaver's. This loom had no crank shaft or connection rods to give motion to the lay; it had only one shaft which was called the wyper shaft, placed in the same position as the wyper shaft is in the common power-loom at the present day, its length being the

(if the cloth was too thick). The spring for the purpose of pulling the lay forward was set to suit the force that was required for putting on the quantity of weft desired. With this explanation, the following description of the uptaking motion will be easily understood:—As will be seen from the drawing at figure No. 45, the beam for winding up the cloth has a wheel on its end, with the worm on the end of the small shaft working into it; on this small shaft was a ratchet wheel with its teeth about half-an-inch long, the teeth of which was made on its side, and the catch for giving motion to it was so arranged as it would take one tooth every pick of the loom just at the instant the lay was at the fell of the cloth, but if the lay moved the smallest space further forward than was necessary, it struck the top end of the catch and prevented it from turning the ratchet wheel, so that when the loom was working without weft, the cloth beam did not move. It will be obvious that the traverse of the lay could be made short or long by the setting of the uptaking motion catch; if it was set towards the breast beam the traverse would be made long in proportion, if it was set back then the traverse of the lay would be made shorter. This was a very simple way of altering the travel of the lay, and it had its advantages as well as its defects. But it will be evident to the reader who is acquainted with power-loom weaving, that this loom could never have been made to make heavy work, unless a very powerful spring had been applied to it to pull the lay forward; and as it had no protector to stop it, when the shuttle, by any accident stopped short in the shed, a strong spring would have broken the warp yarn, but with a proper protecting apparatus, this loom was well adapted for giving the weft shot a double stroke as is done by the hand-loom customer weaver, a thing that has occupied the attention of many in the power-loom trade, and a thing that could be very easily done if it was absolutely wanted. It was only necessary in this loom to make the cams that took back the lay with a double perfory, and then the fell of the cloth would get a double stroke with the lay every shot.

As already stated, the reed in this loom, was allowed to move back a little when it came to the fell of the cloth, so that when the loom went without weft the reed met with no resistance from the cloth, and the uptaking motion ceased to work. Mr. Stone had a patent loom, the reed motion of which was something similar, and he took advantage of this motion of the reed for the purpose of delivering the warp from the yarn beam, with an apparatus the same as was on this loom for the cloth beam; indeed, the moveable reed has been the principal feature in a great number of patents both here and in America.

To prevent any one who may read this from troubling himself about inventing things that has already been done, it may not be out of place to state here a number of things that has been tried in connection with the power-loom, and now all given up, or at least not in general use.

There was a power-loom Mill put up in Glasgow that had no belts at all for driving the looms; it was four or five stories high, and an upright shaft went from the bottom to the top between each pair of looms for the purpose of driving them. The bevel wheels on the upright shafts geared into bevel wheels on the looms, and when the loom was to be put in motion the weaver drew a clutch into gear with the bevel wheel which was running loose on the loom shaft. This did all very well for driving the looms, but when it had to be stopped with the old frog motion it very often broke something about the loom.

Another Mill was built about the year 1824 in a fine airy situation; it was got up with considerable taste and expense; the looms were placed in such a manner that the weavers all looked in the same direction when working; this looked very well, but the arrangement caused expense for double the quantity of gearing. Whatever was the cause, the party that started it did not succeed, and the work passed into other hands.

DOUBLE LOOM.

There was a great anxiety with some of the power-loom weavers at one time for working two Webs in one loom, and one of them made a Vertical Loom for that purpose. The yarn beams were placed next the floor, and the cloth beams at the top of the loom, and the lay or lays went up and down by means of cranks and connection rods; as a matter of course the heddles were placed below the lay horizontally, and were tied across the loom from front to back beneath the reeds; when the sheds were opened, the shuttles began to run along the face of the reed to the other side of the loom. The other movements for pacing the warp and winding up the cloth, &c., need not be explained, as this loom never came into practical use. Another party in the year 1846 got two looms made (for which a patent was obtained), for working two webs in each loom. This loom will be readily understood, as it was just one loom fixed on the top of another arranged to allow the weaver to work them (of course the framing was made to answer this arrangement) with as much facility as possible. As this loom had some advantages (for working plain light work), it deserves a few words of explanation. The top or crank shafts were the same as those in the common loom now in use; the lay was placed on slides fixed at the sides of the loom, instead of being on swords, and the connection rods were fixed to the back of the lay, so as to have the space all clear between the two Webs. This loom had no wyper shafts, and for the shedding motion, which is generally worked off the under shaft, it was mounted with a common heddle roller below the heddles, the same as above, and on the end of one of these rollers was a pinion, which geared into a segment of a wheel that received its motion from the wheel driven from a pinion on the crank shaft. (This shedding apparatus was almost the same as that applied in Todd's patent loom for working the heddles); the crank shaft pinion made two revolutions for one of the wheel, and on this wheel was placed a picking pulley for the purpose of giving motion to the shuttle, in the same manner as what is understood in the trade by the name of dog leg pick. This loom had a wheel and pinion at each side of it, which was necessary for picking the shuttle, and for the purpose of giving the weaver as much space as possible for working the under Web. The breast beam was made of cast iron, hollow below, to allow the cloth beam to be placed as close to it as possible; the uptaking motion for the cloth beam and the pace for the yarn beam were of the common kind. In this double loom the two Webs were perfectly distinct, the one could be working while the other was standing; each Web had its own weft stopper, protector, and driving belt.

The inventor of this loom expected to have got the following advantages from it:—He had a Mill that was put up for four hundred common looms, and the same space filled with the double looms would have woven eight hundred Webs; the same gearing except the drums would have done, and had there been no disadvantages, the saving would have appeared thus:—

For space 400 at 15s. each,	£300	℞ year.
., interest on gearing,	45	,,
,, interest on first cost of looms,..	20	,,
	£365	

But a larger saving was expected from another source, and that was the working of four Webs by one weaver. At the time this loom was brought out, a very strong prejudice existed among the power-loom workers in Glasgow against working four looms, and it was thought they could be got to work four Webs in two looms at a lower price per piece; taking the whole into consideration, it was not at all what may be called a bad idea.

Another loom for two Webs was made about the year 1847, but no patent was taken out for it, and it seemed to have answered the purpose of the manufacturer at the time, as he got a lot of them made after experimenting with two of the looms for some months; for what reason they were given up the writer does not know. This loom was made sufficiently broad so as to take in the two Webs, with room in the centre of the lay for a shuttle box; the two shuttles were picked at the same time. Suppose one shuttle to be in the right hand box, and the other in the centre box; when the loom is set in motion, the shuttle in the centre box is driven to the left hand box, and the one at the right hand is driven into the centre box; the next pick will be the reverse, and so on alternately. It is evident that the centre box will always have a shuttle in it every shot, and the only novel thing about this loom was the protection for stopping it when any thing happened to keep the shuttles from getting into the boxes, and this was managed by a double protecting rod, with a little extra mechanism at the centre box. The centre box had double slots or swells, and unless the shuttle was full in the box to operate on both swells, the loom would be stopped. The working of two Webs in the hand-loom on this plan is very old, and is much adopted in some districts at this present time; but this system of weaving is most profitable where expensive mountings are required, such as those that are used in weaving damasks and brocades.

AIR PUMP PICK.

The driving of the shuttles (or what is called picking) has occupied the attention of many, and many different contrivances has been tried and failed, but only one of them will be taken notice of in this place. The inventor no doubt had in his mind the great expense that power-loom weavers are at for shuttle cords, treadles, and picking sticks, and the annoyance that tentors had in adjusting the shuttle cords—it is a great pity the invention did not succeed. The shuttle, in this loom, was driven by air, and to accomplish this, a small pump was placed at one side of the loom which was driven off the under shaft by means of a crank and connection rod, which gave motion to the piston of the pump that forced the air into a vessel, and from this vessel there was a pipe taken to a small cylinder which was fixed on the under side of the sole of the lay near its centre. The cylinder was similar to the cylinder of a horizontal steam engine, with its piston rod coming out at both ends. These piston rods were made of sufficient length so as to extend to be right under the centre of the shuttle boxes, and on the ends of the rods were fixed the brackets for giving motion to the drivers; the valve of the cylinder was moved by the motion of the lay, and the air was admitted into the cylinder in the same manner as steam is admitted into a steam engine. But it will be evident that the loom would require to be driven for a short time to get up the required pressure of air before the shuttle was put in; the force given to the shuttle was regulated by the pressure of air in the chest or air vessel, and the pressure in the chest was regulated by a safety valve, which allowed the air to escape when it became too strong. The length of stroke in the air pump could be made short or long at pleasure, so as to give just the proper quantity of air required without a waste of power in driving the air pump.

THE COMMON POWER-LOOM.

What is meant here by the Common Power-loom, is a loom for working plain cloth, and a description of one of the best that is in use at the present time will be given in this place. The writer believes that the credit belongs to James & Adam Bullough, of Blackburn, for the introduction of this loom, which has been a great acquisition to the manufacturer of plain power-loom cloth; indeed, before the introduction of Bulloughs' weft stopper and fly reed, the power-loom was (comparatively speaking) very deficient, for without the weft stopper the looms used to run at times hundreds of picks without putting in a single shot of weft, and it was not only the loss of time and power when the loom was working in this way, but the selvages of the Web got all chaffy and out of order when the loom was working without weft, and this also caused a considerable time to be lost in getting the selvage yarn put right again, besides spoiling the cloth. The advantages of the weft stoppers are so evident to any power-loom weaver, that no more need be said about them, for in fact, the half of the weaver's time was taken up in watching the shuttles, so as the loom would not go without weft, knowing well the bad consequences.

THE FLY REED.

When Mr. Bullough introduced his Loom with the Fly Reed, it created quite a sensation in the trade; for before its introduction it was not considered profitable to drive above one hundred and twenty shots per minute, and now they may be driven at two hundred shots per minute, with perfect safety. The difficulty of driving the old loom (as it is now called) at a high speed was caused by the knock-off motion; whenever it was attempted to run the looms beyond a certain speed there was great danger of breaking the swords of the lay, or the connection rods, or something else; even the framing of the loom was sometimes broken, so that the fly reed gave the manufacturer the advantage of driving his looms quick without the risk of these breakages; it also gave him the advantage of having a much lighter loom to do the same work. Another saving that this loom has over the old one, is, that the lay can work with a shorter traverse, and by so doing it is easier on the yarn; and the reason that this loom can work with a shorter traverse, is, that the spike that stops the loom does not take effect on the handle till the lay is within three quarters of an inch off the fell of the cloth; whereas, with the other, it must strike the frog for stopping the loom when the lay wants about two and a half inches from the cloth.

It will be seen from the following what the patentees

themselves say about this loom, and the drawings as shown in Plate No. 5, will illustrate their inventions; the specification is given in full, so that the reader may see the legal form of such documents.

J. & A. BULLOUGH'S SPECIFICATION.

"To all to whom these presents shall come, we, James Bullough, of Blackburn, in the County of Lancaster, Machine Maker, and Adam Bullough, of the same, Overlooker, send greeting.

Whereas, Her present most Excellent Majesty Queen Victoria, by Her Letters Patent under the Great Seal of Great Britain, bearing date at Westminster, the First day of December, in the tenth year of Her reign, and in the year of our Lord One thousand eight hundred and forty-six, did, for Herself, Her heirs and successors, give and grant unto us, the said James Bullough and Adam Bullough, Her especial licence, full power, sole privilege, and authority, that we, the said James Bullough and Adam Bullough, our executors, administrators, and assigns, and such others as we, the said James Bullough and Adam Bullough, our executors, administrators, or assigns, should at any time agree with, and no others, from time to time and at all times during the term of years therein expressed, should and lawfully might make, use, exercise, and vend, within England and Wales, and the Town of Berwick-upon-Tweed, our Invention of "CERTAIN IMPROVEMENTS IN LOOMS FOR WEAVING;" in which said Letters Patent is contained a proviso that we, the said James Bullough and Adam Bullough, or one of us shall cause a particular description of the nature of our said Invention, and in what manner the same is to be performed, to be enrolled in Her Majesty's High Court of Chancery within six calendar months next and immediately after the date of the said in part recited Letters Patent, as in and by the same, reference being thereunto had, will more fully and at large appear.

Now know ye, that in compliance with the said proviso, I, the said James Bullough, do hereby declare that the nature of our said Invention, and the manner in which the same is to be performed, is particularly described and ascertained in and by the drawings hereto annexed, and the following explanation thereof (that is to say):—

These Improvements in Looms for Weaving apply to power looms (whether used for plain or fancy weaving), and consist,—

Firstly, in a certain novel arrangement of apparatus for the purpose of regulating the "letting off" of the yarn or warp from the yarn beam to be used in con-

INSERT FOLDOUT HERE

nection with a positive "taking up" motion, whereby the "letting off" of the yarn is governed by the "taking-up" of the cloth.

Secondly, in a modification of the above, in which arrangement the yarn beam is held fast by means of a friction break whilst the cloth is "beat up," and when being released, the tension of the yarn will cause the yarn beam to let off as much warp as required.

Thirdly, in an arrangement of mechanism connected with the ordinary "taking-up" wheel for the purpose of "letting back" the cloth by hand when requisite, without lifting the taking-up catches.

Fourthly, in a modification of the above motion, which may be made either self-acting or otherwise.

Fifthly, in a swivelling "slay cap," for the purpose of allowing the reed to give way whenever the shuttle stops in the "shed," thereby preventing injury to the cloth, but which is held firm whilst beating up; and,

Sixthly, our Invention consists in the application of a friction break, which is caused to act simultaneously upon the face of the spur wheels which connect the ordinary tappet and crank shaft (and are known as the tappet shaft wheel and the crank shaft wheel), for the purpose of stopping both shafts at one instant whenever the shuttle is absent from both boxes, instead of allowing the tappet shaft wheel to stop itself by concussion of its teeth against the teeth of the crank shaft wheel as heretofore.

These several improvements will be better explained and more readily understood by reference to the Drawing accompanying these Presents, which is of a scale of about two inches to a foot, and has figures and letters of reference marked upon it corresponding with the following description thereof, the new parts being shaded with color for the sake of distinction, and the ordinary parts of the loom being drawn in outline, merely for the sake of illustrating the relative positions of the various improvements.

Figure 1 is a side elevation of a loom with part of my improvements attached thereto, and Figure 2 is a section of a loom exhibiting other parts of the Invention. A, A, is the main framing of the loom; B, B, is the yarn beam; C, C, the crank shaft; D is the slay; E, the breast beam; and F, the cloth roller.

The first part of our improvements is seen best at Figure 2. Upon the ordinary tappet shaft G of the loom is a double tappet a, a, which, as it revolves, causes the lever b, b, to rise and fall. This lever b is connected by a rod c to a small lever d, which has its fulcrum upon cross shaft e; there is also another lever f attached to the same shaft, which has a catch g affixed to it. When the cam or tappet a lifts the lever b, the lever d comes in contact with the lever f, and causes the catch g to take up one tooth of the ratchet wheel h, which being connected to the yarn beam B by the worm and wheel i, i, lets off the yarn. The quantity of yarn let off is regulated in the following manner:—The yarn or warp is caused to pass over a rod or bearer k, which vibrates upon supports fixed at each end. This yarn bearer k is furnished with a weight and lever l at one end for the purpose of keeping the yarn at the proper tension, and at the other end of the same is a pin m, which vibrates between the stops n and o. When more yarn is let off than is taken up, pin m comes into contact with the stop n and projects a small lever p, underneath the lever f, and holds it up out of the reach of the lever d, and thus stops the letting off; but as soon as the tension of the yarn, consequent upon the taking up of the cloth, causes the pin, m to come into contact with the stop o, it will withdraw the lever p, and allows the "letting-off" to proceed as before. Figure 3 is a side view of the ratchet wheel and levers, and Figure 4 is a plan view of the apparatus.

The second part of our Invention is shown in Figure 5. A is part of the framing of the loom, and G is the tappet shaft. When the yarn beam is placed in the loom the boss at the end thereof is placed inside the pulley a, a pin upon the boss fitting between the two projections b, b, so that the yarn beam connot turn without the pulley. Upon the tappet shaft G a tappet c is fixed in such a manner that the instant the reed is beating up the cloth, the tappet c causes the lever d to tighten the friction belt or break e, upon the pulley

a, by means of the connecting links f, f, and thus prevent the yarn beam from "letting-off" any warp whilst the reed is "beating up," but releases it the moment afterwards, the tension of the yarn causing the yarn beam to let off as much warp as is required. The same arrangement of detached pulley may be applied without the break in those looms where friction is applied to the warp beam by a rope coiled around the end of the same and carrying a weight, the principal feature of novelty consisting in having the pulley to which the friction is applied detached from the yarn beam, in order to afford more convenience in re-filling.

The third part of our Invention is shewn in Figures 1 and 6. q is the ordinary "taking-up" ratchet wheel which is loose upon its stud, and has a ring of leather let into its side; there is also a ring of leather let into the boss of the spur wheel r, which wheel slides upon a feather on its stud, and is held firmly against the wheel q by the spring s. The wheel r gears with a pinion t upon the shaft u, which is turned by a hand wheel fixed upon it near to the "setting-on rod," not shewn in the Drawing. Thus it will be evident, that by turning the hand wheel the cloth may be let back without lifting the catches from off the "taking-up wheel" q. If it be thought desirable to have the shaft u stationary while the loom is working it may easily be accomplished by removing about four of the teeth of the pinion t.

The fourth part of our Invention is shewn in Figure 7, which is a plan view of another arrangement of mechanism for letting back. The "taking-up wheel" q has a small pin or tooth v, which takes into the teeth on the face of the wheel w, which slides upon a feather, and is held against the wheel q by the spiral spring x, but may be thrown out of gear by the lever y either by hand or by being connected to the weft motion. When the wheel w is thrown out of gear the tension of the cloth will pull the cloth roller back one tooth at a time, so that any required amount may be let back.

The fifth part of our Invention is shewn in Figures 1 and 2. The "slay cap" 1, which holds the upper part of the reed 2 instead of being bolted to the "slay sword," as usual, swivels upon a pin or stud at each end, so that when the shuttle stops in the shed it allows the reed to give way, as shewn by dotted lines in Figure 2. The "slay cap" is held firm at the moment of "beating up" in the following manner. To one end of the same a small lever 3 is fixed, which lever is connected to the lever 4 by a link 5; the lever 4 at the moment of "beating up" passes above the projecting piece 6, and thus holds the slay cap firm.

The sixth and last part of our improvements is shewn in Figure 1; the ordinary "stop rod finger" connected to the swell in the shuttle box, is shewn at 7. 8 is a break which is supported by the levers 9 and 10. When the shuttle is absent from both boxes the finger 7 remains in the position shown in the Drawing, and coming against the projection upon the lever 9, draws the break 8 into contact with the crank shaft wheel 11, and the tappet shaft wheel 12 simultaneously, thus stopping both shafts at once, and with less concussion than heretofore. In those looms where the ordinary break is applied to the fly wheel we propose to apply a fixed or stationary break attached to the framing of the loom at the opposite side of the wheel to the ordinary break to prevent straining of the crank shaft, and also to gain additional friction power.

Having now described the nature and object of our several improvements in looms for weaving, and the manner of carrying the same into practical effect, I would remark, in conclusion, that we claim as our Invention,—

Firstly, the novel arrangement of mechanism shewn in Figures 2, 3, 4, and 5, for "letting off" the yarn or warp (together with the application of the detached pulley to looms where friction is applied by a coiled rope and weight), and also the method of regulating the same, namely, by the tension of the yarn or warp threads.

Secondly, we claim the apparatus shewn in Figures 1, 6, and 7, for "letting back" the cloth when required without the necessity of lifting the catches from the "taking-up wheel," to be worked either by hand or by the weft motion when the weft breaks.

Thirdly, we claim the swivelling "slay cap" whereby the reed is allowed to give way whenever the shuttle stops in the shed, and also the apparatus shewn in the Figure 1 for holding the same firm whilst "beating up;" and,

Fourthly, we claim the employment or use of a break, as shewn in Figure 1, to act simultaneously upon both the "crank shaft wheel" and "tappet shaft wheel" for the purpose of stopping the loom when the shuttle is absent from both shuttle boxes at once; and also the application of a fixed or stationary break in addition to the ordinary one to those looms where a moveable break is applied to the fly wheel for the purpose of stopping the loom."

> In witness whereof, I, the said James Bullough, have hereunto set my hand and seal, this Thirty-first day of May, One thousand eight hundred and forty-seven.
>
> JAMES (L.S.) BULLOUGH.

"And be it remembered, that on the same Thirty-first day of May, in the year above mentioned, the aforesaid James Bullough came before our Lady the Queen in Her Chancery, and acknowledged the Specification aforesaid, and all and every thing therein contained, in form above written. And also the Specification aforesaid was stamped according to the tenor of the Statute in that case made and provided.

Inrolled the First day of June, in the year above written."

There has been many modifications of the Fly Reed, but the plan that is in general use is the one that allows the reed to go back from the bottom. It will be seen from the drawing of Mr. James Bullough's loom, that the reed flies back from the top; and it is very probable that some one may bring out a loom, the reed of which will go back both top and bottom, which may be easier on the rims of the reed.

The novel arrangement of mechanism, which the patentee claims for the letting off the yarn or warp, although it is his first claim in the specification, has not yet come into much use, and is not likely to do, as better plans than his have been patented and tried before, and did not succeed. But those failures need not keep others from trying to get some novel arrangement of mechanism, whereby the present mode of pacing the beam may be done away with to advantage, for it is decidedly a defect in the power loom, the pacing apparatus as it is in general applied at the present time. Neither has the second claim in this patent come into general use, but the third and fourth are almost in general use, and they were great improvements to the power-loom. Mr Bullough gets great credit in the trade for his invention, and he well deserves it, for he has brought out some of the very best things in connection with power-loom weaving.

TODDS' PATENT LOOM.

About five years ago, a loom for Plain Cloth was brought out, which was known by the name of Todds' Patent Loom; and although a great many of its movements were not new, yet it was a happy combination of working parts as a whole, and was then considered the best out, and perhaps it is so still.

The picking, in this loom, is accomplished by the picking stick coming up through the lay, and by this arrangement no spindles or shuttle cords are required, the end of the picking stick acting direct on the shuttle driver. The picking stick gets its motion from a small upright shaft fixed to the sword of the lay, and on the end of this upright shaft is a small projection like a finger, which comes in contact with another finger as the lay moves back; it is by this arrangement the shuttles are driven. The heddles are fixed to a roller below, in the same manner as they are fixed to the one above, and by moving one of these rollers, the sheds are formed.

The following is Messrs. Todds' own description:—

TODDS' DESCRIPTION.

Our improvements relate, first, to that part of power-looms known as the tappet shaft, and used for actuating the tappets, which give motion to the heddles, and consists in a novel method of driving such shaft, which is accomplished by means of a second shaft, to which a rocking or reciprocating motion is imparted, and at each end of which shaft is a small pulley or drum, to which is attached an endless band or strap of metal, leather, or other suitable material; the strap also passes round and is attached to a loose pulley upon the tappet shaft; this pulley has upon the interior surface of its rim a spring pressing upon a pawl or catch, which acts against a plate secured upon the tappet shaft, and having two or more ratchets or teeth formed on its periphery. By this arrangement, when a rocking motion is given to the pulleys at the end of the rocking shaft it will be imparted to the loose pulley, which will cause the pawl to force round the ratchet, and give an intermittent motion to the tappet shaft as required. This arrangement is applied at each end of the loom, and both driven in the same direction by the straps, being one open and the other crossed, as the pawls are required to force the ratchets alternately on each side of the loom. The motion given to the "yarn bearer" for ensuring the equal tension of yarn is also actuated from the rocking shaft by means of an eccentric in connection with and through the medium of a suitable arrangement of levers.

The second part of this invention relates to the rocking or oscillating shaft above mentioned, and consists in imparting to the said shaft an uniform reciprocating motion, through the medium of which a positive dwell is given to the heddles. This motion is affected by means of a lever or arm, indirectly connected with the crank shaft (from which it receives motion) by an arrangement of levers. One end of this lever is secured to the framing, the other being enlarged to the required size, so as to form a segment of a circle. About the centre of this segment is situated the required number of teeth, leaving the two sides of the segment a plain surface; gearing into these teeth are the corresponding teeth of a disc fixed upon the rocking shaft, the remaining portion of such disc having a plain surface like the segment. Supposing motion to be given to the arm, the teeth thereupon would turn the toothed disc until the plain surfaces came into contact, which would cause a dwell; if, now, the arm moves back as the crank revolves, a plate secured upon the said arm will fit into a corresponding recess in the toothed pinion and bring the teeth again into gear, and so on, at every upward and downward throw of the crank, thus causing the required oscillation or reciprocating motion of the shaft, and positive dwell of the heddles while open.

Lastly, these improvements apply to the part called

the "weft stopping motion," usually in connection with the "swell" of the shuttle box, and consists in the addition and application of a suitable formed spring, situated beneath one of the cranked levers, one of which presses against the swell of the shuttle box, the second being employed to strike the "frog;" this spring is placed under the third, in order to assist in forcing the second on to the "frog," and, by being suitably curved, to release the "swell," and consequently the shuttle from pressure, as it is expelled from the box. A similar effect may also be gained by curving the third lever upwards, so as to come into contact with a stud upon the crank arm, and so fitted, that as the arm moves, the lever may touch the stud, and thus release the swell from pressure, and raise the second finger from the "frog" if the shuttle completes its course from box to box; but should any occurrence interfere to cause the absence of the shuttle, then the first lever would press the swell in, and allow the third one to be raised and struck by the advancing stud, and consequently force the second lever on to the "frog," and stop the loom.

It will be seen from the description given by the patentees, that the positive dwell of the heddles, when the shed is open, is one of the things they claim; but the same thing can be done, and *is* done, by the common wypers better than what it is in this loom. But their last claim for the contrivance that takes the pressure off the shuttle before it is picked, is a very good thing, although it has been applied to power-looms before.

SCOB OR FLOAT PREVENTER.

When the weft passes over a portion of the warp without being interwoven with it, the defect is that the yarn hangs loose at that part, and it is called a Scob, Float, or Flow; and to have a contrivance that would really prevent floats without any other drawback, would be a very good thing indeed for the power-loom; but all the plans hitherto tried has not as yet proved successful.

When a warp thread breaks, and the end of it gets entangled with the other warp threads, it prevents that part of the Web from forming a shed, by holding both halfs of the warp together in front of the reed; the shuttle must pass either above or below this part; if it passes below it will work a float, if it passes above it will do the same, but it is in general thrown out of the loom when it passes above. By putting the tips of the shuttle a little nearer the under side of the shuttle than the top of it, it will always pass under the part of the shed that is obstructed, and in doing so, will receive a certain pressure on the top. After this explanation, the following plans for preventing scobs will be understood without much study.

The first plan was to have the shuttle made with its tips as described, and a small nob like part of a circle projecting a little above the top surface of the shuttle, and this was connected to a lever of the first kind which was placed in the inside of the shuttle, being in the same direction as the skewer. The end of this lever pressed upon a small pin that was placed between the tip and the eye of the shuttle in front, and this pin and lever was so shaped that when that part of the warp which would make a scob, pressed upon the nob, it caused the pin to project from the fore side of the shuttle, and this prevented the shuttle from getting into the box, and the loom was stopped by the common protection.

Another plan (but this one requires to be put on a loom that has the weft motion on it) is to have the shuttle made in the same form as in the other plan, with a cutter that will cut the weft shot at or near the shuttle eye, and when this is done, the loom will be stopped by the action of the weft motion, in the same manner as if the loom was working without weft. It will be obvious to those who know what a shuttle is, and its use, that in applying this apparatus to it, it must be in as compact a form as possible, and all to be inside of the shuttle except the small curved part of the nob that the yarn is to press upon, and to be so placed as not to weaken or destroy any other part of it; also, so arranged as not to be a drawback to the weaver when changing and filling the shuttle.

Some years ago a description was given of a shuttle in the following words:—"The said invention relates to shuttles, and consists in the addition of an improved apparatus for the twofold purpose of preventing the occurence of what is technically termed 'float,' and of retaining the cop on the spindle and preventing its being shaken off by the vibration in the shuttle caused by the blows of the picker. The defect termed 'float' is caused by imperfect shedding, and in order to prevent it, we cause the twist or threads of the warp which obstruct the shuttle race from being insufficiently raised or depressed in the shedding, to press down a small hook or cutter near the eye of the shuttle; and this being done, the loom is stopped by the action of the weft motion, in the same manner as in an ordinary case of broken or exhausted weft. It is proper to mention here, that hooks or cutters of this kind have before been applied, or attempted to be applied for this purpose; and therefore, we wish it to be understood, that this part of our invention does not consist in the use merely of such hooks or cutters, but in the mode of applying and fixing them to the shuttle hereinafter described, the peculiarities of which are, the compact form of the apparatus and its capability of being affixed on the solid part of the shuttle, so as not to weaken the sides thereof—the entire absence of every part of the apparatus from the body of the shuttle, so that it is no longer liable to be interfered with or damaged by the weaver in the act of removing or replacing the cops, and the incorporation with it of the transverse plate hereinafter described, for the double purpose of retaining the cop on the spindle and masking the hook or cutter so that it may not catch the yarn in its passage from the skewer, except when depressed for that purpose, &c., &c." But no more need be said about it, for it is clear that the party who wrote the description was not a practical weaver, and the principle is already described.

THE SHUTTLE CHANGER.

A few words in this place will suffice for a description of this contrivance, but we may have occasion to say more about it in another place. It is an apparatus for changing the shuttle when the weft cop is run done, or the weft thread broken in the working shuttle without the assistance of the weaver. The loom that this apparatus is applied to must have the weft stopper motion, and the brake and the weft stopper fork should be on the side of the loom opposite to the driving pulley; it is also necessary it should have a crank shaft with fly wheels upon it; the brake acts on the fly wheel next the driving pulley. When the weft motion stops the loom, and the swell that is placed on the rim of the fly is so set that it allows the shuttle to be thrown to the driving pulley side of the loom, before it is entirely stopped, for although the weft motion pulls off the handle of the loom when the shuttle is at the opposite side of the lay, the loom has acquired as much force with its fly wheels as carry the shuttle to the other side where the changing apparatus is placed. It will be obvious that the loom will stop always at the very same place, in consequence of the swell on the fly wheel. Suppose the loom is stopped when the lay is about one inch from the fell of the cloth, and the shuttle with the cop in it is placed on a level with the race of the lay, two inches in front of the shuttle box; and suppose the front or fore box side moves down until the top of it is level with the race of the lay, then a pair of fingers from the back box side pushes the empty shuttle over the top of the front box side, and it falls into a keeper placed below the sole of the lay, to lie there till the weaver removes it. The shelf that holds the full shuttle now moves towards the lay, and at the instant it touches the front of it, the shuttle is pushed on to the lay, and the front box side rises up to its original position; when this is done, a small lever takes hold of the shuttle and puts it as far back into the box as the driver will allow, in the same way as the weaver does it with his hand. The shuttle is now changed, and the loom ready to be put again in motion by pushing the handle into its proper position. It is already explained how the loom is stopped when the lay is within an inch of the cloth.

The instant that the weft motion disengages the handle of the loom, it throws the belt on to the loose pulley, and at the same time puts into gear the shifting apparatus which is driven with the loose pulley. On the eye of the loose pulley is a pinion in the proportion of one to three of the wheel that it drives; the wheel is a solid one without arms, and has on its side cams or groves for working the different levers, which are all compactly fitted into a framing that is bolted to the side of the loom right below the driving pulley.

The reader will observe from the foregoing description, that the first movement is the front box side, and one lever takes it down and puts it up; this first lever, as it is named, also pushes the shuttle over the edge of the lay into the keeper; the second lever moves the shelf with the full shuttle towards the lay, and a third lever puts the shuttle into the box and shifts it as far back in the box as the driver will allow. The fourth lever pushes the handle of the loom on, and throws the shifting apparatus out of gear, to stand until the next time the weft shot brakes.

From the time that the loom stops when the weft shot is broken, to the time it is put on again with the full shuttle, is three shots, but it might be managed by the loss of only two shots, and then the pinion on the loose pulley would require to have only one tooth for two that is in the apparatus wheel.

ARTICLES ABOUT A LOOM.

It will be of advantage to the new beginner to know the names of the principle things that compose a loom, as it will enable him to understand the various descriptions given in this work; and before proceeding further, a short explanation of some of them will be given:—

DRIVING PULLEYS

Are the pulleys that are fixed on the top shaft for giving motion to the loom; the loose pulley is the one the belt runs on when the loom is standing.

CRANK SHAFT.

Sometimes called the top shaft, or driving shaft, is the main one in the loom, and has the pulleys on the one end, and a pinion on the other. It is from this shaft that the lay receives its motion by means of the connection rods.

CONNECTION RODS.

The crank shaft has two Connection Rods which are attached to the lay or swords of the lay. In some looms a small rod for working the uptaking motion is known by this name.

WYPER SHAFT

Is the shaft that works the shedding and picking motion, and is driven by the crank shaft with a pinion gearing with a wheel on the end of the wyper shaft; this shaft makes only one revolution for two of the crank one.

YARN BEAM.

That cylindrical piece of wood or iron which is used for holding the warp yarn; on it is placed two flanges, which are set at a distance from each other to correspond with the breadth of the Web. There is also on it an iron pulley at each end, which are called pace pulleys, because a rope or cord is passed round them for pacing the Web. The end of the pace cord is tied to a lever which is called the pace lever, and the weight that is put on this lever is the pace weight. The iron pivots that the beam turns upon are called the gudgeons.

CLOTH BEAM

Is the beam on the opposite side of the loom for winding up the cloth as it is woven; on the end of this beam is a spur wheel which is called the cloth beam wheel; in some looms this beam is covered with emery or card sheets, and then it is named the card or emery beam. When this is the case, a wood roll is used besides, and is called the cloth roll, because it receives the cloth as it is delivered from the card beam. In hand-looms the card beam is not used, and very seldom does the hand-loom weaver use flanges for their yarn beam, as they build the selvages of the Web like a cone.

SWORDS, LAY, AND ROCKING SHAFT.

Swords are those parts of the loom that the lay is fixed to; for power-looms, they are made of cast iron, and are fixed on the Rocking Shaft which stretches from one end of the loom to the other, near the floor. The Lay is bolted on to the upper ends of the swords, and the connection rods are either fixed to them or the lay. The sole of the lay is that part of wood or iron where the race is fixed on, and the shuttle runs upon the race. The top shell is that part of the lay which holds the reed by the top rim, and the under rim of the reed is placed in the under shell, sometimes named flighter. The protecting rod is that round piece of iron which is placed along the lay, either below it or at the back. The box sides are those parts, made either of wood or iron, that keeps the shuttles in their proper places at the end of the lay, after they have passed through the shed. The spindle heads are those pieces of iron that hold the ends of the spindles that are next to the Web.

BREAST BEAM

Is the rail in front of the loom that the cloth passes over as it is woven to the cloth beam. It is on this rail the self-acting temples are fixed; by hand-loom weavers it is sometimes called the slab stock.

PICKING ARM, PULLEY, AND CONE.

The picking arms are those levers that are keyed on the wyper shaft, with a slit in them for the purpose of receiving the studs that carry the picking pulleys; and the picking pulley strikes against the treadle, lever, or some other moveable article that gives motion to the shuttles. Sometimes a bracket of a particular curve strikes against a cone or small pulley called a truck, which is made to pick the shuttle.

CAMS OR WYPERS.

Wypers are those pieces of cast iron of an eccentric shape that are fixed on the under shaft for moving the treadles that shed the Web, and the small castings, with the pulleys in them, that are on the treadles, are named the shedding trucks; the curved plates used for moving the tweeling treadles, are called wypers or cones. Sometimes the picking arms are named cams.

PICKING STICK

Is the piece of wood that has the shuttle cords attached to it for pulling the picker that throws the shuttle; they are made of various lengths and thickness, some of them round and others flat.

UPTAKING MOTION

Is a term given to that piece of mechanism which winds up the cloth on the cloth beam when the loom is in the act of weaving; one kind is called the bell crank motion, which does not take up the cloth regular, the quantity of shots being regulated by the weight of the pace or friction put upon the warp yarn; the other takes up the cloth uniform, and the number of shots or picks is regulated by a pinion named the change pinion. This motion commonly consists of a connection rod attached to the end of a lever of the first kind, and at the other end of the lever is a catch for driving the ratchet wheel; and on the eye of this wheel is put the change pinion which drives the spur wheel on the end of the cloth beam. There is another catch that falls into the teeth of the ratchet wheel, which holds it from turning back.

GEARING.

When speaking of Gearing in connection with a power-loom factory, it is understood to consist of, first, the main gearing, and second, the small gearing. The main gearing are the shafts, wheels, brackets, bushes, and belts that are between the engine and the shafts in the flat or shed with the drums on them for driving the looms, and the shafts with the drums, grounds, hangers, bushes, and bolts, are what is called the small gearing, although the shafts may be both large and long.

INSERT FOLDOUT HERE

CHAPTER V.

CHECK AND DAMASK POWER-LOOM.

This is a loom which requires a considerable quantity of machinery and extra mounting, more than what is required in a common power-loom, as will be seen from the drawings given. It is the most complicate loom that has yet been brought out for fancy work; and if the reader will pay attention to the descriptions which will be given with reference to the drawings, it will be easily understood. A patent was obtained for this loom at the time when it was brought out, so we shall first give the description as given by the patentee, and then explain its different parts in a manner that will enable the workman to mount the loom and work it.

DESCRIPTION OF THE DRAWINGS.

Plate I. In this Plate, Figure 1 is a front view of the loom, showing its connection with the Jacquard machine, also a front view of the apparatus for disengaging the connection of that machine when required, together with the cam barrel and levers for working the heddles in connection with the harness. Figure 2 shows an end view of the loom with the cam and lever for working the Jacquard machine, the supports for the "stenting rollers," and other parts.

Plate II. In this Plate, Figure 3 is a ground plan of the entire loom, of which Figure 4 is a general section. Figure 5 is a side and end view of the disengaging apparatus detached.

Plate III. In this Plate, Figure 6 is a front view of the loom, in which are shown the shuttle box of the lay, and the details of the apparatus for working it. Figure 7 is an end elevation of the same.

Plate IV. Figure 8 in this Plate represents an elevation of the loom, as seen from the back. Figure 9 is a general section shewing the internal arrangement of the levers for working the shuttle box, &c. Figure 10 is a ground plan. Figure 11 is a vertical section through the shuttle box, showing the gearing by which it is shifted. Figure 12 exhibits the details of the weft protector detached.

The main frame of the loom marked A is similar to that of other power-looms in common use. The motive power is communicated to the working parts in the usual manner by a band from a drum on one of the leading shafts of the factory passing to the pulleys B, B, one of which is fast and the other loose upon their common axis (*a*), as in other power-looms. The reciprocating motion of the lay is derived from two cranks on the pulley shaft (*a*) by means of two connecting rods C, C, attached by pin joints to the lay swords D, D. On one extremity of the shaft (*a*) is fixed a wheel E, which is in gear with the wheel F on the corresponding extremity of the second shaft (*b*). The ratio of the wheels E and F is as 1 to 2, so that the shaft (*b*) makes exactly one revolution for every two picks or shots thrown. On the same shaft (*b*) is fixed the cam or wyper G which works the Jacquard treadle H of the loom when employed in producing fabrics requiring the use of that apparatus. The motion of the cam G. is transferred to the Jacquard lever I, which communicates with the treadle H by means of the small rod (*c*), and is supported by a stud on a bracket J, attached in any convenient manner over the loom. The action of these last-mentioned parts are as follows:—When the cam G revolves, it depresses the treadle H, and consequently the end of the lever I to which it is attached by the rod (*c*). This action necessarily raises the opposite end of the lever I in connection with the Jacquard machine, but immediately on the treadle H being depressed by the cam it is brought under the control of the "disengaging apparatus," to be hereafter described, and which keeps it down, and consequently causes the Jacquard lever to maintain its elevated position, until the required number of picks or shots pertaining to the card of the machine at the time being passed is thrown, when the treadle rises, and the cam G comes again into action. The treadle H is made to project in front of the loom to enable the weaver to turn back the cards of the Jacquard machine when any derangement takes place, and it is required to open out any number of picks. By this arrangement the weaver avoids the inconvenience of working the loom empty, that is, without weft, for the purpose of bringing the proper card into position. The conditions necessary to be observed in forming the cam G are as follows :—First, the part of the periphery which comes first into contact with the treadle H ought to have a curvature of large radius so as to cause the Jacquard lever I to commence its rise slowly, and gradually accelerate its motion until it has attained half the required elevation, when its motion ought gradually to decrease until it has risen to the highest point of elevation necessary. By thus regulating the motion of the lever any undue vibration of the leads of the harness is avoided during their rise, and the cards are less liable to be deranged on the barrel of the Jacquard machine. When the lever has remained up during the time requisite, it is again slowly lowered by the action of the cam becoming gradually less, until it finally ceases to act upon the treadle H, in consequence of the hollow portion of its periphery being brought opposite to the point of contact with the treadle. The succeeding lift is regulated in the same manner as above described. To regulate the number of shots or picks on the cards of the Jacquard machine, the following arrangement is adopted:—A small pinion (*a*) on the shaft (*b*) gives motion to the wheel (*e*), formed with a hollow projecting boss on which is fixed a change pinion (*f*), gearing with the wheel (*g*), carrying one, two, three, or more small studs, as the pattern may require. On these studs are carried the small friction pulleys (*h, h* . . .) which coming round on the under side act on the lever (*i*), causing one extremity of it to descend. In this extremity is a hole through which a cord is made fast, and which communicates with the bell crank lever (*j*). The purpose of this is to keep the treadle H depressed when the cam G has acted upon it; and again, when the lever (*i*) is pressed down, it necessarily pulls the cord attached to the bell crank lever, and takes this out of contact with the treadle H, at the instant the cam G begins to act upon it, thereby letting down the needles of the Jacquard machine with the same kind of gradual motion as they were raised. When the machine is ready to take another lift, the small spring (*k*) by contracting pulls the bell crank lever (*j*) into contact with the treadle H, and the action proceeds as before described.

The mode of working the heddles may be understood

from the following description in reference to the Drawings:—A shaft carrying a series of cam plates (marked L) is driven from the shaft (b) by a bevil pinion (l) gearing with the bevil wheel (m). The ratio of this pair of wheels is properly adjusted to the tweel which is required to be put upon the cloth at the time worked. The cams are so formed and set in relation to each other that the heddle leaves all stand steadily in one position, except the two leaves in action at the particular time. The projection marked 1 on the cams is for sinking the heddle leaves, and that marked 2 is for raising them, while the circular parts marked 3 are for keeping those leaves steady which are out of action. These cams are so pitched or set as to work in unison with each other and with the Jacquard machine and the lay D^1 while the loom is in action. When the point 1 comes round to the part of the treadle at 4, it causes the treadle (u) to descend at the point, and the cord marked 5 being attached to the extremity of the treadle (u), and also to the heddles (marked o), it makes the shed downwards; and the treadle (u^1) being acted upon simultaneously with the treadle (u), and the cords marked 6 being attached to the contiguous extremities of the upper levers (p), these extremities are depressed by the action of the cords when pulled; but the levers being suspended on an axis at or near the middle of their length, the depression at one end is necessarily accompanied by the corresponding elevation of the contrary end, which being attached by cords to the heddle leaves, the effect is to cause those acted upon to shed upwards, and the other heddles being connected in the same manner, the cams to which they are respectively related retain them in a middle position, neither up nor down, until by the motion of the common axis of the cam barrel L they are brought into action, and those previously engaged thrown idle. This arrangement of parts, and the motions above described, are principally adapted to working two, three, four, five, or six thread harness more or less, as may be required, and can be applied to work four, five, six, seven, eight, nine, or ten heddle leaves, and the advantage of it is that the cams keep the idle leaves steady when the others are shedding. The tweeling cams may be formed of simple plates cut to the required shape, or they may be formed with loose marginal pieces made to fit upon permanent centres. They may also be formed with rollers at the projections marked 1 and 2. The stenting rollers (q), shown in Figures 2, 3, and 4, are carried in bearings acted upon by springs, to allow the yarn to yield, yet remain tight when the heddles or harness is acting, without subjecting it to unnecessary strain, which it would be were no such provision made for its stretch when the heddles are shedding. There is one of these rollers for every leaf in the set of heddles employed, and the springs marked (r) are so adjusted in tension as to keep the yarn at the degree of tightness required for putting on the requisite number of shots or picks on a given length of the warp yarn. In the Figures referred to above, the arrangement of parts is adapted to a five-leaved set of heddles, but may be extended to any number, more or less, as may be required for the particular kind of fabric to be woven; the yarn passing through the eyes of the heddles of any particular leaf passes over one of the rollers, and that particular roller yields to the yarn when the leaf of heddles through which it passes is forming a shed, producing a similar effect as if the yarn were elastic in itself. The brackets (s) carrying the rollers and springs are fixed on the two side frames of the loom in any convenient manner. The yarn beam M, the pace pulleys (t), the pace weights N, the picking treadle O, the picking stick P, are similar and similarly applied as in other power-looms.

I will now describe the selvage protector, the use of which is to prevent the warp yarn from being broken by the weft shot drawing it too tightly. The small pins (u) at each side of the web, work up and down alternately, each being down for the shot, on that side from which the shuttle is thrown. The two cams (v) on the shaft (b), (see Figures 8, 9, and 10,) are formed with recesses to allow the levers (w) to fall. These last are fixed in brackets at the back rail of the loom, and the small pulleys marked 6 in the levers (w) lift

INSERT FOLDOUT HERE

the levers (x) which are suspended on axes at (y), so that when the recesses in the cams successively come round, they allow the pins (u) to fall into position at the selvage, taking hold of the selvage threads, and the weft of the successive picks turns upon them, thus preventing all unnecessary strain on the selvage yarn. The cams are so made and set in relation to the movements of the loom, that whenever the shuttle is in the box of the lay at the contrary side, the pins (u) rise out of contact with the yarn, and move slightly back to allow the lay to drive up the weft shot to the fell of the cloth without touching the pins.

I will now describe the apparatus for working the shuttle box Q, when three or more shuttles are employed for the purpose of putting in different kinds of weft into the web. The Drawings marked Plates III. and IV. show an arrangement for six shuttles, and the mechanism is so constructed and adapted that any number of shots of one kind of weft from two upwards, may be thrown in any order whatever of the shuttles answering to the particular pattern to be woven. When the box Q is to be shifted to change the shuttle, one of the cords marked 7 attached to a spring marked 8 is pulled up by the Jacquard machine, and this cord being attached to one of the bell crank levers (z), provided with a toothed segment at one extremity, makes the small tumbler (a^1) to rise in its place in the lever or treadle R, and this tumbler (a^1) being moveable on a centre in the treadle, when the cam S on the shaft (b) comes round, and depresses the treadle, the two chains at its extremity are so adjusted as to act upon the pulleys (b^1) to which they are attached on the rod T. On this rod are also two wheels ($c^1, c^1,$) gearing with the racks ($d^1, d^1,$) see Figure 11, which cause the box to shift to the position required. Immediately on this being effected, the cam S passes over the tumbler (a^1), and touching the bell crank (z), throws it back, thereby causing the tumbler to fall into its place in the lever R, and so on for every subsequent shift of the shuttle box. Every shuttle has its own lever, tumbler, and pulley; and the cam S making one revolution for every two shots thrown, it is always ready to shift the box Q to whatever position the Jacquard machine shall indicate. To this end the pattern must previously be all completely arranged upon the cards of the Jacquard machine. The shaft T is supported in bearing, attached to the swords of the lay, and therefore partakes of their reciprocating motion. I wish it also to be observed that the treadles or levers being each attached by two chains, one on each side of the pulley (b^1) of that treadle, they can every one act independently of the others. That the box Q may shift freely, the cam U on the shaft (b) is so pitched as to allow the small pulleys marked 9 to come out of the notches in the racks ($d^1, d^1.$) When the box has been shifted to its proper position, the cam U turns its full side to the pulley and the lever W, and pulling the connecting rod (e^1), which is flexibly attached to the small horizontal lever (f^1) at the bottom of the lay sword, it causes the upright lever (g^1), centred on or near the middle of its length, to act upon the spiral spring (h^1), which, pulling the frame carrying the small pulleys marked 9 into the notches of the racks (d^1, d^1), holds the box firmly in its proper place until the instant for shifting again arrives. The reason for having all the levers working at the rocking-tree shaft X is, that at that point there is the least motion of the lay. The weight of the shuttle box is counterpoised by the weight Y, to render it more easily shifted. The weight is suspended by a cord or chain from the top of the box passing over the pulley Z; and to prevent the motion of the lay from communicating to it a swinging motion, it is controlled by a small guide rod attached to the contiguous sword of the lay. The protecting rod (i^1), shown at the back of the lay in Figure 8, is similar to that in other power-looms.

I will now describe the mode of stopping the loom, when it happens from any cause during its working, that the shuttle driver is not taken back to its proper position, it being understood that the driver or picker (k^1) ought always to be back when the box is shifted, to touch the small curved lever (j^1) shown in front of the shuttle box Q, and send that end of it back also. The effect of this is to raise the other end of the lever, and consequently the lifter (l), clear of the frog; but when any derangement occurs to prevent the driver from getting back, the lifter is not raised, but striking on the frog or moveable catch (m^1), this last is brought into action upon the upright lever (n^1), and pushing it forward transfers the motion along the rod A^1 in front of the loom to the opposite end, at which is the lever (o^1) connected with the handle B^1 for stopping the loom. To secure the correct shifting of the shuttle box, before picking the first shot of the shuttle shifted to, an apparatus called the protector is provided, the character and action of which may be understood from the following description with reference to the Drawings. The small pulleys marked 9 on the brackets V, enter the notches of the racks (d^1, d^1), when the box Q is in its proper position, and the bracket V pressing on one end of the lever (p^1), at the back of the shuttle box, causes the other end to press on the rod descending from the back tongue of the protector, and lifts it over the notch of the frog (m^1) (see Figure 7); but if not lifted, the tongue (l^{11}) strikes the frog when the lay is going back, and a pin in the frog pushes the lever (q^1) back, and this being in connection with the lever (n^1) and the rod or shaft A^1, pulls the handle B^1, and stops the loom.

The weft protector, which I now proceed to describe, is similar to that in common use on the side of the loom contiguous to the driving pulleys B, B; but it is also applied at the side of this loom where the shifting

INSERT FOLDOUT HERE

shuttle box is situated, to allow the loom being stopped whenever any of the weft shots fail. To accomplish this, I employ an apparatus of the kind depicted in the Drawings, and which may be understood from the following description:—A frame (r^1) is fixed to the sword of the lay on that side at which the protector is to be applied, and in this frame is a lever (s^1) carrying a small fork at its extremity for lifting the weft of the idle shuttles out of the way of the weft stopper forks (t^1.) The lever S^1 is lifted by a wyper or cam C^1, on the shaft (b), and allows the shuttle to pass below it from the single side of the lay. After it has passed into the box Q the wyper E^1 acts upon the hanging lever (v^1), which pulls the lever (w^1) hung upon the frame (r^1) or sword of the lay. This lever is provided with a friction pulley, and being pulled back *di*sengages the small wires holding up the threads of weft, and allows them to fall to the race of the lay, when the wyper C^1 acting upon the lever (v^1) allows the lever (S^1) to fall to the bottom of the slit provided for it in the race of the lay. This done, the wyper E^1 allows the spring or weight (x^1) to pull the lever (s^1) with its fork under the weft shots, when the shuttle has passed to the single side of the lay, and thus lifts all the weft shots by the wyper C^1 acting on the lever (u^1), as before described. When the weft of any shuttle is run out or breaks, the fork (t^1) is not lifted, and the arm F^1 on the shaft (b) acts in consequence upon the lever (y^1), and thereby communicates motion to the hauling catch (z^1), which pulling the lever G^1 pushes forward the upright lever (n^1), and this acting upon the handle of the loom stops it, in the same manner as the other proctectors before described.

Having thus described the nature of my Invention, and the means employed by me for carrying the same into effect, I would have it understood that I do not confine myself to the details shown and described, so long as the peculiar character of any part or parts of my Invention is retained. But what I claim is,—

Firstly, the particular shape or form of the cam or wyper G on the shaft (b) for working the Jacquard machine.

Secondly, the form and position of the treadle H, whereby it is made to project in front of the loom, for the purpose of enabling the weaver to work the Jacquard machine independently of the loom.

Thirdly, the peculiar apparatus for disengaging the Jacquard machine.

Fourthly, the application of a series of cams or other like mechanism for steadying the idle heddle leaves when the other leaves are working or in action.

Fifthly, the application of what I have called stenting rollers for keeping the yarn at proper tension, at the same time that it is allowed to yield to the working heddle leaves.

Sixthly, the apparatus depicted and described under the name of selvage protector.

Seventhly, the mode of working the shuttle box when three or more shuttles are employed.

Eighthly, the mode of applying apparatus to stop the loom from the double box side of the lay when the weft fails.

Ninthly, the mode of stopping the loom when the shuttle driver is not taken sufficiently back. And,

Tenthly, the mode of stopping the loom when the shuttle box is not properly shifted.

TO MOUNT A HARNESS LOOM.

The first thing that should be learned about Damask Weaving, is designing the Patterns; indeed, this is required for all kinds of figured weaving, and a great deal depends upon the selection of the patterns, but more will be said about this under another head; the remarks here will be confined to what is required for the Mounting and Starting of a Harness Loom.

The figure to be woven is first painted on design paper (see design paper), which must be of the proper proportion for the warp and weft, and the card-cutter cuts the cards from this painting; also the weaver or harness tyer, finds the number of tail cords that will be required for the pattern from this paper. After the quantity of tails are found that will make the harness, the workmen will require the following articles before he proceeds to mount it.

MAILS

Are in general made out of sheet copper of an oblong shape, with three holes in them, and they answer the same purpose as the eyes of heddles, the warp of the Web being drawn through the centre hole. They are made in a variety of shapes and sizes to suit the kind of work they are used for.

INSERT FOLDOUT HERE

LEADS

Are from seven to twelve inches long, and may be made by casting small rods, and then drawing them in the same manner as iron wire, through holes of different diameters, until the proper size is got; they are used as weights in the harness, and are connected with twine to the mails. The weight of the leads to be employed will depend upon the weight of the work they have to do; for a full harness and light work, they may be made as light as to have about one hundred of them in the pound, but the weight of them must be increased in proportion to the weight of cloth. For a split or four thread (if not a pressure one) harness, about thirty in the pound will do, but if it be a four or five thread pressure harness, such as is used for table-covers, &c. &c., then they will require to be as heavy as to have only ten to sixteen in the pound. The leads in the centre of a Web may be lighter than those at the border, as their action is more direct, and with gathered ties, the leads can always be used lighter than in those that are not gathered.

HARNESS TWINE.

This Twine is used for tying the leads to the mails, and forming what is called the Sleepers, and Neck of the Harness. It should be made from some substance that has little or no elasticity in it, at the same time flexible; it is generally made from flax yarn, with as many threads twisted together as will make the twine up to the strength that will be required for the kind of work that is to be woven. For full harnesses with light work there is no use in putting in twine heavier than six ply of eighteens, as it would be adding expense to the mounting for no purpose; but when the harness is a pressure one, with four or five threads in the mail, and with leads, that each one will weigh two ounces, then the twine requires to be very strong, and this strength can only be got by putting in more plies of yarn. At the sides of broad Webs, the harness twine undergoes a great deal more friction than in the centre, and it might be profitable to use two sizes of twine, putting the lightest in the centre. However, much of this must be left to the discretion of the manager or workman.

SLABSTOCK.

The Slabstock is a piece of wood about six inches longer than the loom is broad, it is five or six inches broad, and one inch thick, with a grove made on the edge of it, for the purpose of holding the ends of the mails, when the harness is being tied. The use of the slabstock will appear in the explanation given for mounting the loom.

HARNESS OR HOLE BOARD.

The Hole Board is made of plane-tree wood, or some other hard, smooth material, and is made as long as the loom is broad. For a full harness, the hole board must have at least as many holes in it as there are threads in the Web that is to be woven, but they are scarcely ever made so as just to be the same set as the reed, because each part in the harness should begin with a full row in the board. Suppose the tye to be 360, and the board bored with eight holes in the row, this tye would fill exactly 45 rows, and the reed and hole board might be the same set; but if the tye was 350, it would fill forty three rows and six holes; this would leave two holes empty in each part; consequently, it would require the hole board to be finer than the reed. In fancy work there is always many changes, and manufacturers find it better to have the hole boards made fine in the set, and when a coarser set is required than what the hole board is, they order so many holes to be left empty, in the same manner as heddles are set when they are finer than the reed. The rows of holes run in oblique lines across the board, and that obliqueness depends upon the fineness of the set; in fine boards each row of holes embosom each other, to keep them from being too much crowded, and that the mails may stand as near as possible opposite to their respective intervals of the reed. In a full harness where two threads are put in one split of the reed, the two mails should just take the same space as one split, and when four threads are in one mail, it should take up the space of two splits, and so on, in proportion to the quantity of threads in one mail.

Hole boards used to be made by dividing them off with a pair of compasses, and was a matter of taste as to the number of holes in the rows across the board, but now they are made by machinery, and in general have eight holes in the row, and can be divided to have holes to suit any reed, as the apparatus for dividing the board is almost the same as what is used by the reed makers for regulating the set of the reed.

STANDERS

Are articles which are required for holding the Slabstock in its proper place in the loom, when the harness is being tied up. They are either made of iron or wood, about three or four inches broad, with a slit in the side of them, as wide as to allow the slabstock to get in.

TO PREPARE THE HARNESS.

The first thing is Stringing the Leads (the name given to this operation), and it is in general done by children. The flax yarn used for this purpose is cut into pieces called hangers, in lengths about twelve or fourteen inches long, and laid on a small bench or table opposite the operator; the mails and leads are also put on this bench. The person takes one lead with the left hand, and with the right hand puts the hanger through the hole in the end of it, and then through the under hole in the mail; the two ends of the twine are then tied together, and hung on a rod with the mail uppermost; this operation is repeated until there is a sufficient quantity of leads and mails strung to make the harness. They are now taken off the rods in handfulls, by slipping the hand between the legs of the hangers, and allowing the leads to hang down, and are in this position put on the slabstock, and spread along it.

The next thing that is required is a piece of flat wire, a little longer than the harness is broad, which may be got from any reed maker, and on which the mails are placed one by one; the mails will now be all right above the grove in the slabstock, with their top eyes above the flat wire. The slabstock with the leads and mails are now put into a frame like the letter H, which is made of wood, the ends of it going into slits that are made in the sides of the frame for that purpose. The slabstock is moved up towards the cross bar in the frame, and when it and the cross bar are about fourteen inches apart, and parallel with each other, it is fixed in that place, for the harness to be what some weavers denominate "cast," which is, connecting the mails to the sleepers. Sleepers are made from the same kind of yarn as the hangers, in the following manner:—The yarn is first wound on bobbins, and one of these bobbins with the yarn on it is placed at the side of the frame upon a wire or spindle. The boy or girl, or whoever is to cast the harness, takes the end of the yarn that is on the bobbin and puts it through the eye of a common needle, and goes to the opposite end of the frame where the casting should begin; the needle is now put through the top eyes of fifty or sixty of the mails and the twine drawn along with it. After this is done, the end of the twine is taken out of the needle, and fixed to a nail or wire that is in the cross bar of the frame. These nails should be arranged along the cross bar, not more than four or five inches from each other, to prevent unnecessary loss of twine.

The caster now takes a piece of small wire, or drawpoint, and inserts it in between the end mail and the one next it, below the harness twine, and lifts the harness twine up to the nail in the cross bar. The drawpoint is next inserted in between the second and third mail, and the twine put upon the nail as before, and so on with the remainder of the mails that the sleeper twine has been put through, till finished. The foregoing operation is continued until the harness is all cast. It will be evident that in winding the yarn on the bobbins, it will not do to have any knots on the twine, as they would not pass through the eyes of the mails. The next thing is to take the sleepers off the wires, and cut them in the exact place where the wires were in.

Now that the harness is cast, the next process is to draw the sleepers through the holes in the harness board; and for illustration, we will suppose the tye to be a 400, the Web to be put in a 12^{oo} reed, and the yarn to fill as near as possible 38 inches of the reed. As will be seen from the table of splits in a Web, that there is 1232·43 splits in a 12^{oo} 38 inch, which will make, with 2 threads in the split, 2464 ends (keeping out the fraction) in the warp of the Web; take off 16 ends for selvages, and the number will be 2428, which is divided by the tye, namely,—

$$400)2428(6 \text{ times over.}$$
$$\underline{2400}$$
$$28$$

This 6 times over, means that the tye in this Web is repeated 6 times, and there is 28 ends over, which must be left out, unless the pattern be very small, but in this instance, the whole 400 is required to complete the pattern; therefore, the 28 ends are left out, which will make the Web about three-eights of an inch narrower. This quantity, 2400, represents the number of sleepers that are to be taken through the harness board, and the holes in the board must be divided off, so as the harness will occupy exactly 37⅝ inches, the space that will be filled in the reed by the warp of the Web. After the holes in the board have been marked that are to be filled, it is hung up a little above the slabstock. If the person who is to draw the sleepers into the board be standing in front, the drawing must begin at the left hand side, with the back hole in the board; there being 8 holes in each cross row of the board, the tye will fill 50 rows, and it being 6 times repeated, as stated before, the harness will fill 300 rows exactly; but if the tye had not divided by the number of holes in a row (viz. 8), but left a few holes in the last row of the repeat, these holes must remain empty, as every repeat of the tye must begin with a full row.

The harness board, with slabstock, mails, leads, and sleepers, are now taken to the loom, and placed in the position as seen at (c), in Plate III, Figure 7, which is an end view of a power-loom, with a full harness; (figure 6 being the front view of the same), as will be observed, it is very near the front of the loom; indeed, a common full harness should be as near to the back of the lay as just to be clear of it, when it is full back. If the harness is to be put up in a loom that has got no arrangements in it for allowing the harness board and jacquard machine to be shifted, after the harness is tied, the harness board in this case must be firmly fixed in its place, not to be shifted, after the harness is tied, in any direction whatever. And although there are arrangements made in power-looms for shifting the jacquard machine and harness board to any position that may be required, still it is better to have them as near as possible fixed in their place where they are to remain when the loom is at work. To find the proper height for the mails, the lay is placed half way back, and a small straight edge put across the race, with the end of it projecting as far back as to reach the slabstock; the under edge of the straight edge where it crosses the top of the slabstock is the proper height for the mails, the slabstock being fixed in brackets which are bolted to the sides of the loom; the mails can be brought to their position by shifting these brackets up or down. After the slabstock is secured in its proper place, the hole board is next fixed in its place, which is about seven inches above the top edge of the slabstock, thus allowing the sleepers to be about eight inches above the hole board, and about seven below. The harness tyer now takes pieces of cord and ties them round the slabstock at a distance of three or four inches from each other, for the purpose of keeping the flat wire with the mails on it close down to the slabstock during the time that the harness is being tied. When this is done, the sleepers are gathered into bunches, with four hundred in each bunch, and a piece of string put round them to keep each four hundred distinct. The jacquard machine is now set in its proper position, which is right above the centre of the harness board. The usual method for placing the jacquard machine is, to take one of the leads and attach a piece of harness twine to it, and hang it to one of the cords in the centre of the machine, which is then shifted till once the lead is exactly above the centre of the harness board.

The harness is now ready for beating and tying up, and the most expeditious way to do it is to have two or three persons to leaf the harness, and one to tie it, which is done in the following manner:—Having ascertained the length of the neck twine (which is the twine that connects the sleeper to the tail cords in the jacquard machine), and supposing them to be five feet long, a piece of wood, such as a heddle shaft, is taken, and two pins put into it, two-and-a-half feet apart, and the twine is reeled on to the pins for the neck, which will give the length required, by cutting it in the centre. Each person who is to beat the harness, gets a quantity of this twine and knots it to the sleepers, beginning with the back hole in the row on each part ; and suppose there are only two beaters, each will hand up three ends to the harness tyer, who will tie them to the cord that is next the jacquard machine barrel in front of the machine; this is what is called the first cord, and attention must be paid to the design to see that the flower is drawn to answer this ; the tail cord next to this one in the cross row of the machine is the second, which the harness tyer takes next, and so on with all the four hundred tail cords, taking them in regular rotation. The knot used here is a matter of choice; if the snitch knot is employed at all it should be between the neck twines and the sleepers, for the purpose of adjusting any of the mails that may be too high or too low, but the harness tyer should be very careful to have all the neck twines equally tight, and the knots on the tail cords all the same distance from the jacquard machine, for if the knots be not all in the same horizontal line, the heck for guiding the neck twines cannot be properly set.

When the harness is brought forward to this stage, the workman proceeds to take away the brackets that are bolted on to the sides of the loom for holding the slabstock, and for the purpose of keeping a lease in the harness, he ties a cord to the end of the slabstock, which is drawn through the legs of the sleepers when the slabstock is pulled out. This lease is to preserve the order of the harness, so that the person who is to draw the warp into the mails may get them in regular succession. The slabstock and brackets having been removed, a boy commences with the first lead at the side of the harness and brings the knot on the hanger down to the eye of it, proceeding from one to another until he goes over the whole of the hangers. The brackets for holding the harness board are now put on, in the same place where the brackets were that held the slabstock, and the harness board fixed in its place. The harness is now ready for dressing; that is, putting a sort of varnish on to the hangers and sleepers, and that part of the neck twine that will rub on the heck when the harness is working, but care must be taken that the varnish is thoroughly dry before the drawing of the warp into the mails commences. The drawing of the warp into the mails of a full harness is the same as drawing a plain Web, which is explained at page 76.

The Web being now in the loom, and the harness board fixed in its proper place, the tenter's next duty is to see that the yarn is in its proper position, which is just to be touching the race when the lay is half way back; if it be too high or too low, he moves the jacquard machine up or down, as the case may be, till once the mails of the harness are at their proper place. The rod (c), as shown in Plate III., Figure 7, also in Plate IV., Figure 9, is now to be connected to the lever I. which works the jacquard machine, and in doing so, care must be taken not to have the shed too large. It will be seen from the drawing that there are a number of holes on the lever for the purpose of regulating the size of the sheds. After this is done, he puts his foot upon the treadle H., and depresses it, and by doing so, the brander of the jacquard machine, along with the whole harness and warp of the Web, is raised, and it is kept in this position until the workman puts four cards on the barrel, which cards have been previously cut for making plain cloth. The brander and harness are now lowered, and the plain cards coming in contact with the needles of the jacquard machine, one half of them will be pressed back, and the next time the brander is raised a plain shed will be formed, when the first lease rod may be put into it. The next tread will make the other plain shed, when the second lease rod can be put in, then the loom will be ready for making plain cloth; and to make good plain cloth with the jacquard machine, the different articles about it require to be nicely adjusted, which will now be explained.

JACQUARD MACHINE.

The position that the Jacquard Machine occupies in regard to the loom, will be seen in Plate III., which is right above the loom, and it should be as near to the ceiling as it can be got, for the purpose of giving the harness twine as little angle as possible. If the machine is properly made, the upright needles should stand perpendicular when the brander is down, if they are not pressed back by the cross ones. The hooks on the upper end of the upright needles should be $\frac{3}{8}$ of an inch above the blades of the brander. If the needles press too much on the blades of the brander, the trap board is shifted a little towards the front or barrel side of the machine, if they are not near enough to the blades, the trap board is shifted back. As very much depends on the setting of the trap board to have a good going machine, the workman should be very particular to have it right done. The box at the back of the machine which contains the small spiral brass springs, should be so set, as not to press too hard on the cross needles; this can be adjusted by putting a small slip of wood, or paste-board between the spring box and the standers of the machine, for if they are allowed to press too much, the points of the needles will have a greater tendency to pierce holes in the cards.

To get the barrel properly set also requires great care, and in doing this, the workman takes a card which has been previously cut, and places it on one of the sides of the barrel, when he will see if the pegs will suit to keep the card in its proper place; if the holes in the card are all opposite the holes in the barrel, it is right, but if not, he shifts the pegs till once the card is brought to the position required. After he has examined all the four sides of the barrel, and made them right, the cards for working plain cloth are again tied on the barrel, and put into the machine, when the brander is allowed to come down. He next sets the bracket that moves the lay of the jacquard machine, so as it will bring the barrel as close on the needles as to make all the upright ones stand clear of the brander blades, except those that are to be lifted. It does not do to have the barrel coming too close to the machine, because it puts unnecessary strain on the cards, and that must be avoided.

The rod (c) that connects the lever I (that lifts the brander) to the treadle H, should have a screw upon it, for the purpose of making it short or long at pleasure; by this screw the tenter adjusts the fall of the brander. If the brander be allowed to come down and rest on the machine every shot, when the loom is in full motion, it will have the same effect as if it was struck with a hammer, which makes a disagreeable noise, and has a very bad effect upon the whole of the harness, such as turning and bending the needles, causing the leads to have a swinging motion, and destroying the regularity of the shedding; and to avoid this, the rod (c) is screwed up to that extent, that the weight of the brander will always hang upon the cams G, as shown at Figure 9, Plate IV.

MAKING CLOTH.

When all the little parts about the jacquard machine are properly adjusted, and the harness brought forward, as has been explained, the loom is ready for weaving; and as plain cloth will show the working of the harness better than any other, a few inches of it should be woven before the flowering cards are put on.

In Plate III., Figure 6, the cards are shown at K, and it will be observed that they are hung on two curved iron rods, the curves of them being made so as they will be suitable to hold either a small or large set of cards.

After having woven a few inches of plain cloth, the set of cards that is to work the pattern wanted is hung upon these curved rods, the cards having been all previously laced and arranged on wires for supporting them on the rods. The four plain cards are now taken off the barrel, and the flowering cards put on, which completes the mounting of a full harness power-loom. The method for regulating the quantity of shots to be put on the cloth has been explained in Chapter III.

When the weaver is obliged to turn back the cards to find the suitable one, from any cause that may happen, such as taking out a quantity of shots, that cord which is attached to the upper catch for turning the barrel, which will be seen in Figure 6, Plate III., is taken hold of, and pulled downwards; and as both catches are connected at their points, it is evident that when the top one is taken out of gear, the under one will be raised, and come into contact with the barrel, which will turn the barrel backwards along with the cards, when the weaver depresses the treadle H. The treadle H is depressed by the weaver's foot, and to prevent the harness from being lifted too high, a guide is placed on the under edge of the treadle for that purpose, which enables the weaver to work the jacquard machine with the greatest ease.

To keep the wooden frame that guides the upright needles steady, there are four small spiral springs used; two of them are shown in Plate III. (right above the word, Figure 6, and below the jacquard machine), the other two are placed at the opposite end of the machine, and not shown in the drawings. These springs are in general made of brass wire, or some other material that will not be affected by dampness.

PRESSURE HARNESS LOOM.

Those Harnesses that work in conjunction with the heddle leaves, which leaves force the warp of the Web into a shed, are denominated Pressure Harnesses. In a pressure harness the warp threads in each mail vary from two to seven, and sometimes more; but for many kinds of cloth, it is not necessary to have an equal quantity of threads in each mail, although it is better to have them as near as possible equal, as it makes the turnings in the figure more regular.

This mode of weaving has been applied to the making of many different kinds of goods, such as shawls, ladies' dresses, table-cloths and covers, napkins, bed-mats, &c.; and to make the principle of this plan of weaving understood, the reader is requested to look at Plate II., Figure 4, where an end view of a loom, with a pressure harness mounting, will be seen. It will be observed that the warp threads cross each other between the heddles and the harness. For illustration, suppose the warp of the Web to be white, and the weft red, and that none of the warp is lifted by the harness, the heddle leaves in this case would make tweeled cloth, according to the quantity of leaves employed, which in this loom are 5; and as there is never more than 2 leaves working at the one time in a pressure harness, the consequence will be, that only a fifth-part of the warp is lifted each shot, and the upper side of the cloth will be red, and the under side white, or nearly so. If the loom be allowed to work two inches of cloth in this way, and then work two inches with the whole harness lifted, only a fifth-part of the warp will be sunk, and the colours will be reversed. It will be obvious that if the loom was to work for some time in this manner, a red and white stripe would be woven, each stripe two inches broad; but suppose that cards cut for plain cloth were to be put on the machine barrel, every alternate mail would be raised, and along with them half the warp; and if the heddles were allowed to stand idle for a short time, and the machine to work every shot, this would make plain cloth the same as a full harness, if each mail had only one thread of warp in it; but in this harness each mail has four warp threads in it, so the shuttle will pass above and below four threads alternately. Suppose now that the harness is kept up for four shots at a time, and the heddles put in motion, and the loom allowed to work for a little, the cloth produced will have the appearance of a four-and-four red and white check; because the heddles will press up and down a fifth-part of the warp threads from each half of the harness, every shot.

The reader will understand from the foregoing explanation, how any flower or figure that is within the compass of the tye can be woven. As already stated, the number of threads in each mail will vary, a harness with six threads in each mail will make a figure double the size of one with only three, if both harnesses have the same tye; also half the quantity of cards will do, for in general the same number of shots are woven for each shift of the card, as there are threads in the mail. For example,—A three thread harness will have three shots for each lift of the harness, a four thread, four shots, and so on for every thread in the mail, one shot more for each card.

A description of how a harness should be prepared is given under the head, "Full Harness," so it need not be repeated here, the only difference being, that the mails and leads are larger, and the twine stronger, than what is required for a full harness.

The mounting now to be described, was for working linen damask table-cloths, and was applied to the loom from which the drawings were taken that are given in Plates I. and II. For these table-cloths a gathered tye of 612 was employed, and the space occupied in the harness board was nearly 76 inches. What is meant by a gathered tye, is, in tying the harness, the operator takes two ends, one from each half-part, and tyes them to the tail cord, and whatever the figure is on the one half, it is the same on the other, reversed. In some figures it is necessary to take only one end from the centre of each part for the first tail cord; this is to make the centre of the figure neater, by having only one mail for the figure to turn on. But all the other tail cords, as stated before, must have two ends, one from each half-part. However, the tye for this table-cloth had only one whole-part on it, which will be apparent as we proceed with the description.

The harness, being prepared and ready for the loom, the slabstock with it is fixed in its proper position, which is shown at the words, "Harness Leads," Plate II., Figure 4. In this loom the distance between the harness and fell of the cloth was 22 inches, but this may be different in other looms. The proper distance for the mails to be from the fell of the cloth, in a pressure harness, can be found from the traverse of the lay. Let the heddles be kept as close to the lay as just to allow them to work clear of it; and suppose the distance from the fell of the cloth to the centre leaf to be about ten inches, then from the centre leaf to the centre mail in the harness should be ten inches also.

The jacquard machine having been fixed right above the centre of the slabstock, the harness tyer begins his operations by taking the two ends, forming the neck twines of the two mails that are in the centre of the harness, and the first tail cord in the machine, and tyes them together. He goes on tying two of the neck twines to each of the tail cords in regular rotation, until the whole 612 are tyed. Of course the last tail cord will have tyed to it the two outside mails, one from each selvage. It will now appear that this tye can work any figure that will come within the range of 1225 mails, or $612 \times 2 = 1224$, the number of mails in the harness; but the figure must be so drawn, that when the two halves are put together they will join without any defect, and make one complete figure.

Suppose the harness is now ready for the warp of the Web to be drawn into it, divide the whole number of ends in the Web by the mails in the harness, and this will give the number of ends or threads for each mail. The Web being a 12^{oo}, with 4920 ends in it, (which makes it nearly 76 inches wide), the threads in each mail will be 4, as will be seen from the example, after allowing 12 ends for each selvage.

EXAMPLE.

1224)4920(4 Threads in Mail.
4896
———
24 for Selvages.

When the Web is to be drawn through the harness, it must at the same time be drawn through the heddles, and the heddles are placed in the loom, in front of the harness. The drawer begins by taking the first end through the mail and heddle next the selvage; the second end is taken through the same mail, and through the second heddle; the third and fourth ends are taken through the same first mail, and through the third and fourth heddles, and so on with all the rest, four ends in each mail, taking the heddles in regular succession, until all the Web is drawn. This will take all the warp in the Web, except 24 ends, which are allowed for the selvages, and 2 or 3 mails are hung at each side of the harness board, for the selvage ends that are not lifted by the harness. If all the 12 ends for the selvage are put in one mail, a lead sufficiently heavy must be hung to the hanger, to keep them down, so that the pressure of the heddles will not be able to lift the lead.

After the Web is drawn into the harness and heddles, it is knotted up in the same manner as a common Web, but the mounting of the heddles is rather different. The eyes of common heddles are about $\frac{3}{8}$ of an inch long, but for a pressure harness the eyes must be at least 3 inches long, to allow the yarn in the harness to form a shed independent of the heddles; as 3 of the leaves out of the 5 will be at all times in a mid position, neither up nor down, while the other two are forcing the tweel shed, one of the two will take down the fifth part of the warp that is lifted by the harness, and the other will raise a fifth part of the warp that is not lifted. So when tying up the heddles the under end of the eyes are to be brought nearly on a level with the race of the lay; and when this is done, a piece of wood is put on the top of the jacks at P. P. P., Figure 1, Plate I., and firmly tyed down upon them, to keep them parallel with the heddle shafts, for the time being, when the workman is connecting the heddle shafts to the jacks and treadles with cords, which cords are represented at 5 and 6, Figure 1, Plate I.

When the heddles are mounted, the piece of wood is taken off the jacks, and two or three inches of cloth is woven with the heddles, the harness being allowed to stand idle. By doing this, the workman will see if the sheds are properly formed, better than if both the harness and heddles were working. If the jacquard machine and harness board have been adjusted, according to the direction given under "full harness," the loom will be ready for the flowering cards; and if the Web is to be woven with the same quantity of weft as warp, then the set of cards will contain 1224 flowering cards, and 6 blank or uncut ones, making in all 1230; but to this should be added other ten tweeling or blank cards, to allow room for a hem on each end of the table-cloth. It will be seen from the position of the heddles in the loom that the harness requires to make a shed double the size of what is made by the heddles, (see dotted lines, Figure 4,

Plate II.), so as to have the sheds that are made by the harness and heddles both the same size in front of the reed where the shuttle runs. The shed made by the harness is regulated in this loom in the same manner as in the full harness one.

In the same Plate, at Figure 5, will be seen a drawing of the disengaging apparatus, which apparatus is for regulating the quantity of shots the loom works for every change of card.

It is common in the trade to say so many shots on the card, as four shots on the card, five shots on the card, &c., which means that the loom works that number of shots for each card, and for this table-cloth there was four shots on the card, and as the set contains in all 1240, including the blank and tweeling ones, that number multiplied by 4 will give 4960 shots for one table-cloth. The reader will understand from this that any figure or pattern can be woven up to that quantity of shots.

To save expense in cards, manufacturers in designing for table-cloths, very often makes the pattern of the one end of the cloth the same as the other; when this way is adopted half the cards will do, by working them back for the second half of the cloth.

Suppose, that it is wanted to have 15 shots on the cloth, instead of 12, and to keep the table-cloth the same length, and to have no more cards in the set, the disengaging apparatus is made to put five shots on the card instead of four; because if four gives twelve, five will give fifteen. This is accomplished by changing the pinion S on the boss of the wheel, c, c, at Figure 5. If the wheels and pinions in this apparatus are properly proportionated, any degree of wefting can be put upon the cloth with far more accuracy than with the hand-loom weaver, because it will not forget, as a weaver might do, the number of shots for each card. For example, if the weft that is wanted on the cloth be equal to $4\frac{3}{4}$ shots on the card, then 3 cards would require to have 5 shots, and one 4, which will make 19 shots for 1 revolution of the stud wheel in the disengaging apparatus. It will be observed that there are 4 studs in the wheel shown in the figure, but they are set to work only 4 shots on each card, and 4 times 4 being 16, a pinion will be required to be put on, so as the wheel will make 1 turn for 19 shots. Suppose again, that the cloth wanted is to be equal to $3\frac{1}{8}$ shots on the card, this example will show how any nicety can be attained by this apparatus. To find the pinion required for the different shifts,—first find how many shots will be required for one revolution of the stud wheel, and it will be found by multiplying the number of shots on the card by the denominator of the fraction.

EXAMPLE.

$3\frac{1}{8}$ Shots on Card.
8
———
25 Shots for 1 turn of the Wheel.

It will be evident that the wheel will require to have 8 studs in it, for the $3\frac{1}{8}$ shots on the card, which will be equal to 7 cards with 3 shots on each, making 21, and 1 card with 4 shots, which makes up the 25. After this explanation, with the description given at page 157, it will be easily understood how the apparatus should act.

STENTING ROLLERS.

At page 159 there is given a short description of the use of these rollers, and it will be well for the reader to look at the drawings again, and the description there given.

The little or no elasticity in linen yarn has always been a drawback to the weaving of it in a pressure harness, because the heddles have to force the yarn from the harness shed to form the tweeling sheds; therefore that part of the warp which is pressed sustains the whole strain or weight of the pace; and the consequence is that the rest of the warp in the harness does not form a proper shed, by it becoming slack. When experimenting with the pressure harness in the power-loom, the greatest difficulty we had to contend with was to keep the warp yarn at its proper tension, and this led to the introduction of these rollers, which are represented in Plate II., Figure 4. The dotted lines at q, q, q, show the position of the different portions of the warp yarn for each respective leaf; that portion of the warp which passes over the roller nearest the yarn beam, is taken through the back leaf of the heddles, the yarn passing over the next roller, through the next leaf, and so on with the others in regular rotation. When any of the leaves begin to force the shed, the spiral springs of the roller yield to the strain put upon them, and by this means the warp yarn in the harness that is not pressed is kept at a proper tightness, by the pace on the yarn beam not yielding to the pressure of the heddles. To keep the different parts of the warp distinct, it is necessary to have each roll placed a little below the one immediately behind it, as shown in the Drawing; which also shows, that the whole of the warp yarn is brought to the same level with the common warp roll, which is placed behind the harness.

By using these rollers, the following advantages are obtained:—The Web can be woven with a lighter pace, and consequently will be easier on the yarn; the cloth is made more perfect, by being free from what is called skipped warp, caused by the warp yarn being slack; the weaver's time is economised by being able to work with larger shuttles and pirns; and there is a saving of power in driving the loom, because the warp yarn does not press so much upon the shuttle, being enabled to work with larger sheds which allows the shuttle to be driven with a lighter pick.

It is essential to have the rollers strong at the

same time light, and small in diameter. They must have as much strength as not to bend in the centre, when the pressure of the yarn comes upon them, for that would destroy the regularity of the shed; they must be small in diameter, so as to take up as little room as possible; and they must be light, so as the springs will not be too much burdened with their weight. To have these three requisites, the rollers should be made of sheet-iron tinned, similar to a cylinder of a throstle frame, but on a much smaller scale.

SHEDDING.

It has been explained how a common Web is shedded, and a few words will show the difference for the shedding in this loom. As will have been noticed, the eyes of the heddles for a pressure harness is at least 3 inches long; and as the heddles must move the length of the eye besides the depth of the shed, it will be necessary to take this into calculation in making the patterns for the tweeling barrel and treadles; for if the shed wanted be 3 inches deep, and the eye of the heddle be 3 inches, then the traverse of the points of the tweeling treadles must be 6 inches, to make up for the length of the eye. But the shed must not be so large as the eye of the heddle, or the warp yarn will press upon the eyes of those that are not in the act of shedding, and put unnecessary strain on the Web.*

CHECK POWER-LOOM, WITH SIX SHUTTLES.

Checked Cloth is made by having stripes in the warp and weft; and these stripes may be formed by putting in so much coarse, and so much fine yarn, alternately, in the warp of the Web, and the same way with the weft, which will make a check. But checks are mostly made, by having the warp and weft striped with different colours, which stripes form the checks, according to their arrangement.

It is an easy matter, to have the warp striped with as many colours as may be chosen; the warping of which has been explained at pages 61, 62, and 63. But it is a very different matter with the striping to be made in the wefting; which will be apparent from the description given at page 161, about the working of the shuttle boxes.

We may also state here, how patterns are got up at first. A pattern drawer may paint on paper, from his own imagination, or from the suggestion of the manufacturer, as many as will make a pattern Web; and if the checks are small, there may be 10 or 12 of them put in it. The use of the pattern Web, is to show the effect the different colours have when woven into cloth;

---

* At page 153, where this chapter begins, on the fourth line from the top, for the word "complicate" read "complete."

for very often, the patterns that look best on paper, have very little appearance in cloth. Suppose that a Web is warped 4 or 5 yards long, with ten of these patterns in it, the weaver works over each pattern, with wefting the same as the warp, which will give each pattern in the warp 9 different weftings, besides its own. And when all the 10 patterns are woven over, there will be 10 of them regular, and 90 irregular; or what is called chance patterns. All the 100 patterns are cut separate, and put in some convenient place to be examined; those that are considered fair, are put aside for a second examination, the others are thrown into the waste basket; on the second examination, if any one is found good, it is given to the Warper. The pattern Web being still in the loom, any little alteration can be made in the different patterns, that may be suggested, until the whole length of the Web be consumed in trials.

Having fixed upon a pattern, that requires 6 different colours in the wefting, it will require a lay with a six shuttle box to make it; and our object here, is to explain how these can be made to work in the power-loom, and to make the description more readily comprehended; also, for the benefit of those who wish to try their inventive faculties at making a complete power-loom for check work, the following hints are given. The number of plans that have been tried in connection with check-looms, are astonishing; and by far the largest number of them did not succeed; so the remarks given here, may be of use to the inventor and loom-maker.

When the hand-loom weaver requires to use more shuttles than 5, he in general works with a single shuttle lay, and has the number of shuttles lying on a board, at the side of the loom, which he picks up with his hand, as they are required to be changed, according to the pattern; but in the power-loom, this has all to be done by machinery.

To have a complete power-loom for making the various kinds of checks used in tartans and fancy dresses, the apparatus used, as an index for the pattern, must have an extensive range, such as what may be obtained by using the jacquard machine for that purpose.

It should have a weft stopper motion that will stop the loom the first shot, and this will cause the use of a fork at each side of the Web, or some other thing that will act upon the loom whenever the weft is away, not allowing it to run one shot afterwards, as is the case with the common weft motion.

The mechanism for shifting the shuttle-box should be so made, that any shuttle can be brought into play so as to make any pattern that can be imagined. A contrivance for stopping the loom when the shuttle-driver is not properly taken back at the double-box side of the lay; for if the driver happens to be in the box at the time it should be shifted, either the box or the driver will be broken, perhaps both.

If the box is not brought to its proper position when shifted, there should be a protector to stop the loom to prevent damage being done to the picking or shuttle box.

As mistakes sometimes occur by putting in the wrong colour, and thus spoiling the pattern, some mechanism should be applied that will prevent the loom from working if the proper coloured pirn be not in the shuttle; and as it would be difficult to make the loom distinguish colours, the pirns that the weft is wound upon could be made with different shaped heads, each colour having its own kind of pirn; and if the shuttle is filled with a wrong pirn, the loom will not work, because the proper pirn is not in the right shuttle.

As stated at page 161, the Drawings marked Plates III. and IV., show an arrangement for 6 shuttles, which will answer for the pattern fixed upon; and the pattern given at page 64 will do for an example in the arrangement of shuttles, supposing the slate colour is understood to be wefted with white.

It will be seen at page 64 that the first of the pattern is 60 of Brown; and suppose, for the sake of reference, that the shuttles are numbered 1, 2, 3, 4, 5, and 6, No. 1 being the shuttle in the top box, the others to be in regular rotation to No. 6, the shuttle in the bottom box. To work this pattern, the box will require to be shifted as under:—

60	of	Brown,	...	1st Shuttle.
2	,,	Red,	...	2nd ,,
2	,,	Orange,	...	3rd ,,
2	,,	Yellow,	...	4th ,,
8	,,	Green,	...	5th ,,
2	,,	Brown,	...	1st ,,
20	,,	White,	...	6th ,,
2	,,	Brown,	...	1st ,,
8	,,	Green,	...	5th ,,
2	,,	Yellow,	...	4th ,,
2	,,	Orange,	...	3rd ,,
2	,,	Red,	...	2nd ,,
10	,,	White,	...	6th ,,
10	,,	Brown,	...	1st ,,
10	,,	White,	...	6th ,,
4	,,	Red,	...	2nd ,,
14	,,	White,	...	6th ,,
14	,,	Brown,	...	1st ,,
4	,,	Green,	...	5th ,,
2	,,	Orange,	...	3rd ,,
20	,,	Brown,	...	1st ,,
20	,,	White,	...	6th ,,

On examination of this pattern, it will be observed, that the shuttles cannot be taken in regular succession, by working the box up or down, without missing some of the shuttles; and to obtain this, each shuttle must be at the control of the index for the pattern, which in this case is the set of cards working on the jacquard machine.

What is called a 400 jacquard machine has, in general, 51 rows of needles, with 8 in each row, which in all makes 408; and the tye of the "full harness" which has been described is, 400, which leaves 8 needles not required for the harness; 6 of these 8 are taken for regulating the movements of the shuttle box; as the wefting was one shot above, even with the warp, the set of cards were 440, for the complete pattern of the flowering; the checking pattern, being just half the size, it is twice repeated on the set of cards, as it only required 220 shots to complete the check pattern. The ends of the cards right opposite the needles, set aside for the checking, are not cut, except when the shuttle box is to be shifted, and then 1 hole is punched in the card, to correspond with the shuttle, which is to be brought into play. It will be seen from this pattern, that only 22 cards will require to be cut for 1 repeat of the checking, the remainder being all left blank at their ends.

After the pattern is arranged on the cards, the workman will require to adjust each shuttle box to its respective lever, or treadle; and this is done by turning the cam S, Figure 9, round, until the full part of it presses upon the tumbler, then screwing up the chains at X, to have both of them the same tightness, when the shuttle box belonging to that lever is in its proper place. After this has been repeated upon all the 6 levers, the 6 needles in the jacquard machine are connected with cords to the bell cranks that work the tumblers in the levers; and care must be taken to have the proper needle attached to the lever that is to work the shuttle corresponding to the pattern. It will be observed in Plate III., Figure 7, that there is a spiral spring (marked 8) for each of the 6 cards, but only 1 is shown in the drawing; and as the jacquard machine may be lifted higher at one time than another, these springs yield to the over-lift, which saves the cords from being broken, and the needles from receiving any undue strain.

It will also be observed at the back of the rack ($d^1 d^1$) Figure 11, that there is a projecting casting, with 6 hollow curves, 1 for each shuttle box; these curves are used for keeping the shuttle box steady, at the instant the shuttles are being picked. As the cam S makes 1 revolution for every two shots; the shuttle box is relieved every second shot from the strain put upon the rack, so that the box can be shifted every second shot if required. Another thing that these curves are used for is, that if the chains do not bring the sole of the box exactly level with the race of the lay, the small pulley (g) being pressed into the curve, by the cam S, makes them exactly level. But if one of the chains breaks, and the box stops when the small pulley (g) is opposite one of the projections, then the protector for stopping the loom, when the shuttle box is not properly shifted, takes effect and stops the loom.

The shuttle cord at that side of the loom where the shifting box is placed, must be so adjusted as to allow the driver, when taken back, to touch the lever, J J, shown at Figure 6, Plate III., or the loom will not work, because this lever acts upon the apparatus for stopping the loom when the driver is not taken back to its proper position. When the weft stoppers and other parts about the loom are all properly set, the loom will be ready for making cloth. And although this check-loom that we have been describing has also a harness, the description given will answer for any kind of checked work; for if the harness be not required for the kind of work to be woven, a small machine, made on the principle of the jacquard machine, will do for an index for the pattern. But if the manufacturer has already got jacquard machines, he can use them for that purpose with an old set of cards that may have the number in it for the pattern, which will save the expense of getting new ones.

CHAPTER VI.
LAPPET WEAVING, &c.

To represent flowers and figures on the surface of woven cloth has been a work or an amusement to females in every age, generally known by the name embroidery, which was commonly done by sewing; using, for the sewing thread, a different kind of yarn from what the cloth was woven with. This difference might either consist in the sewing thread or yarn being coarser, or in the colour of it; so lappet weaving is just to make representations of different kinds of flowers, birds, and other things, on the surface of woven cloth, although this is not sewing, but a mere imitation of it.

Articles of dress, ornamented with sewed work, have long been held in esteem; and the prices paid for some of them were astonishing, which may have been the reason for so many different inventions for the purpose of making sewed work cheaper, and the introduction of machinery for imitating needle work, which enables the manufacturer to bring that class of goods to the market at a low price. Among those machines, may be classed, the tambouring frames, the embroidering machines, and the different kinds of looms that have been used for that purpose; the lappet loom is one of them which will now be explained.

The ground of lappet cloth may be either plain texture, or gauze, or it may be both, by having stripes of gauze work interspersed with the plain cloth. But the descriptions given in this place, will be to show how the "whip" is put upon the surface of the cloth, to form the figures.

Whip is the name given to that kind of yarn which is used for making the figures in lappet weaving, and it is made by twisting together so many ends of common yarn, in the same manner as sewing thread is made. The twist put upon it depends entirely upon the kind of work it is to be used for. A very large quantity of the whip used in lappet weaving, is made from 40s and 50s; but the following list will show some of the varieties that are used:—

				White.	Red.	Blue.	Orange.	Other Colours.
2	Ply	of	No. 18s,	,,	,,	,,	,,	,,
3	,,	,,	18s,	,,	,,	,,	,,	,,
2	,,	,,	20s,	,,	,,	,,	,,	,,
3	,,	,,	20s,	,,	,,	,,	,,	,,
2	,,	,,	24s,	,,	,,	,,	,,	,,
3	,,	,,	24s,	,,	,,	,,	,,	,,
2	,,	,,	30s,	,,	,,	,,	,,	,,
3	,,	,,	30s,	,,	,,	,,	,,	,,
2	,,	,,	40s,	,,	,,	,,	,,	,,
3	,,	,,	40s,	,,	,,	,,	,,	,,
4	,,	,,	40s,	,,	,,	,,	,,	,,
2	,,	,,	50s,	,,	,,	,,	,,	,,
3	,,	,,	50s,	,,	,,	,,	,,	,,
4	,,	,,	50s,	,,	,,	,,	,,	,,
3	,,	,,	60s,	,,	,,	,,	,,	,,
4	,,	,,	60s,	,,	,,	,,	,,	,,

Besides the preceding, there are many other sizes used, and the twist put upon them varies according to circumstances; however, the whip must always have as much twist put upon it, as to make it stand the strain it has to undergo in the process of weaving. When the merchant wishes his goods made with very soft whip, it is very difficult to hit upon the exact twist, as a great deal depends upon the quality of yarn the whip is made from, and the twist must be found out by experiment.

It is important that the manufacturer should have his whip made from good yarn; many make great mistakes in buying low-priced whip, considering it cheap; but it is a delusion, for some of the trashy stuff that is sold for whip is dear at any price to use it for lappets; because the weaver can neither make quantity nor quality to remunerate the manufacturer if the whip is not good.

LAPPET LOOM.

The framing of a power-loom for weaving Lappets is nearly the same as the framing of one for plain cloth, the stretch being rather longer to allow room for the whip rolls and the extra traverse of the lay; the shedding, picking, and a number of other things, are similar to those in the common loom, and will not be taken notice of here; but before beginning to explain the different articles that are required extra for the lappet loom, it may be stated, that the crank and wyper shafts should be so placed as to give ample room for the lappet mounting to work without coming in contact with any other parts about the loom, and the cranks should be made with a throw sufficiently large to give the lay nearly 7 inches of a traverse. The space that the needle frames take up in the lay is the cause of this large traverse. It will also be necessary when putting up the gearing for driving the looms, to take into consideration the extra space they will occupy, compared to what is required for common looms.

LAPPET WHEEL.

The pattern to be woven is drawn upon design paper, from which the wheel-cutter works. The wheels for lappets are in general made of plane-tree, being previously well seasoned, but they may be made from any other kind of hard wood that is close in the grain, and not liable to cast by change of the atmosphere.

The diameter of the wheel will depend upon the size of the pattern, although for very small patterns, such as the honey-comb, it is not advisable to have the wheel so small as just to have the pattern once on its circumference, because the grooves are very soon worn with the peck, and this will spoil the neatness of the figure; therefore, for small figures it is better to have the pattern repeated three or four times. After the diameter of the wheel has been fixed upon, and the number of teeth that will be required for the pattern, the piece of wood is put into a lathe, for the purpose of being turned to its proper size. On the side of the wheel where the groove or grooves, as the case may be, are to be cut, a number of circular lines are made for the guidance of the workman when cutting the pattern; these lines may either represent the space of 1, 2, or 3 splits of the reed of the intended Web, and the workman will cut accordingly. Steel combs can be got any pitch required for making the circular lines on the wheel all at once; there is also a small groove cut in the wheel, near its circumference, for the pace cord.

After the wheel is turned, the next process is to divide its circumference into as many divisions as will make up the number of teeth required; this is done by an index which is fixed on the spindle of the lathe, or by a dividing machine, the number of teeth having been ascertained from the pattern on the design paper. When these divisions have been marked for the teeth, a straight line is drawn from each mark to the centre of the wheel. The circular lines represent the warp of the Web, and the straight ones the weft; for each straight line there will be two shots of weft, and for each circular line there may be two, four, or six threads of warp, according to the fineness of the comb.

The workman will now draw on the face of the wheel

those parts that are to be cut for the groove, and the design paper will show him how many threads of the warp will require to be traversed by the lappet needle to form the pattern at each tooth of the wheel; and to this space must be added the space that the peck will occupy. When he has got the piece cut out for the first tooth to correspond with the first line on the design paper, he takes the next line for the second tooth, and so on for the round of the wheel.

Suppose, for illustration, that before the wheel was taken out of the turning lathe a groove had been cut in it half-an-inch wide, and suppose the peck to be a quarter of an inch, then it would follow that a straight stripe of whip a quarter of an inch broad would be woven on the face of the cloth. Now it will be evident that if the groove be made wider at any part of the wheel, the stripe will be made broader in proportion at that part. It is upon this principle of widening and contracting the groove, and changing its position on the face of the wheel, that any figure which will come within the range of the lappet loom may be woven.

Every new pattern requires a new wheel, and although not very expensive, at the end of a year the wheel-cutter's account amounts to a considerable sum, which has caused some manufacturers to consider whether some plan could not be devised, so that one wheel would answer for any pattern; but as yet no such wheel has been constructed, although a near approach to it was made about sixteen years ago. This wheel was made of sheet iron, was fully 22 inches in diameter, and had 180 teeth of $\frac{3}{8}$ pitch. On the face of it the circular lines were marked to correspond to the splits of a 10^{∞} reed, and opposite each tooth there was a slit about 6 inches long, into which a pair of small bolts with thin flat heads were placed, the heads projecting from the face of the plate about a quarter of an inch, to form the sides of the grooves for the pecks. These small bolts being moveable, they were shifted to any place in the slits of the wheel to form the pattern wanted.

The wheel having 180 teeth, would have a range for a pattern containing 360 shots of weft, but it will be obvious that this wheel would not answer for any pattern; for the number of weft shots contained in the given pattern must be a number that 360 will divide by; perhaps this was one of the principal reasons manufacturers had for not adopting this wheel.

LAPPET NEEDLES AND PINS.

Lappet Needles are made from brass or iron wire; iron ones are the best and cheapest, but sometimes it is necessary to use brass where the iron has a tendency to rust. The length of the needles is about $3\frac{1}{2}$ inches, and their diameter depends upon the kind of work to be woven. When the wire has been cut into lengths to form the needles, one of the points of each wire is flattened, and into the flattened part is put the hole for the whip; the other end of the wire is merely rounded a little. It is important to have the ends of the needles where the whip goes through, made very smooth, and well pointed; otherwise they would break the yarn. The pins are made of wire the same as the needles, but stronger and shorter, with no holes in them; their use will appear further on.

LAPPET LAY.

The Lappet Lay for a power-loom is similar in many respects to a common lay, and what has to be explained here is the apparatus attached to it, for the purpose of making it a lappet lay. In the first place, the reed requires to be placed about 2 inches back from the race, to allow room for the frames to work in front of it; and as the whip has to come through below the reed, a thin iron groove is bolted on the lay, for the pupose of holding the under rim of the reed. To answer this position of the reed, the top shell is bolted on to the back of the swords of the lay, instead of the front.

The pin frame, which is very like a heddle shaft, is made to work as near the race as it can be got, and is kept in its position by brass slides fixed on the swords. The use of the pin frame is to guide the shuttle along the lay, in absence of the reed. On the sole of the lay, 2 cast iron brackets are hung, for the shifters to work in. These brackets have small friction rollers in them, for the edge of the shifters to bear upon. The shifters are made of wood about $1\frac{1}{2}$ inch broad, and $\frac{3}{8}$ thick, the length of them being regulated by the breadth of the lay, and opposite the reed space, are placed 2 brass uprights on each shifter for guiding the needle frames. The needle frames are also $1\frac{1}{2}$ inch broad, and $\frac{3}{8}$ thick, with brass tips on their ends made to fit the uprights on the shifters.

For illustration, suppose that the lay be made for working 3 frames, then it will require 3 shifters; and on the top of each stump or sword will be fixed a small brander, with 3 slits in each, for the points of the uprights to work in. The needle frames are made to fit exactly in between the uprights of the shifters, and they must slide up and down easily, without having any play endways. If this is not attended to, the figure made on the cloth with the whip will not be properly formed.

The frames being all fitted, as far as the moving parts of them are concerned, the next process is, the marking off on the edges of the needle shafts how the needles are to be arranged. After having ascertained the number of splits the flower will occupy, and the number of times it is to be repeated on the breadth of the cloth, the workman makes a mark for each needle with a pair of small dividers, which are set to answer the figure. When the same figure is to be woven in a number of looms, it saves time to mark off one shaft correctly, and keep it for marking the rest from; this is done by catching the shafts that are to be marked along with the pattern shaft, in a vice, and taking a small square and applying it to the pattern shaft, when a line can be drawn across the whole of the others, and these lines will show where the needles are to be driven into the shaft. When the quantity of needles that are required have been driven into the shafts, each shaft is put on to its respective shifter, and the pecks which work in the grooves of the wheel are set. On the end of each shifter there is a small brass nob with a pinching pin, for the purpose of holding the pecks; it is by this pinching pin that the frames are adjusted endways.

The wheel and the frames being placed in the lay, the articles employed for shifting the frames can now be applied; and the different plans that hand-loom weavers have for this purpose are very numerous, which does not require an explanation here, as the movements will be readily understood, when they are described for the power-loom; suffice it to say, that what is done by machinery in the power-loom the hand-loom weaver performs with his hands or feet; indeed many of the things used in the first power-looms for lappets are very similar to what are employed by hand-loom weavers.

In making arrangements for the different movements, it must be taken into consideration the time that the movements should take place, and also the proportion of time they should occupy. In the best made lappet looms the wyper shaft extends from the one end of the loom to the other, and on each end of the wyper shaft there is a cam for working the needle frames endways; these cams are so fixed on the shaft, that when the full edge of one is up the other is down. For each shifter there is a small iron lever, the weight of which is sufficient to shift the frame; attached to the end of each lever is a leather strap or cord, which passes up and through the cast iron bracket on the sole of the lay, and the other end of the strap is fastened to a shifter with a small screw-nail. The straps are adjusted so as the levers will hang with their weight upon them when the full part of the cam is down.

When the reed comes forward to the face of the cloth, all the needles must be down below the level of the race of the lay, and this is the time the needle frames are shifted endways, the needles being all clear of the warp of the Web. If the lay has seven inches of a traverse, the needles should be full down when the reed is half an inch from the fell of the cloth, and they should not begin to rise until the reed has receded from the fell of the cloth another inch.

Many of the lappet looms are very defective in not having a proper apparatus for lifting the needle frames; most of them being lifted by the motion of the lay; and although this mode is simple in itself, that accuracy, which is necessary for the movements of the needles cannot be obtained; for the needles will not be at their highest point of elevation until the lay is full back, whereas they should be full up at the instant the shuttle begins to enter the shed. It is an easy matter with the movement of the lay, to have the needles sufficiently high before the shuttle enters the shed; but they will continue to ascend, while the lay moves back, which will put unnecessary strain upon the whip, therefore, it is better to have them lifted by a wyper or cam made for the purpose.

To make a cam for lifting the needles, first draw a circle on a piece of wood which has been planed smooth, say 7 inches in diameter, the circumference of which will be 22 inches, divide this circle into 88 equal parts, then draw a line from each part to the centre of the circle; and as stated before, the needles should be down when the reed wants half an inch from the fell of the cloth, and remain down until the reed has receded another inch, which will make $1\frac{1}{2}$ inch. The cam being placed on the under shaft, which makes one revolution for two picks, it will require to be similar in shape to the cam G, in Figure 2, Plate I.; consequently, one revolution of the cam will lift the needles for two shots. It will be evident that for one revolution of the top shaft, 44 parts of the 88 will have passed a given point, and as the needle frames should remain up for the time that the top shaft will take to make a half turn; this will take 22 parts, and 6 parts for the needles, to remain down, will leave 16 parts; 8 to lift the needles, and 8 to allow them to fall, making in all 44; the other half of the cam is divided in the same way, which makes up the whole 88 parts.

Suppose, now, that a circle be drawn on the piece of wood $3\frac{1}{2}$ inches in diameter inside the other circle; this will leave $1\frac{3}{4}$ inch for the lift of the cam, which is divided into 8 equal parts on one of the radius lines, making a mark for each division. A pair of dividers are now taken, and one leg placed in the centre of the circle, and the other on the first mark in the radius line; the dividers are now turned round, and a mark made on each of the first lines in the four divisions, and so on with the others. When this is done, each mark can be joined by drawing a pencil line from the one to the other, which will give the proper curves for the cam. The foregoing description shows the principle upon which all cams or wypers are made. The same principle will do for drawing hearts for winding and dressing machines, and it will be obvious to the practical weaver, that nothing can be better adapted for lifting the lappet needles than a cam drawn upon this plan, as they can be made to work to any amount of accuracy.

The cams for lifting the levers that move the frames endways, are of a different shape from the one that lifts them, and may be understood from the following observations. Let the reader remember what has been stated before, that the frames must be shifted endways, exactly at the time when the needles are clear of the warp yarn, and, that that time cannot be more than the seventh part of the time, which is occupied by one revolution of the crank shaft, and from this data the form of the cams will be found.

The lappet wheel requires to be moved forward one tooth every second shot, which is done by an article called a "stamper;" this is a flat piece of iron placed in slides facing the edge of the wheel next the Web. The power applied for shifting the wheel is in general a spring of the spiral kind attached to the slide, which spring is adjusted to give just as much power as turn the wheel. The wheel on the end of the wyper shaft is cast with a slit in it, into which is placed a small pulley for working the lever that lifts the stamper. When the cams that work the levers for shifting the frames endways, are in a mid position, neither up nor down, this is the time the lappet wheel should be shifted, because at this point the strain of the pecks on the grooves in the lappet wheel is taken off. The reason for not shifting the lappet wheel direct from the loom is, that if any obstruction takes place to retard its motion it is not forced round beyond the power of the spring.

STARTING THE WEB.

The Web is put into the loom, and plain cloth made before the whip is drawn through the eyes of the needles. Below the yarn beam, on each side of the loom, the brackets are fixed for the gudgeons of the whip rolls to run in; each needle frame requires a roll for itself; and the number of needles in the frame, gives the number of ends that is required to be put on the roll. After the whip rolls are put in their places, the ends are taken under and over the spring cords, and through between the legs of the heddles at the proper intervals, and then under the rim of the reed, and through the eyes of the needles. A small cord is put round each roll for the purpose of pacing the whip. When the needle frames are lifted, a quantity of whip will be drawn off the rolls; and when they descend at the time the reed comes forward to the cloth the whip would remain slack if the spring cords did not act upon it, and the spring cords must be so adjusted, that they will yield to the lift of the needles, and at the same time have spring enough to take up the slack of the whip.

The loom can now be put on, and a few inches of cloth woven; this is the best time to see that all the things are properly set. The mounting of the heddles is done in the same manner as if it was a plain Web; the sheds should not be large, and the eyes of the needles when raised should not be higher than the upper half of the shed, to avoid unnecessary strain being put upon the whip, but they must be raised as high as to allow the shuttle to pass freely under the whip.

Having explained how common lappet cloth is made, and the different parts and movements for accomplishing this, a description of some of the varieties will now be given. It will readily be understood from what has been stated, how any figure of a running nature can be made; but when figures that stand detached from one another are to be woven, a different arrangement requires to be made; for instance, if a sprig is to be woven on the cloth, and each sprig to stand at a distance of half an inch; then the frames will require to be put out of gear, or what is called in the trade, dropped. This is managed in the following manner:—Upon the back of the lappet wheel near to its circumference, is fixed a piece of wood or iron, of sufficient length to occupy the space for the number of teeth that will be required for the half inch of cloth which intervenes between the sprigs. This piece of wood or iron is made to project about three-quarters of an inch from the wheel, and in some convenient place a small lever is attached, in such a manner that the projection on the wheel can act upon it. This lever may be made to work either in a perpendicular or horizontal position, whatever way the form of the loom will suit best. At the point of this lever is affixed a cord, which acts upon the apparatus for dropping the needles.

As already observed, the needles and also the pin frame for guiding the shuttle, rise every shot, and suppose all the 3 needle frames are to be dropped at the same time, it will be obvious that the pin frame must continue to work, so provision must be made to allow the needle frames to discontinue working while the pin frame works on. This is done by having an intermediate crank or catch, which is attached to the lifting rod for each frame; and so long as the lappet wheel does not indicate that the frames are not to be lifted, they continue to rise; but when the wheel comes round to that part where the frames are to be dropped, this catch is drawn to one side and does not act, and the needle frames are not lifted so long as the wheel presses upon the small lever. But after the loom has made the number of picks necessary for the interval of half an inch between the figures, the catches are allowed to go into their former position, and the frame again rises and continues to work until the time arrives that they should again be dropped.

When flowers are to be woven which have different colours in them, and some of the parts being detached from the main figure which continues to work; in this case some of the frames will be dropped, while the others will continue to work. It is by arranging the frames in this manner, that many of the different varieties may be woven.

GAUZE STRIPES, &c.

Gauze stripes are frequently made in lappet cloth, which goes under a great variety of names. The principle upon which they are all woven is nearly the same, which is to cross the warp threads, and this is sometimes done by the heddles behind the reed, and sometimes it is necessary to have the heddles before the reed; and in this case they move backwards and fowards with the lay.

Plain gauze may be said to be the foundation of all the other kinds; and when it is properly understood to comprehend the other kinds, is comparatively easy. Suppose a plain Web drawn upon 2 leaves of heddles, and the leaf next to the lay or fore leaf to be cut away, and the back leaf, with half of the warp of the Web in it, fixed up in a position so as the warp threads will be high enough for the top shed; this part of the warp will be the top shed for every shot of weft. Now, suppose the yarn that was in the fore leaf, to be drawn into what is called doups, (which is the under part of the heddles); these doups to be on 2 heddle shafts, what is on one shaft is to pass over the warp threads from the right; and what is upon the other from the left, so as the warp will form a shed for the shuttle to run through, first on the one side, and then on the other, alternately, and this will make plain gauze. To weave gauze in this manner, it will be necessary that the back leaf be placed at a sufficient distance from the doups, so as to allow the warp threads to cross without being too much strained.

Needles may be used for making gauze, and for some kinds very advantageously, if two needle shafts, such as is used for lappets, be taken, and each shaft to have as many needles in it as will contain half of the warp that is in the Web, and if these shafts be placed in a frame immediately behind the lay, one shaft with the points of the needles up, and the other with the points of the needles down, and if these needle shafts are made to move up and down, and one of them to move a little endways, (at the time the two halves of the warp are clear of each other,) for the purpose of crossing the warp threads; if the top shaft with its needles descend $1\frac{1}{2}$ inch, and the under one ascend $1\frac{1}{2}$ inch, a shed will be formed of $2\frac{1}{2}$ inches, allowing half an inch for the yarn in the eyes of the needles to be clear, at the time the frame is shifted endways.

By adopting the needles and frames for working gauze in the way described, it will be easy to imagine how any kind of gauze or net work may be woven, as all the different varieties depend upon how the warp threads are crossed; and that crossing just depends upon how the needle frames are shifted endways, which can be done with a very simple apparatus, such as a lappet wheel, or barrel. And for extensive patterns, such as those used for shawls and scarfs, the use of the jacquard machine may be taken advantage of, for regulating the shift of the needles, when there would be no end to the variety that might be produced. But it must be understood, that when more threads are to be crossed than what is contained in one split, the needle frames must be made to work before the reed, and behind the race of the lay. It will also be obvious, that if a number of these needle frames be employed in the same manner as heddle levers are, for tweeling, a still greater variety of patterns may be woven.

In working with a number of needle frames where the crossings of the warp are unequal, it will not do to have all the warp of the Web on one beam, so that the workman will require to consider the extent of the shift for each frame, and get beams warped for these frames; which require more or less warp than what is required for the common crossings. It may be difficult to get at the exact length of the warp for each frame, when starting a new pattern; but after the first Web is woven, it will be easy to find the proper quantity for each beam by keeping a note of the length first warped, and then measuring the yarn that is left on the beams, after the whole of the yarn has been woven off one of them; (that is, when one of the beams is out).

The plan or method of working the needle frames is

as follows:—To shift the frames endways, has been already explained, which is done in the same manner as the needle frames for lappets. The sinking and rising of the frames can be best done by having a roller above and one below the needle shafts, and the shaft attached to these rollers in the same way as common heddles; so that when the one rises the other will descend. To accomplish this every shot a wyper can be put on the end of the crank shaft, which makes one revolution for every shot, or a double cam or wyper (of the same kind as shown at G, in Plate I., Figure 2,) can be put on the under shaft, which makes only one revolution for every two shots, and this cam will work a treadle, to be put in connection with one of the rollers, that when the treadle is depressed by the cam, the shed will be formed. But as there is only one treadle to work the frames up and down, a spring or weight must be used to close the shed, or bring the frames back to the position they occupied before the shed was formed. If the spring or weight be objectionable, and in some cases it may, then a cam can be put on the shaft that will work the treadle both up and down.

When the Web is very fine great care must be taken to have the needles properly set into their frames, for if this be not attended to, the figure will not be formed according to the design.

It has already been stated, that the jacquard machine might be employed for gauze work. We will now endeavour to explain how it can be applied both for gauze and lappets. Suppose, for example, the figure requires the frames to have a range of 10 inches endways; and at the end of the lay, where the lappet wheel is usually placed, instead of the wheel, there is fixed a pair of hole boards, of the same set as the reed or Web that is to be woven. These hole boards are fixed with their edges towards the lay, and the one above the other about half an inch apart, and their holes right opposite. If the Web to be woven be a 10^{∞}, there will be 270 holes in each board, that is allowing each hole to occupy a space equal to a split in a 10^{∞} reed. Into each of the holes in the top board is put a piece of wire like a lappet needle, with its eye up, which is allowed to drop into the hole directly below in the under board; the under board having a piece of thin wood fixed on its under side, for the purpose of preventing the wires from falling through. The jacquard machine is placed in any convenient part above the loom, and small cords are attached to each of the wires, and then tied to the tail cords of the jacquard machine in the same manner as in tying a harness, each wire having a tail cord for itself. Consequently, there will be 270 of the needles of the jacquard machine employed.

In this arrangement, a peck is used for guiding the frames, similar to those used with the lappet wheel; but that part of it which works in the groove of the wheel is made much longer, as the length of it must be equal to the breadth of the boards that hold the wires. The figure to be woven must be drawn on design paper, in the same manner as it is drawn for lappet weaving, and the cards cut, so as the wires will be lifted to form the space for the peek to work in, in the same manner as forming the groove in the lappet wheel. The principle of the lappet wheel has been already explained. However, in working lappets with the jacquard machine, the length of the figure will depend upon the number of cards used, and any quantity can be employed, if there be room to hold them. The machine will require to be lifted every second shot, and remain up for the two shots; the same length of time that the common lappet wheel stands unmoved by the stamper. How to accomplish this will be understood by referring to the description given of the disengaging apparatus, at page 157, also page 192.

SEWING FRAMES FOR LOOMS.

There is a species of figured work done in the loom with what is called sewing frames, which may be very appropriately explained in this chapter, although it does not come under the name of lappets. To persons unacquainted with weaving, some of the figures done in the lappet loom look very like those done by the sewing frames, but they are very different, and the name given to this kind of weaving (sewing frames), implies that it comes nearer to sewed work done by the hand than any other done in the loom.

Many a contrivance has been planned, and put into operation, for this species of weaving; but before describing any particular one, it will be better to explain the principle upon which this kind of sewing is done. It is a matter of choice what the ground of the cloth should be where the figures are to be sewed on; it may be either plain, or tweeled, or both. But suppose it to be a plain ground, and the figure to be sewed a small spot or sprig, which will occupy a space on the cloth of a quarter of an inch, and the sewing thread to be all on the one side of the cloth; in this case one thread of the warp, or at most two, is lifted at each side, where the edge of the spot or sprig is to be formed, and the sewing thread put through, below them. After this the plain shed is formed, and a shot of weft is thrown for the plain ground, then the warp threads at the edge of the spot or sprig is lifted again and the sewing thread put through, then a plain shot of weft, and so on alternately. If the sewing thread is to be shown on both sides of the cloth, then as much of the warp is lifted as will make the extent of the figure, which, in this case, is a quarter of an inch, and the sewing thread is put through below it, then the plain shot of weft is put in, next the sewing thread is put above the same warp threads as it went below before, and so on alternately; this is the principle upon which sewing is done in the looms.

A description will now be given of some of the plans that have been adopted for putting in the sewing thread. In this kind of weaving it has been found advantageous, in almost all instances, to use the jacquard machine for forming the figures, and, for simplicity, it is better to use it alone, allowing both the ground of the cloth and the figures to be made by the jacquard machine. This plan may cause a little more expense for harness twine and cords, but it is by far the most simple way for the weaver, as he has only to work the one treadle; whereas, if a separate mounting was put up for making the ground of the cloth, he would have to work the extra quantity of treadles which that ground may require. The figure having been drawn on design paper, and the extent of the tye fixed on, the cutting of the cards and the mounting of the harness is proceeded with in the same manner as for a full harness, which is explained under "Full Harness," the only difference being that the ground cards, and those used for the figures, will require to be laced in such a manner that a figuring and a ground card will act upon the needles of the jacquard machine alternately, so as the warp of the web will be raised to answer both for the ground and the figure when required.

One kind of sewing frame consists of a flat rod of

wood placed in front of the top shell of the lay, on which are fixed the small brackets for holding the shuttles with the sewing thread. These brackets are arranged to suit the number of figures which is to be sewed on the breadth of the cloth, and between each bracket a space is left of sufficient extent for the range of the figure. The bracket itself is a little broader than the shuttle is long, but the size of both the shuttle and bracket, and also the space that is between the brackets, depend on the size of the figure to be woven, and also the quantity of figures in the breadth of the cloth. When the weaver has formed the shed for the sewing shuttles, the lay is put back, and the sewing frame depressed so as to allow the small shuttles to be thrown through the shed, from one bracket to another; this is done by shifting another rod endways, which is placed along the top shell, all the shuttles are moved simultaneously, each having a lever attached to the rod. The frame is now raised out from the warp, and the lay brought forward to the fell of the cloth, and the shed made for the ground shot, which is next put in, then the shed for the figure, when the frame is again depressed as before, and the small shuttle thrown back into the brackets they were first moved from, next a ground shot, and so on, a shot for the figure and one for the ground alternately. If the sewing thread is to appear on both sides of the cloth the same, the small shuttle, after being thrown through the shed and raised up from the warp, is shifted back to the other bracket before the frame is again depressed for the next shot.

Another plan of the sewing frame is, instead of the brackets and small shuttles, to have a number of small copper pieces, about $1\frac{1}{4}$ inch in diameter, and one-eighth of an inch thick, hollow in the centre, and formed like a half moon, or the letter, C; into the inside of the copper circle is put the sewing thread, and the warp threads being also brought up into the inside, or hollow part of the circle, through the opening in its edge, the copper is made to make one revolution, and by doing so takes the sewing thread under the warp threads. The circles or copper pieces are made to turn by a rack fixed on the top shell of the lay, the teeth of the rack gearing into small pins that project from the sides of the copper pieces. When the weaver is working he shifts this rack with the same hand as he works the lay, in the same way as a check weaver changes the shuttle box, and with as little trouble; as there is a stopper fixed on the top shell to prevent it from going too far, either to the one side or the other, but just to allow it to have as much traverse as to turn the circles once round. This plan does not admit of having the sewing thread shown on both sides of the cloth.

There is another method, which in some respects is very like the one first explained, It is superior to any of the others for working spots. When the space between the spots is not more than one inch, instead of a small shuttle being used, as in the first plan, a small brass tube is employed, made in shape similar to a common bottle, the neck of the bottle answering for the eye of the shuttle; the sewing thread is put into the tube at the opposite end of the neck, and then the end closed up, by screwing in a small piece of brass plate. These tubes lie loose on the small brackets, which are depressed into the warp, and are made to roll through the shed, from the one bracket to the other; the brackets are made a little hollow, so as the tubes will not fall off them by the vibration of the lay. By using the tubes the spots can be shown on both sides of the cloth, if required.

It may be noticed here, that this kind of weaving has not yet been applied to the power-loom with any advantage; and from the nature of the work, and the low price of hand-loom labour, it is not likely to be a profitable job for the power-loom for a long time to come, unless some plan be invented very different from any of those kinds known at present. All the different movements that are required in this species of weaving can easily be done in the power-loom, but the difficult part is, to get some contrivance which would keep all the small shuttles working properly, and stop the loom the instant that any one of them requires to be refilled with the sewing thread; even this might be accomplished, but then the small quantity that each shuttle holds would cause the loom to be so frequently stopped, that it would not pay. However, no one knows what may be done.

CHAPTER VII.
MOUNTING FOR TWEELS, DIAPERS, &c.

What is meant here by mountings is the articles or apparatus used for moving the heddle leaves to form the sheds of the web, such as wypers, cams, barrels, rollers, &c.

In Chapter II. a number of draughts are given, and the treading for the same, of different kinds of tweels and diapers. A description will now be given of some of the best mountings for working the heddles, commencing with the three leaf tweel. If the cloth to be woven is of that nature which does not require the warp to be spread (that is, all the warp threads standing at equal distances from each other), then a common wyper, with three arms, will do for working the treadles; but if the warp is to be spread, then the wyper requires to be made so as at least one of the heddle leaves will be always down. How to obtain this, and make it understood, it will be requisite to make a few remarks about the speed of the tweeling shaft.

The shaft for a three leaf tweel makes one revolution for every three picks or shots, or one for three of the top shaft; but the tweeling shafts are in general driven from the under shaft, which makes one revolution for two of the top one, so the wheel and pinion will require to be in the same proportion as two to three. For example, if the pinion on the under shaft has 40 teeth, the wheel on the tweeling shaft will require to have 60 teeth. The proper time for the shed to be full open, is the time the top will take to make a half turn. It is explained in the last chapter, how the proper curve is found for cams and wypers, and it has only to be stated here the number of parts that will be required to form the circle of the wyper.

To find the proper form for a wyper of this kind, divide a circle into twelve equal parts of a given diameter, which diameter will depend upon the size of the wyper wanted; 4 parts of the twelve will be required for each shot (or one revolution of the top shaft), 1 part to open the shed, 2 parts to keep it full open, and 1 part to close it. But for this kind of cloth there is at least always one of the heddle leaves down, and for this purpose the wyper will require to have 6 parts of the circle for its largest circumference, the other 6 parts divided into their proper proportions for opening and shutting the shed, and the small circle of the wyper. All the three wypers are made alike, and may be cast in one piece, if thought proper. However, some people prefer having all the three a little different, for the purpose of making the middle leaf rise a little higher than the fore one, and the back leaf a little higher than the mid one, but there is no use for this difference, as the object can be better obtained by the treadles.

The best position for the tweeling shaft is in front of the low shaft of the loom, right below the heddles, and as far off the centre of the loom as will allow the points of the treadles to come fair below the centre of the heddle shafts, where the treadles and heddles are connected. The tweeling shaft will, in this case, be driven by bevel gear.

The top mounting for this three leaf tweel, consists of 2 rollers, the one above the other; the top one has a wooden or iron pulley on each end, like a cone with two steps, the small diameter of the cone is $1\frac{1}{2}$ inch, the large one is 3 inches, and it is hung in brackets from the top rail of the loom. On to the small parts of the cone are fixed leather straps, with hooks for hanging the under roller, which is just the same as those used for plain cloth, two of the heddle leaves are hung from the under roller in the usual way, the other leaf is hung by straps which are fixed to the large part of the cone on the upper roller; from the nature of this top mounting, the warp in the heddle leaf, which is lifted, will rise through double the space of what the warp in the sinking leaves will descend. If the shed wanted be 3 inches, when the two leaves have been depressed 1 inch the other leaf will have risen 2 inches; so the person who puts the web in the loom will require to take this into consideration when mounting the heddles.

Many other kinds of mountings are used for working three leaf tweels, which will be taken notice of farther on, but the one explained is considered among the best for that kind of cloth which requires to be spread.

MOUNTING FOR A FOUR LEAF TWEEL.

By refering to No. 5, page 82, the tread of a four leaf tweel will be seen, and what is said there about it will show how the wypers (we are about to explain) should be placed on the tweeling shaft.

For stout cloth such as sheeting, it is better to use wypers than the common barrel, and they are made on the same principle as the three leaf wyper, with this difference, that the heddle leaves are allowed to come even every shot. The form of the wyper will be found by dividing a circle into 16 equal parts, and following the directions already given for drawing cams and wypers.

The tweeling shaft with its wypers is placed in the loom, in the same position as that explained for the three leaf tweel, and is driven by a bevel wheel and pinion of the proportion of 1 to 2, because the tweeling shaft makes only 1 revolution for 4 of the top or crank shaft. In the example given for the three leaves, the pinion has 40 teeth and the wheel 60, and if the same pitch of teeth is to be kept in both mountings, then the nearest number that can be got is 33 teeth for the pinion and 66 for the wheel, which does not come out exactly, the one pair having 99, and the other pair 100 teeth.

The best top mounting for this tweel is three rollers, one of them hung from the top rail in the same way as if it was for plain cloth, with a wood or iron pulley on each end of it. On these pulleys are fixed straps, with small gabs or hooks sewed to their ends, for the purpose of suspending the other two rollers, about 3 inches below the top one. The first and second leaves are hung from one of the suspended rollers, and the third and fourth from the other. Suppose that the heddles are now connected to the four treadles below, the wypers will require to be so arranged on the tweeling shaft that 3 leaves will be down and one up, every shot in the same order as shown at page 82, under the head, "Four Leaf Tweel."

No. 6, page 83, is a different draught for a four leaf tweel of the same kind as has just now been explained, and to preserve the tweel the same, the wypers are arranged on the shaft so as to produce the treading, as described under No. 6, page 83. The top rollers remain the same for both draughts.

When the cloth of a four leaf tweel is to have an equal quantity of weft and warp on both sides, by sinking 2 leaves and raising 2, in the same manner as described at page 84; only two rollers are required for the top mounting, and they are both hung on brackets from the top rail of the loom. But different wypers will be required for this tweel, as will be evident by refering to the example, and the figure, No. 7, given in page 84.

The four leaf tweel can be treaded in a variety of ways, and the manufacturer who wishes to have a mounting that will answer for any of them, should adopt that kind of mounting called the barrel and springs.

A very simple barrel, for a four leaf tweel, is made by having two cast-iron flanges keyed upon the tweeling shaft, about 3 or 4 inches apart; between the flanges are placed a number of pulleys, which act upon the treadles. The quantity of these pulleys used will depend upon the number of leaves that are sunk for one revolution of the tweeling shaft. The pulleys are supported by pins, which extend from one flange to the other, and the pulleys are made as broad that 4 of them will fill the space that is between the flanges, and their diameter is so large as to allow sufficient traverse for the treadles to form the shed without pressing on the pins. These pulleys can be arranged on the pins to work any tweel that four leafs and four treads will produce. When the workman is placing the pulleys upon the pins to suit the tweel wanted, wherever a pulley is not to be put on, in place of it he puts on the pin a small cut of an iron tube to keep the pulleys in their proper position; for instance, if only 1 leaf is to be sunk the first tread, only 1 pulley is put on that pin and 3 of the iron tubes; if the second tread is to sink two leaves, two pulleys are put on and two tubes, and so on;—1 pulley for each leaf that is to be sunk, and one tube for each leaf that is to rise.

For the top mounting it is always better to use rollers instead of weights or springs, but in some instances it cannot be done, therefore recourse must be had to some other contrivance for lifting the heddle leaves. With hand-loom weavers it has been a very common practice to employ a complication of levers called marches and jacks for raising the heddle leaves, but for the power-loom this is not necessary; for by using a small spiral spring for each leaf, for raising the heddles, the whole movements of the heddles are regulated by the tweeling barrel, as the springs will yield whenever any of the treadles are pressed upon by the pulleys in the barrel. Perhaps the using of these marches with the hand-loom weaver is more convenient for him, for by using springs there is always a quantity of power lost in the hand-loom; but it is not so with the power-loom, for if the treadles and barrels are properly made, the power expended upon the extension of the spring is to a certain degree given back in the contraction. The springs can either be applied to the leaves direct, or connected to the ends of the levers, and the opposite ends of these levers attached to the heddles. Therefore, the springs make a very simple top mounting for raising the heddles.

DOUBLE BARREL.

If the fabric to be woven requires much power to form the shed, a double barrel is used, one half of it for sinking the leaves, and the other half for raising them. What is meant here by a double barrel, when used for a four leaf tweel is, one that will work 8 treadles, instead of 4; 4 treadles to pull the leaves down, and 4 to pull them up. In this case the flanges that form the sides of the barrel will occupy double the space, so as to have room to hold eight pulleys instead of four, and that part of the barrel which is to raise the leaves must be as far back from the front of the loom as will allow the rising cords to come up at the back of the heddles, to be connected to the levers above, in the same manner as shown at P, P, Figure 1, Plate 1. But sometimes it is objectionable to have the cords coming up through the yarn, and this is avoided by taking them up at the side of the loom, clear of the warp yarn. This can be done in a variety of ways. One is to have 4 long marches, with their fulcrum, at one end of the loom, and their points at the other; the points of these long marches being connected with the top levers, and the points of the treadles connected to the centre of the long marches. Another way is to have the points of the 4 treadles, which raise the leaves, turned towards the end of the loom, and their fulcrum in the centre of the loom. This does away with the long marches, as the points of the treadles are connected direct to the top levers. When the double barrel is used, the pulleys should be arranged in it from a draught made out on a piece of paper. If the tweel be the same as No. 18, at page 88, and the black squares the sinking leaves, the white squares must be the rising ones, so the pulleys must be placed in the barrel to correspond to the design paper.

The barrels made with pulleys and flanges, on the plan just now explained, although easily made, are not nearly so good as some of the other kinds, which will require to be described for working the larger tweels, diapers, double cloth, &c.

MOUNTING FOR A FIVE LEAF TWEEL.

For illustration, take No. 8, in page 85, and although it is the general rule in treading a web to sink the greatest number of leaves and raise the fewest, in this case we will reverse it, for the purpose of having an opportunity of explaining a simple plan of a barrel. In the Figure, No. 8, it will be seen, that there is one black square and four white ones, which represent the five leaves; the black are those that are to be sunk, and the white those that are to be lifted. If the tweeling shaft be placed in the loom, in the same way as it is for the three leaf tweel, the pinion for driving it will require to have 2 teeth for every 5 that is in the wheel; if the wheel has 70 teeth, the pinion will require to have 28, the two added together making 98, which number makes the nearest approach to the same pitch as the three and four leaf tweels.

As only one leaf is to be taken down at a time, all that is necessary to put on the tweeling shaft is a small projection for each treadle, arranged on the shaft in the form of a scroll, in such a manner as the one follows the other in regular succession, which projections depresses the treadles. The top mounting being made with springs, all the leaves will be held up, except the one that is taken down with the treadle that is depressed by the barrel; and to prevent the leaves from rising any farther than what is necessary to form the shed, an iron guide is placed above the points of the treadles for that purpose, which can be set to give the size of shed wanted.

When a different treading is required for a five leaf tweel from that just now explained, another kind of barrel is employed; and one of the best kinds is made up of five flanges, or plates (called "stars" in the trade), all the five being alike, only one pattern is made which is drawn in the following manner.

Before beginning to draw the form of the star, the size of the shed, the length of the treadles, and the part of the treadle where the barrel is to act upon, must be understood. The space that the points of the treadles traverse will determine the size of the shed. Suppose that to be $3\frac{1}{2}$ inches, which will be sufficient for an ordinary web, making allowance for the eye of the heddles and the stretch of the cords; say the length of the treadle is 24 inches, and the part of the treadle that is acted upon by the barrel to be 8 inches from the fulcrum or heel, from these figures (by the rule of proportion) will be found the traverse of the treadle at the barrel, which will determine the throw of the star.

If 24 inches give $3\frac{1}{2}$, what will 8 give?

EXAMPLE.

$$24 : 3\frac{1}{2} :: 8$$

$$8$$

$$\overline{24}$$

$$4$$

$$\overline{24)28(1\frac{1}{6}}$$

$$24$$

$$\overline{4}$$

$$24$$

The diameter of a barrel for 5 leaves, with its tapets in, need not be more than 10 inches, so a circle is first drawn 10 inches in diameter, then another $9\frac{1}{17}$ inches in diameter, also another $8\frac{3}{8}$ inches; after this is done divide the 10 inch circle into 20 equal parts, with a pair of dividers, and from each mark made by the dividers draw a radius line to the centre of the circle; this will give 4 parts for each tread, 1 to open the shed, 2 for keeping the shed open, and 1 to close it. The 2 parts for keeping the shed open will be part of the circle, which is 10 inches in diameter, the other 2 parts will be a curve made from the 10 inch circle to the $9\frac{1}{17}$ inch one. From the $9\frac{1}{17}$ inch circle, to the circle which is $8\frac{3}{8}$ inches in diameter, will form another curve of one part, the next two parts have the circle of $8\frac{3}{8}$ inches, so that there will be a curve made from the 10 inch circle, which will make a uniform motion for the movement of the heddles from the $8\frac{3}{8}$ circle to the 10 inch one. When all these lines are drawn upon the piece of wood that the pattern is to be made from, the form of the tapet will be got from the marks made above the line, which is $9\frac{1}{2}$ inches in diameter, and after it is got the workman begins to make the pattern for the star, by cutting away all the wood that is above, making it exactly $9\frac{1}{2}$ inches in diameter, and then cutting it out by the marks down to the circle which was drawn $8\frac{3}{8}$ inches in diameter. When this is done the star is formed, so far as its circumference is concerned.

Into each of the five divisions on the star, there is made a recess for the tail of the tapets to go into, and the 5 bolts that hold the stars together also serve for keeping the tapets in their places, therefore the bolt holes require to be cast in the centre of this recess.

When the stars are all cast, and ready for forming the barrel, they are placed on the tweeling shaft, and screwed close up to the back of the bevel wheel with the bolts. In general there is a ring cast on the back of the bevel wheel for the purpose of screwing the stars to. When putting the tapets into the barrel, the workman is provided with a piece of paper with the draught of the tweel upon it, and from this paper he sees where they should be put in, or left out; only one bolt is taken out at a time, for if all the five bolts were made loose at once, the stars would be liable to get out of position.

By using a tweeling barrel made with the stars and tapets, along with the springs for the top mounting, it has the following advantages over the one previously explained. First, the tapets can be arranged to answer any tweel that comes within the range of 5 leaves and 5 treads; and second, the heddles meet in a mid position every shot, consequently, the shed is made by the heddles rising to form the top shed, an equal distance to those that sink to form the under one; thus keeping an equal strain upon the yarn in both, which cannot be accomplished by the other barrel with any degree of accuracy.

TWEELING TREADLES.

The treadles for this kind of barrel should be made of cast iron, and the small pulleys in them, that are acted upon by the tapets, should be set a little lower than the point and heel of the treadle. This can be done by making the treadle the form of a bow, instead of it being straight.

Before going on to explain the mountings for the larger tweels and diapers, a description of the treadles that are generally used for diapers and large tweels is deemed requisite in this place, which will save any further remarks about them when explaining the different barrels.

For some kinds of work it is not convenient to use the brander for guiding the points of the treadles, and if the brander be done away with, some other mechanical contrivance must be substituted for keeping the treadles in their proper place. One of the plans employed for that purpose is to have the two outside treadles with long bearings at the treadle heel pin, and the inside of the outside treadles made broad and flat, for about 5 or 6 inches at the heel; the centre treadles being made in the same way, except that their bearings are no longer than the thickness of the treadle, in this way the treadles are kept from moving either to the one side or the other if they are properly fitted. Instead of having the flat part of the treadles the 6 inches all to the front of the heel, it is better to have 3 inches to the front and three to the back of the heel, if there is room for this way in the loom. When no brander is used in front of the barrel, the workman gets easier at the points of the treadles to adjust the sheds, and to get this advantage some made the treadles to project away back from the heel a sufficient distance, so as to employ a brander at the back of the barrel.

Sometimes the treadles (or rather levers when used in this way) are placed above the barrel, with their fulcrum at or near their centre. The one end of the lever is made to come to the centre of the loom, right below the heddles, where the heddles and levers are connected, the other end to be fair above the centre of the barrel, and on this end is fixed the pulley for the tapets to act upon. As the barrel revolves, the tapets cause that end of the lever to ascend, which is in contact with the barrel, the other end descends, and being connected to the heddles, pulls them down to form the shed. That end of the lever which is connected to the heddles, will describe part of a circle when moving, which will cause the heddles to move a little endways, and to prevent this, a small segment is cast on the end of the lever for the cord to work upon, which connects the heddles to the levers. These levers have moveable fulcrums, which can be shifted at pleasure to suit the size of the shed. They are supported by two castings, which are bolted to the framing for holding the barrel, and as the levers must always be in the position that their ends will answer for the barrel and heddles, the two castings which support them require to be shifted along with the fulcrums of the levers.

Another way to use the lever above the barrel, is to have two sets of them, and the barrel placed in the centre of the loom; each pair of levers are connected with a joint right above the centre of the barrel, and their opposite ends to the heddles. This plan is better adapted for heavy work, because the heddle shafts can be corded at two different points, whereas, in the other way, the heddle shafts are only catched in the centre with the under cords, unless small jacks be used.

These levers are sometimes employed with the barrel placed outside the loom, at the opposite end from the driving pulleys, and in this case one set is put above the heddles, and another set below them; so arranged that one end of the lever will come to the centre of the loom, and their other end to the barrel; and their fulcrum is at or near their centre, which is made moveable like the others; but in this case there is a set of treadles used along with the levers, and the points of the treadles are connected with cords to the top and bottom levers. This kind of mounting was at one time extensively used for weaving that class of goods called moleskins and corduroys.

MOUNTING FOR A SIX LEAF TWEEL.

A barrel can be made for working a tweel with six leaves from the same rules which have been given for making the five leaf barrel, and by adding one division more to the star, and one star more to the barrel, that will make the barrel to contain six stars, and each star will have six divisions. What is meant here by the word "division" is that part on the circumference of the star, which is required to make one tread. It is common for tradesmen to say, when speaking of tweeling barrels, it is a barrel for "so many leaves," "with so many treads;" for instance, if only three of these stars were put on a tweeling shaft, it would be called a barrel for three leaves, with six treads, &c.; for every star that is put on the tweeling shaft, one leaf more, and for every division in the star, one tread more; and it is plain that if stars are put on, with six divisions to make the barrel, it could work a three leaf tweel by repeating the treading for it twice on the barrel.

No. 10, at page 85, will show how the tapets are

arranged on the barrel for a regular tweel, and No. 11, at page 86, for a broken one. The top mounting for this tweel can be made with the springs, as already explained.

This barrel will make 1 revolution for six picks, and if driven off the under shaft the same as the others, the pinion will be as one to three of the wheel; and if the same pitch of teeth is still to be preserved the pinion will have 25 teeth, and the wheel 75, which is 100 for both, making the pitch exactly the same as the three leaf tweel. It will be readily understood how the treadles are made and placed, from what has been said before.

MOUNTING FOR A SEVEN LEAF TWEEL.

A barrel is made for this one by putting on 7 stars, each star with 7 treads, and the tapets put into their places in the same order as shown by No. 12, at page 86; No. 13 is the broken tweel; the pinion for this one will be in the same proportion as 2 to 7 of the wheel, the pinion having 22 teeth, and the wheel 77, making 99 in both. The top mounting and treadles for this tweel may be the same as the others.

To find the proper proportion for the number of teeth in the wheel and pinion for driving the barrels for these simple tweels,—First ascertain the number of treads the barrel will make in one revolution, then fix a number that will divide by the number of treads, and divide the number fixed upon by the number of treads, and if the barrel be driven off the under shaft, which makes one revolution for 2 shots or picks, multiply the dividend by two, which will give the number of teeth for the pinion.

For illustration take the seven leaf tweel, the barrel makes 7 treads for 1 revolution, and the number of teeth fixed upon is 77, because that number will divide by the number of treads, viz., 7, and the number of times that 7 can be got from 77 is 11, so 11 multiplied by 2 makes 22, the number of teeth in the pinion.

EXAMPLE.

7 | 77
———
11
2
———
22   Number of teeth in pinion.

Again—Suppose an eight leaf tweel with eight treads, and the number of teeth fixed upon to be 96, then 96 divided by 8 (the number of treads), will give 12, and 12 multiplied by 2 will give 24, which is the number of teeth for the pinion required.

EXAMPLE.

8 | 96
———
12
2
———
24   Teeth for the pinion.

But if the same pitch of teeth be kept for the eight

leaves as for the others, then the number of teeth for the wheel must be 80, and 80 divided by 8 gives 10, and 10 multiplied by 2 gives 20, the number of teeth for the pinion.

EXAMPLE.

```
8 | 80
    10
     2
    ──
    20   Teeth for the pinion.
```

MOUNTING FOR AN EIGHT LEAF TWEEL.

A barrel for working eight leaves is made with 8 stars, each star having 8 treads. The wheel and pinion for driving this barrel is already given, and the arrangement for the tapets for a regular and broken tweel will be seen at pages 86 and 87. It will be evident, from what is stated under "Six Leaf Tweel," that a four leaf tweel can be woven with this barrel by putting in the tapets, as shown at No. 6, page 83, for a regular tweel. It will also do for No. 18, shown at page 88, in both cases the tweel will require to be repeated two times on the barrel. This mounting will also work four shots of plain, and four shots of tweel alternately, by arranging the tapets, as shown in No. 51, on four of the stars, and keeping the draught the same as No. 6.

FOUR SHOTS OF TWEEL AND PLAIN, ALTERNATELY.

No. 51

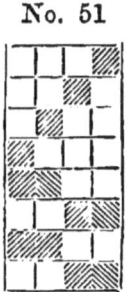

At one time the demand for this kind of cloth was very great, which caused some of the power loom weavers to turn their attention to it, and the result was that many different plans were adopted for working plain and tweel stripes. When the tweel stripe is to be made thicker than the plain one, it is necessary to have an apparatus to make the cloth beam move slower when the tweel stripe is working, which need not be explained in this place.

This barrel can also be made to work plain and tweel stripes in the warp, by employing six leaves, 4 for the tweel, and 2 for the plain, the tapets being arranged in the barrel, as shown at No. 52.

PLAIN AND TWEEL STRIPES IN THE WARP.

No. 52.

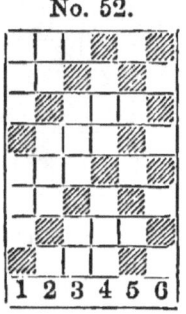

The figures, 1, 2, 3, and 4, represent the tweeling leaves, and 5 and 6 the plain ones. The size and variety of these stripes depend upon taste, but the tweeling stripes should always have as many threads as will make a full draught, which is four, so that the tweel stripes will require to be 4, 8, 12, 16, or any other number that will divide by 4.

DIAPER AND PLAIN CLOTH.

By turning to page 92, it will be seen that the five leaf diaper, No. 26, can be woven by this mounting. No. 28 and No. 29, in page 93, No. 31, in page 94, and No. 32, in page 95, come all within the range of this barrel. If plain cloth is to be woven along with any of these diapers, all that is required is to put in other two leaves, which will make seven, two for the plain and five for the diaper, as shown at No. 53; the diaper part of it is the same as No. 28.

No. 53.

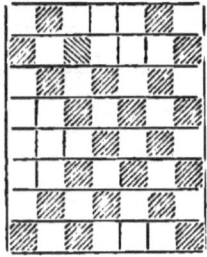

This shows the principle upon which plain and diaper stripes are woven.

MOUNTING FOR A TEN LEAF TWEEL.

The barrel for this mounting requires 10 stars, and each star 10 treads. The number of teeth for the wheel and pinion will be found by the rule given under "Mounting for a Seven Leaf Wheel." No. 21, at page 89, gives one arrangement for the tapets; and some of the other kinds of cloth that can be woven by this barrel will appear further on.

MOUNTING FOR A TWELVE LEAF TWEEL.

When a tweel requires more than ten leaves to work it, the heddle shafts are in general made much thinner, for the purpose of taking up less space in the loom. If the ordinary shafts that are used for a four leaf tweel (each shaft five-eighths of an inch thick), were taken for a twelve, the space they would occupy would be 9 inches, that is allowing one-eighth of an inch of clearance for each leap. To make this space less, the heddle shafts are made as thin as the nature of the cloth will admit of, and if the shafts are made to take up less space, the barrel must be made to correspond to the heddles. But it is found in practice a very difficult thing to keep each respective treadle working properly with its respective star, if the stars that compose the barrel be as thin as the heddle shafts which are employed for large tweels, and to avoid this difficulty the points of the treadles are contracted. The star should not be made thinner than five-eighths of an inch, and twelve will occupy a space of $7\frac{1}{2}$ inches. If the heddles are made to work in the space of 5 inches, the points of the treadles must be made to work in five inches also; and the way to manage this is to make twelve different patterns for the treadles. The 2 treadles for the centre of the barrel are made almost straight, the point of the one bent a little towards the left hand, and the point of the other a little towards the right, the next 2 treadles are bent in the same manner, having a little more bend than the first two, and so on, with each pair of treadles, over all the twelve, giving each treadle a little more bend than the one next it, so that the difference between the space occupied by the points of the treadles from what they occupy at the barrel, will be $2\frac{1}{2}$ inches.

Before commencing to make the patterns for treadles

of this kind, a ground plan of them and the barrel should be drawn the full size, showing the space that each treadle will occupy, and from this drawing the exact bend of each treadle will be seen; it will also show the exact thickness for the brander blades.

The driving of this barrel is different from those previously explained, on account of its size in circumference, it making only 1 revolution for 12 picks. Like the others, it has 1 star for each leaf, each star having 12 treads; and if it was driven in the same way, the wheel would be so large, that it would be inconvenient to have the barrel placed in the loom to answer the heddles; and in order to have it placed in the position most suitable for the heddles to be corded in the same manner as the others, the following alterations are made. Instead of the stars being bolted to a bevel wheel, they are bolted to a spur one on the opposite end of the tweeling shaft, so as to allow the barrel to get close to the under shaft of the loom; this is necessary, in consequence of the bends that are made in the treadles. This spur wheel is driven by a pinion, which is keyed upon the end of a small shaft that revolves in front of the barrel; and this small shaft has a bevel wheel on its other end, which is driven by a bevel pinion that is on the under shaft of the loom. If the small shaft in front of the barrel makes one revolution for six picks, the bevel pinion will be in the proportion of 1 to 3 of the wheel, and the spur pinion as 1 to 2 of the spur wheel.

Some of the barrels we have yet to explain are driven in the same way as this one for the twelve leaves, and the same pattern for the spur wheel may do for a number of them, if the number of teeth be fixed at 120, and, although the stars be of different diameters, for the different barrels, the ring on the spur wheel may be made to answer the different sizes of stars. Let the bevel pinion on the under shaft have 20 teeth, and the bevel wheel 60, and the proper speed to the twelve leaf barrel will be given by putting a spur pinion of 60 teeth on the end of the small shaft which works in front of the barrel.

TOP MOUNTING FOR LARGE TWEELS.

The top mounting for tweels with more than ten leaves requires a different arrangement from those of a less number, and one of the best kinds can be fitted up in the following manner:—

Have 2 cast iron rails, in place of 1, for the heddle-bearer, or top rail, let them be fitted up, so that the space between the two will be exactly the same as the space occupied by the heddles. At that side of the loom where the springs are to be placed, have a small bracket bolted to the upright for holding them by the ends. The springs are so arranged in this bracket, that they will all be clear of each other when working; the other ends of the springs are attached with wires or cords to the levers above, which levers work between the two top rails; the thickness of the levers will depend upon the size of the heddle shafts that are used. To prevent the springs from being too much stretched, the levers are made, with their fulcrums near to the end where the springs are attached. For medium cloth, if the shed be 3 inches, the springs may be made to yield $1\frac{1}{2}$ inch.

When the web is narrow, 1 set of levers will do for lifting the heddles; but if the web be a broad one, it is better to use 2 sets; and when that is the case, the first set, or those that the springs act upon, have an extra arm cast on them right above their fulcrum. The other set is made in the form of a bell crank, and the two sets are connected with wires, so that both are acted upon by the springs simultaneously.

The levers being hung upon pins which pass through the top rails, they are not likely to get out of order, as these rails keep them in their place when once properly fitted. The only objection to the employment of levers for lifting the heddles is, that they do not move up and down perfectly perpendicular; but that objection can be entirely removed, as stated before, by having the ends of the levers properly made; when so made, this top mounting will be found more simple to work, and take less power to work it, than those that are fitted up with the small pulleys and cords.

No. 22, at page 89, shows the arrangement of the tapets for a twelve leaf fancy tweel; and any other tweel, either regular or broken, that comes within the compass of twelve leaves and twelve treads, can be woven by the barrel and top mounting we have just been describing; it is also suitable for working a number of the diaper patterns.

MOUNTING FOR A SIXTEEN LEAF TWEEL.

The barrel and top mounting for this tweel can be made exactly on the same plan as the one for the twelve leaves, but of course will require sixteen stars, each star with sixteen treads. The driving gear will also be on the same principle as that described for twelve leaves, and the same bevel wheel and pinion will do; also the spur wheel for the barrel; but the spur pinion on the end of the small shaft, in front of the barrel, will require only 45 teeth, instead of 60, which is the number of teeth in the other.

To find the number of teeth that is required in the pinion for driving this barrel, first divide the number of teeth in the spur wheel, which is 120, by the number of treads, which is 16, then multiply the product by the number of picks the loom makes for one revolution of the small shaft, which is 6, and the answer is the number of teeth for the pinion.

EXAMPLE.

16)120(7½ × 6 = 45   Number of teeth for the pinion.
112
———
  8
———
 16
———

Another way is to multiply the number of teeth in the barrel wheel, by the picks made during one revolution of the pinion, and divide by the number of picks made during one revolution of the barrel; in this way there is no fraction.

EXAMPLE.

120
  6
————
16)720(45
   64
————
   80
   80
————

No. 23, at page 90, shows the arrangement of the tapets, for what is called a full satin tweel. It is seldom used, except for very fine goods, and then it is used along with a harness for the ground of the cloth.

MOUNTING FOR DIAPERS.

Those mountings that consist of the barrel formed with stars, and the springs for raising the heddles, which have been described for tweeling, will do for a number of the diapers; and it will only be necessary to state the different barrels that are suitable for diapers, as we proceed, beginning with the three leaf diaper.

MOUNTING FOR THREE LEAF DIAPERS.

It will be seen at page 91, No. 24, B, how a three leaf diaper is treaded; and that it requires 6 treads to complete the pattern, so that either the barrel for the six leaf tweel, or that for the twelve will do for it. In each barrel only three of the treadles are used, but the barrel for the twelve leaves will require to have the pattern repeated twice upon it. If the web be finer than a 10^{00}, six leaves of heddles should be used, each pair can be fixed as one, and attached to one treadle. This keeps the heddles from being too crowded upon the shafts, and makes it easier on the warp.

MOUNTING FOR A FOUR LEAF DIAPER.

A four leaf diaper can be woven with the same two barrels that has been pointed out for the three, because it only requires 6 treads for the pattern, which will be seen by turning up No. 25, at page 92.

MOUNTING FOR FIVE LEAF DIAPERS.

The barrel which works an eight leaf tweel will do for any diaper with five leaves, when they have not more than eight treads for the pattern; such as No. 26, at page 92, and Nos. 28 and 29, at page 93, also No. 31, at page 94, and No. 32, at page 95. All these and many more can be woven with the same barrel, by arranging the tapets to suit the pattern.

If any other pattern be wanted which can be woven with five leaves and eight treads, all that requires to be done, is to draw the pattern wanted on design paper, the full size, and from it will be seen how the tapets should be arranged in the barrel. For illustration we will draw No. 26 full size, to show how the arrangements for the tapets are got. The part of the pattern, No. 54, which is taken for the arrangement of the tapets in the barrel, is that part right above the figures, 5, 6, 7, 8, and 9, it being a diamond draught; the other part does not require to be taken.

No. 54.

In drawing small diaper figures, it is better to draw on the design paper two or three repeats of the pattern, so as to prevent any blunder being made in the cloth, where the figures join.

MOUNTING FOR A SIX LEAF DIAPER.

The barrel taken notice of for a ten leaf tweel, will do for any diaper with six leaves, and ten treads; consequently, it will answer for No. 33, in page 95, also Nos. 34, 35, and 36, in page 96, and Nos. 37 and 38, in page 97, by arranging the tapets to suit the different patterns, as shown by the respective drawings under their numbers.

MOUNTING FOR A SEVEN LEAF DIAPER.

No. 39, at page 97, is a seven leaf diaper, with twelve treads, so that the barrel for working the twelve leaf tweel will also suit to work this diaper by arranging the tapets to answer the pattern; and, although only one pattern is given for the seven leaves, with twelve treads, many more can be woven with the same number of leaves and treads, as will be readily understood from what has been previously stated under "Mounting for Five Leaf Diapers."

MOUNTING FOR EIGHT LEAF DIAPERS.

Nos. 40, 41, 42, and 43, at pages 98 and 99, show the treading or arrangement of the tapets for four different kinds of eight leaf diapers, with 14 treads. The barrel for working these patterns, is made upon the same principle as the barrel for working the twelve leaf tweel, the only difference being that 8 stars will do, and that each star will require to have 14 treads. It will be evident that none of the mountings previously explained, will answer for these diapers, because of them having 14 treads; therefore, the small shaft that works in front of the barrel, will require to make 1 revolution for $5\frac{1}{4}$ picks, and that speed can be got for it, by putting a bevel pinion on the under shaft, with 16 teeth, to drive a bevel wheel, on the end of the small shaft, which will require to have 45 teeth. The spur wheel and pinion, used for the sixteen leaf tweel will do for this diaper; namely, 120 teeth for the wheel, and 45 for the pinion.

EXAMPLE.

$$\begin{array}{r} 120 \\ 5\frac{1}{4} \\ \hline 600 \\ 30 \\ \hline \end{array}$$

14)630(45   Teeth on the pinion.
  56
  ―――
   70
   70
  ―――

MOUNTING FOR A TEN LEAF DIAPER, WITH THIRTY-SIX TREADS.

When a pattern requires more than sixteen leaves, and 36 treads, it is not advantageous to use the barrel, although barrels have been made to work as many treads as 96, and its diameter was not more than 32 inches, however, the barrel mounting does very well for 36 treads, such as No. 44 pattern, given at page 100.

The spur wheel with the 120 teeth will also do for this barrel, and the shaft in front of it, to make 1 revolution for 6 picks; the spur pinion will require to have only 20 teeth, which will be seen from the calculation.

EXAMPLE.

$$\frac{120}{6}$$

36)720(20   Teeth on the pinion.
72
———
00

When any fabric requires a large number of treads to complete a pattern, and that pattern can be made with less than 20 leaves, it is sometimes found cheaper not to employ a harness, but some of the other plans, which have been adopted for working heddles. Some of these plans will be taken notice of in this place.

There is one plan for working the heddle leaves with what is called a skeleton jacquard machine, placed above the loom, in the same way as shown at Figure 6, Plate III. For each leaf that is to be employed, there is an upright wire put in the machine, in the same manner as in the common jacquard machine, and to this wire is hung the heddle leaf; and, suppose that 20 leaves are to be used, then 20 of these wires are put in the machine; they can be lifted with a single brander blade, but it is better to have 2 rows of wires, with 10 in each, and 2 brander blades, which will take less space and material.

The heddle leaves can be taken down, either with springs or weights, and they are raised by the small jacquard machine, in the same way, and by the same appliance as described for the full harness in page 180. In this way the warp yarn will be lifted from the race of the lay to form the shed, which is in some respects an objection, and, to obviate that objection, some of these machines are made, so as the leaves that form the under shed will sink as far as the others rise to form the top one; this is done by allowing the under-board of the machine, where the needles rest upon, to descend when the brander that lifts the needles is in the act of rising. To accomplish this movement, instead of using one lever, as shown at Figure 1, Plate I., there is another put below it, which is made to descend by the motion of the top one ascending. By using this kind of machine it is thought the shedding is easier on the warp yarn, but it will be evident that it is not so simple as the other.

Like all the other mountings for figured work, the pattern has first to be drawn upon design paper, and if the pattern is to be regulated by cards, the holes are punched in them to answer to the drawing, just in the same manner as setting the tapets in the barrel. Sometimes, instead of cards, small slips of wood are used, with pegs fixed upon them, to act upon the needles of the jacquard machine, and these pegs are arranged on the slips of wood to suit the pattern that is to be woven.

Another plan is to have the small jacquard machine placed at the side of the loom, which has the advantage of being got at with less trouble when changing the pattern. There are many modifications for working the heddle leaves by the barrel and jacquard machine placed at the side of the loom, and a description of one of the best will be sufficient to lead to a knowledge of the others.

For illustration, suppose the number of leaves in the web to be 20, then place above the heddles 20 sets of levers, in the same manner as those explained for diapers, also 20 sets below the heddles, and to the ends of these levers, that project over the side of the loom, there is attached a rod with a hook or catch to each of them. This gives 20 for raising the heddles, and 20 for sinking them. Each heddle leaf is connected to a lever above and one below; and the lifting and sinking of the leaves of heddles, is by means of two iron bars, which rise and fall to form the shed. The fulcrum of the iron bars is placed at front of the loom, right below the lay, in a line with the fell of the cloth; by having them placed in that position, each heddle leaf forms a shed larger than the one immediately before it, without any alteration in the cording being made for that purpose.

The hooked rods that are attached to the levers, are made to take hold of the iron bars by means of springs, and at the point of action, before the bars begin to move from each other, the barrel or card puts out of gear the hooks that are not to be employed to raise or sink the leaves. The bars receive their motion from a cam or wyper, which is made to give the proper size of shed. It will be obvious that any length of pattern can be made by this mounting, if cards are used, but they must be all of the diced or draught-board pattern. This mounting is also well adapted for an index for the patterns of check work, where more shuttles than one are used. Instead of cards, or the common round barrel being employed to make the pattern, some use an endless chain, which is made to revolve on two small drums, the drums being made with notches to correspond to the links of the chain.

When cards of a similar kind to those used for the common jacquard machine, are employed for the skeleton machine, it is better to get them made of thin iron, when the pattern is one of those that is not likely to go soon out of fashion, as they will last much longer than the paste-board ones.

DICED WORK.

Many different kinds of patterns can be made with heddle leaves, which come under this heading. The principal thing to be attended to is drawing the warp into the heddles. The most simple pattern is what is called the draught-board; a sketch of it, on the smallest scale, is given at No. 55. It will be seen that the pattern is made by reversing the tweel, and although

No. 55.

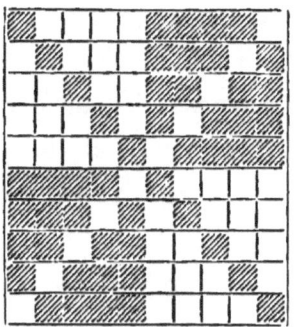

the draught is given only once over, any size of pattern can be made that the web can admit of, the whole depending upon how the web is drawn. No. 55 is a five leaf regular tweel, but in most kinds of cloth the broken tweel will answer best; however, this will show how the patterns are made. If the web to be woven be 36 inches wide, and the tweel a five leaf one, then ten leaves are required, and they are made spaced to suit the pattern, otherwise, the heddles must be set to answer it. The web being 36 inches wide, the largest pattern that can be woven on it, of the draught-board kind is 18 inches, and the smallest 5 threads, which is once over the draught; but any intermediate size of pattern, between the 5 threads and 18 inches, can be made, provided that the pattern fixed upon will repeat, a given number of times, in the breadth of the web.

By employing 15 leaves of heddles, which would make 3 sets for a five leaf tweel, the opportunity of making a larger variety of patterns is greatly increased, and some very complicated things can be done, but they have always that stiff appearance, which is unavoidable in figures made by heddles. There is nothing yet so good as the full harness, for making neat figures on cloth, and the only thing that keeps it from being generally employed, is the expense that it takes to make large patterns with it.

DOUBLE CLOTH MOUNTING.

What is meant here by "double cloth," is the combination of two warps, with their wefts. For some kinds a very simple mounting can do for them, but for other kinds they require a harness.

The principle upon which double-cloth is made is as follows:—If the fabric is to be of a plain texture, four leaves of heddles will do, two for the one warp and two for the other. Although two warps are named here for the sake of distinction, the whole warp yarn may be put on one beam, when both sides of the cloth are to be made the same.

The warp will require to be drawn through the heddles, in the same order as shown at No. 56. The letters, A, B, C, D, represent the leaves, and the figures, 1, 2, 3, 4, 5, 6, 7, and 8, show the order of

No. 56.

	5	1	A
7	3		B
	6	2	C
8	4		D

the draught. If the two leaves, A and B, were to be raised and sunk alternately, allowing C and D to stand still, plain cloth would be produced, and the warp yarn drawn into C and D would either be above or below the cloth, but more likely it would be both above and below, as the shuttle would be driven through that part of the warp, at random. If the leaves marked C, D, be taken down every shot, when A and B are working plain cloth, then all the warp in C and D will be under the cloth. Again—if the leaves C and D be taken up every shot, when the leaves A and B are making plain cloth, then all the warp in C and D will be above the cloth. If A be raised, and the other three sunk for the first shot; C sunk, and the other three raised for the second shot; B raised, and the other three sunk for the third shot; D sunk, and the other three raised for the fourth shot, and this repeated for several times, the whole warp will be woven into two pieces of cloth, which will only be joined at the selvages. Let this be properly understood, and the method for making double cloth will be readily comprehended.

It will be seen from No. 57 how the tapets should be arranged in the barrel to produce this kind of cloth; the same arrangement also answers for how the cards should be cut, if the jacquard machine is used for it;

No. 57.

and for some kinds of work, although it be plain cloth, it is necessary to use the jacquard machine.

When weaving double cloth in the hand loom, one or two extra treadles can produce a large variety of patterns, as the weaver can remember when the extra ones are to be brought into use; but in the power-loom the mounting requires to be as large as to complete one repeat of the pattern. The pattern given at No. 57 can be woven in the power-loom with a barrel with 4 treads, but the cloth will only be joined, as stated before, at the selvages. If the pattern to be woven requires 100 shots, the same as described for No. 57, and then 12 shots to join the two webs, that would make in all 112 shots for one repeat; so 112 cards will require to be used, if woven in the power loom, whereas, in the hand loom two extra treadles would only be required to produce the same effect.

TUBE WEAVING.

Woven tubes are used for many different purposes, such as those employed by brewers and bleachers for conveying their liquids from one place to another; they were also made at one time to answer for the small paper tubes, put on the spindles of spinning frames, to form the bottom of the pirns. For common grey yarn the paper ones answer very well, but when the yarn is to be bleached in the cope, the paper ones give way, and waste the yarn to a certain extent. It was to save this waste that cloth ones were brought into use, and an explanation of how they were woven will give the reader an idea how any other kind of tubes can be made.

The most difficult thing in weaving small cloth tubes, when they must be all of the same diameter, is to keep them to the proper size, because the least alteration in the wefting, alters the size of the tube. A very simple contrivance keeps them all the same size, but, before it can be understood, it will be necessary to explain first how these tubes are woven.

In weaving tubes for long lengths, it is requisite to have the yarn that is to compose the warp of each tube on a reel or bobbin, and these bobbins are put upon an arber, which is placed in the loom in the same position that the yarn beam occupies; each bobbin is paced by a separate cord or spring. If the loom they are to be woven in has a reed space of 42 inches, and allowing 3 inches for each tube, then 14 tubes can be made at the same time; and the heddles will require to be divided into 14 divisions, to suit the bobbins that hold the warp, After the warp is drawn into the heddles, in the order as shown at No. 56, it it is taken through the reed at regular intervals. The arrangement for the tapets is shown at page 274, under No. 57.

The lay is made much in the same manner as a common power-loom lay, without the ends for the shuttle boxes, and it has no protecting apparatus to stop it when any defect takes place, as it is not required, the warp yarn being double, it is sufficiently strong, that, when the shuttle stops in the shed, the pace on the bobbin yields to it without breaking the yarn. On the front of the lay is fixed 2 brackets for a wooden slide to work in, and on this slide is bolted a small brass driver for each shuttle, and one more, which makes 15 drivers in all for the 14 shuttles; this slide is driven from the common picking treadles, and, as it moves from one side to the other, it drives the small shuttles from right to left, and from left to right, through the sheds.

The shape of the shuttle is like the letter D, half round, the straight side is kept to the reed, and if the brass driver does not send it wholly through the shed, the other side being part of a circle, when the shuttle comes to the cloth part of the tube, it is forced to take its place for the next shot. When there is about an inch of cloth woven, in each tube there is placed a round piece of wood of the same diameter as the internal size of the tube, which is kept always as far forward as the reed will touch the end of it every shot, this piece of wood keeps the tube at its proper size, and the wood is prevented from moving forward with the cloth by a piece of thin iron fixed on the breast beam, through which iron, the cloth that forms the tube has to pass in a flattened state; this iron is so set that the end of the round piece of wood is always kept forward to the face of the cloth.

The weft used for these tubes is double yarn, the same as the warp, and it is wound upon small bobbins made to suit the shuttle; the weft passes through a small eye in the centre of the circle of the shuttle, and is kept to the proper tightness with a small spring, which presses on the weft bobbin.

After the tubes are woven, they are put on brass

wires, about 5 feet long, and the wires with the cloth on them are submerged into boiling starch; after they are dry, the wires are taken out, and the tubes cut into the lengths required. By putting them through this process, the tubes all stand open, which enables the spinner to get them on the spindles without difficulty.

In weaving tubes of a larger diameter, such as water-pipes, where the yarn requires to be coarse and strong, the common power-loom is not so applicable; therefore, looms are made for the purpose, the lay of which is very strong, and for each shuttle (or weft bobbin) a small frame is made, which slides into grooves made in the lay. These frames are made sufficiently long, so that the ends of them will enter the opposite groove, before it is half out of the other groove.

Some of these tubes are woven with a four leaf tweel, for the purpose of getting more weft on in a given space, than what can be got on with plain weaving. In this case eight leaves are required, which makes 2 sets of a four leaf tweel; the warp is drawn through the heddles in each set, the same as a common four leaf tweel, and No. 58 shows how the tapets are arranged in the barrel, the black squares represent the leaves that are lifted to form the shed.

No. 58.

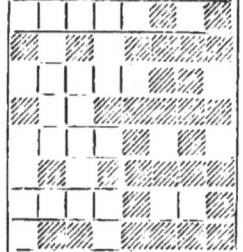

It will be obvious, that a barrel with 8 treads will be required for this.

RICE AND SUGAR BAGS.

In the common power loom, bags for holding sugar are made with the same tweel as shown at No. 58, and it will be observed, that 2 leaves are raised, and 6 sunk for the first shot; 6 raised, and 2 sunk for the second shot, and so on alternately. The best ones are made with double warp and weft, which makes a very strong fabric; they are also used for holding rice. For this sort of work only one shuttle is required, there being only one bag woven at the same time. The advantage of having them made in this way is, that they have no seam, consequently, they are much stronger, and keep the sugar better in. The weaver, for this kind of work, requires to be very attentive, to see that none of the warp threads, when broken, are allowed to remain in the shed; otherwise, the two fabrics may be woven together at that part where the thread is in the shed, and this would spoil the bag.

In general these bags are sewed at the bottom, in the common way, but they can be made so as no seam is required at all, by using the jacquard machine, instead of the barrel for working the heddle leaves. It is requisite in starting a web of this kind, to have it treaded, so as the tweel will run regularly round the bag, and not to allow it to have the appearance of a reverse tweel at the selvages.

From what has been said on this subject, it will be apparent that many other things might be woven without a seam, such as pillow and bolster slips, bedding, petticoats, &c., &c.

BED AND TOILET COVERS.

Some of the very best covers, for beds and toilets, are made on the principle of double cloth weaving, and if the reader will look at what is stated under the head, "Double Cloth," he will more readily comprehend what follows.

It altogether depends upon the quality of the cover wanted, what set of reed, also what kind of warp and weft should be used. The most common kind of covers is made with four leaves, without any figure, the one side of which is made with finer yarn than the other, and are woven together by having the tapets arranged in the barrel, as shown at No. 59; the draught is the same as a plain web.

No. 59.

C and D are the two fore-leaves, with the coarse warp drawn into them; A and B are the two back ones with the fine warp; the figures, Nos. 1, 2, 3, 4, 5, 6, 7, 8, represent the different treads; the black squares are the leaves that are to be raised, and the white ones those that are to be sunk. No. 1 tread makes the first shed, and the shuttle with the coarse weft is put through it, which makes the first shot for the top side of the cover. No. 2 tread makes the shed for the shuttle with the fine weft, and when it is put through the first shot is made for the under side of the cover. No. 3 tread makes the shed that lifts all the coarse warp and sinks the fine; the coarse weft is put through this shed. No 4 tread makes the shed which joins the two warps, and the fine weft is put through it. The treads, Nos. 5, 6, 7, and 8, are just another repeat of the same; and by continuing to work in this way, a cover will be produced with one side fine and the other coarse.

All the variety of figuring is produced upon these covers by fixing the two warps together, according to the pattern wanted, upon the following principle:—

No. 60.

A	B	C	D	
			▨	1
▨		▨		2
		▨		3
	▨	▨		4
	▨		▨	5
▨		▨		6
			▨	7
▨		▨		8
		▨		9
		▨	▨	10
	▨		▨	11
▨		▨		12
		▨	▨	13
▨				14

Suppose No. 60 to be treaded according to how it is shown at the figures, 1, 2, 3, and 4, until the loom has woven 108 shots, and 10 shots of weft (Scotch glass) put on, on each side of the cover, this will give one inch of cloth for each side, without putting any coarse weft between the two warps. When the leaves C and D are treaded, coarse weft is put in; and when the leaves A and B are treaded, fine weft is put in. The treads 5 and 6 join the two fabrics; and it is done by putting in fine weft. Then the treads, Nos. 7, 8, 9, and 10, are repeated for the same number of shots as the figures, 1, 2, 3, and 4, which will make another inch of cloth, and the treads 11 and 12 are those that join the fabrics. If this treading was continued, a stripe one inch broad would be produced without putting anything between the two warps; but if coarse weft is to be put in between the two warps for filling, then the heddles are treaded for that purpose, in the same manner as shown by the figures 13 and 14.

To make this very simple pattern in the power loom, it will require at least 218 cards, or two different barrels (or shedding gear), which can be brought into, or put out of motion, by an index whereon the pattern is arranged; but the cards with the small jacquard machine is the most simple way of doing it. In the hand loom it can be woven with a few treadles and marches. There are many small patterns that can be woven on bed and toilet covers, with heddle leaves, by employing as many as 16, and varying the draught; but when a fine flowery figure is wanted for the centre, and a border all round the cover, a harness must be used to produce the patterns; and, by taking advantage of the harness and heddle leaves, any figure can be woven to the extent of the cover, and how that can be done is fully explained in Chapter V., page 153. The only alteration that requires to be made, is in the tweeling barrel that works the heddles, and a double box put at each side of the lay.

Like any other figured work, the first thing to be done, is to put the figures on design paper, and consider what kind of tweel is for the under side of the cloth, and what is for the upper. The harness being employed to form the figure, and to fix the two fabrics together; and the heddle leaves for weaving the grounds, which can be either plain or tweeled, or the one plain and the other tweeled. It will be plain to those who have studied what has already been written, that any kind of figured bed-cover can be woven, by using this kind of mounting, by whatever name they may go under; such as diamond quilt, waved quilt, Marseilles quilts, and fancy quilts, with any colour that may be thought proper to be put in, either in the warp or weft. With all those opportunities, some very beautiful things may be woven on bed and toilet covers.

WEAVING BROAD CLOTH IN A NARROW LOOM.

CRUMB-CLOTHS.

Crumb-cloths are, in general, either made of linen or worsted yarn, and are used for putting on the top of carpets for the purpose of keeping them clean. They are considered better to have no seam in them, and suppose one is wanted six yards wide, it would require a loom with at least 19 feet of reed space to weave it, which comes to be very expensive; to obviate the expense of such a large loom they can be woven in a loom two yards wide, on the double-cloth principle, in the following manner :—

Let the fabric be equal to a 10^{00}, and the shrinkage be one in twenty, then the space that will require to be filled in the reed will be 222 inches, if woven in the common way; but in an eight-fourth loom, with six threads in the split, the space required will be only 74 inches; and all the warp that is required will be put on the beam, so as to answer this space (viz., 74 inches), the quantity of which is 12,000 ends for the warp in the web. For the purpose of making our explanation better understood, we will suppose the ground for the crumb-cloth to be a four leaf tweel, and to accomplish this, twelve leaves will be required, as there is in reality three webs on the one beam, and each web requires four leaves.

The web that is to be uppermost can be drawn on the four leaves that are next the lay, the centre web drawn into the four centre leaves, and the under web into the four back leaves.

The first shot that is thrown is for the top web, the second for the centre web, and the third for the under web. If the first shot be thrown from the right hand, the top web will be joined to the centre one at the left hand, as the second shot must be thrown from the left, and the third shot being thrown from the right, the centre web and the under one will be joined at the right hand; the fourth shot is put through the under web from the left hand, which forms the selvage for that side of the crumb-cloth; the fifth shot is put through the centre web from the right, and the sixth shot through the top web from the left, and back again through the top web, which forms the other selvage of the crumb-cloth; and this is repeated for the whole length of the web.

Examples are already given how a four leaf tweel is drawn and treaded, and the main thing to be attended to in drawing this web, is to draw each set the same as any other four leaf tweel, taking one thread on each set alternately. It will be apparent, that a barrel with 24 treads will be required to work this cloth, as it takes six shots to make one repeat of the wefting, and four shots to make one repeat of the tweel; so that 6 multiplied by 4 is 24, the number of treads required.

The explanations given here will only do for a cloth with a plain or four leaf ground, but if figures are required, a harness, or larger mounting, for working the sheds, will be necessary, which can easily be applied even to this kind of work. When the cloth is woven, and taken off the loom, it will measure three times the breadth that it stands in it, whatever that breadth may be.

CARPETS.

Many of the carpets that are sold at the present time are woven upon the double cloth principle, and are called two ply and three ply carpets. If the warps are to form the flowers, they may be woven with one shuttle, and the heddles (or harness) are made to lift that portion of the warp which is requisite to form the flower. The colours that are introduced into the flowers, will depend upon the arrangement of them in the warps. Suppose it is a three ply carpet, and each warp to be all one colour, one red, one blue, and one orange; the designer will have only these three colours to work upon in drawing the patterns. They may be drawn so as one flower may have all the three colours in it, or just the one, that will depend entirely upon what is wanted; the scope for variety with one shuttle, when there is three warps employed, is greatly increased over the two ply carpets, as one set of flowers may be all red, one set all blue, another set all orange, another set red and blue, another set red and orange, another set orange and blue, and another set red, blue, and orange, besides all the imaginable arrangements of the colours that may be introduced into the different warps in the shape of stripes. When only one shuttle is employed, and that shuttle to throw in blue weft, the figure will be brightest where the blue weft crosses the blue warp; but, so as the colours may all be as bright as possible with the one wefting, the warp of the web is made much coarser than the weft.

Another way of making two and three ply carpets, which makes a superior article, is to have as many colours in the weft as there is in the warp. This may cause the use of a great number of shuttles, but it brings up fine bright flowers where the same colour of weft and warp are made to cross each other; this is done by observing what card is made to lift the harness for the different colours, and putting in a shuttle with the same colour of weft as the warp which it is to cross, to form the flower.

In designing patterns for this kind of work, particular care must be taken to have the design painted, so as the card cutter will know what parts are to be cut, and what are to be left blank on each card. For, in reality, there will be three different sets of cards required for a three ply carpet, although they are all laced together as one set for the weaver.

For some of the more simple kinds of carpets, with small figures woven on them, instead of using the jacquard machine for working the harness, a barrel is placed above the loom, whereon the pattern is arranged. It is something similar to the barrel of an organ, and the small pieces of wires that are fixed in it to play the tune, are made to move that part of the harness which is to be lifted to form the figure, the particulars of which need not be explained here, as the movements are similar to those described under tweeling mountings, the wires being arranged in the same manner as the tapets are in the tweeling or diaper barrels.

Mr. Morton of Kilmarnock, at one time made these barrels, to a considerable extent, for weaving carpets; but the cards for the jacquard machine can be made much cheaper now, which, to a certain extent, supersedes the use of Mr. Morton's barrel, even for small patterns. This barrel does for other kinds of figured work as well as for carpets; and it may be observed that it requires to be divided into as many divisions as there are lifts of the harness in one repeat of the pattern, and that the wires or pegs are put in according to the figure on the design paper.

We have given in this chapter an explanation of mountings for working the different kinds of tweels, from a three to a sixteen leaf. In that explanation, the wyper, the pulley, the scroll, and the star kinds have been taken notice of for sinking the heddle leaves, also different plans for lifting the heddles, such as weights, springs, and the jacquard machine. We will finish this chapter by briefly noticing a few other plans for working the heddle leaves; for to make remarks on all would take up too much space.

Mr. Patrick Robertson, of Rutherglen Weaving Mill, took out a patent some years ago, the principle of which was to control the movements of heddle leaves for certain kinds of work, and his plan was considered a very good one; however, our remarks, under the following head, will not be entirely confined to this patent, but will embrace different ways how the same kind of work can be woven.

PLAIN AND TWEEL, WITH WEFT CORDS.

It is shown at page 254, how four shots of plain and four shots of tweel cloth, alternately, can be woven. When the patterns are small (for any that will be completed under 37 shots), the tweeling barrel is the simplest mounting that can be used; but if a pattern, the same as the one given under No. 61, requires to be woven, then it cannot be made with the barrel.

No. 61.

7	shots for	a cord.
24	"	plain cloth.
7	"	a cord.
49	"	tweel cloth.
7	"	a cord.
24	"	plain cloth.
118		

This pattern is woven with four leaves, the warp is drawn through the heddles, in the same order as for plain work; and for making the plain cloth part of the pattern, the common wypers are used, and for the tweel part of it a common four leaf barrel. The four leaves of heddles are corded to the four tweeling treadles in the usual way, but the two plain treadles are corded so as the leaves are at liberty to be moved by the tweeling barrel when it comes into motion; both the plain treadles and tweeling ones are so arranged that they can be put in and out of gear at pleasure. A ratchet wheel may be employed as the regulator of the pattern, and for this one it will require 118 teeth. The first part of the pattern is a cord which is made by putting in 7 shots of weft into the same shed; this is accomplished by keeping the plain shed open for 7 shots, the weft being made to turn upon one single thread at each selvage; the selvage threads may be made to perform this part independent of the heddle leaves. The second part of the pattern is 24 shots for plain cloth. The third part of the pattern is again 7 shots of weft for a cord. The fourth part is 49 shots for the tweeling. The fifth part is again 7 shots for a cord; and then for the sixth part 24 shots for plain. This makes one repeat of the pattern, which is all arranged on the ratchet wheel. On the one side of the wheel there is placed nobs or pins, for putting the shedding motion into gear; the pins on the other side are used for putting the shedding motion out of gear.

It will be evident, from what has already been stated, that, instead of a ratchet wheel for the regulator of the pattern, the jacquard machine, and the endless chain, used for working the heddle leaves, will answer the same purpose; however, the wheel will answer in this place for the illustration of the other parts.

The regulator of the pattern should be got at, with the least possible trouble to the weaver, and easily shifted to its proper position when any derangement takes place in the pattern. This has not been attended to in any of the looms which has come under the notice of the writer, but in some plans the very reverse, by putting the index or regulator of the pattern away below the loom. To any person at all acquainted with power-loom weaving, it will be apparent that the best place is to have it at the handle side of the loom, right opposite the weaver, on the upright of the heddle-bearer. Suppose it placed in that position, all that is required to be in connection with the ratchet wheel is two small levers; these levers when acted upon, put in motion the apparatus for shifting the treadles or wypers; for the object to be attained, can be done, either by shifting the wypers from off the treadles, or by allowing the treadles to fall out of gear from the wypers. If the wypers are to be acted upon, they are made to slide upon their respective shafts to one side, to be out of gear with the treadles. This is accomplished by having a long key made fast on the shaft, and a key seat cut in the wypers to correspond to it. The proper time for the wypers to be shifted, is when the heddle leaves are close; and when the one set goes into gear the other must go out at the same instant.

When the wypers are to be kept always in the same place upon their shafts, and the treadle to be acted upon for changing the shedding motion, a small arbor is placed for each set of treadles, right below the treadle heel pins. These arbors are fitted with an eccentric on each end, for supporting the treadle heel pin, and a slit is made in the treadle heel, for the purpose of allowing the pin to move up or down. When the arbor is turned, so as the full side of the eccentrics are up, the treadles will be in gear with the wypers, and that set of treadles will be put in motion for shedding the heddles; the reverse will take place when the full side of the eccentrics are down. The same appliance which can shift the wypers, can be made to turn the arbors, and that may consist of either a spring or weight, or a lever brought into contact with a cam, put on the under shaft of the loom for that purpose.

The arrangements just explained, place the wypers for we .ing the plain cloth on the common wyper shaft : it, by making suitable wypers for the plain cloth, y may be fixed on the same shaft with the tweel ones, and, in many instances, this is the preferab ay of doing it.

TAPE CHECKS, MADE WITH ONE SHUTTLE.

Tape checks are now very common; they were originally made in the hand-loom, but now mostly made by power. The ground of the cloth is similar to that of a jaconet, and they are striped in the warp and weft, by putting in coarser yarn, or a number of plies of fine, to form the stripes. They are taken notice of here for the purpose of explaining how they are made with one shuttle; and for the guidance of those unacquainted with this fabric, it may be of use to state what numbers of yarns they are made of:—

For a 10^{00} 60s Warp, with 80s weft.
,, 12^{00} 70s ,, ,, 90s ,,
,, 14^{00} 80s ,, ,, 100s ,,

The sizes of yarn given here are those that are commonly used, but some tape checks are made with much finer yarns, for the purpose of making the ground of the cloth more transparent. Suppose the pattern to be 2 inches of fine and 12 shots of coarse weft alternately, the coarse yarn being two ply of 40s, and the fine 80s single, the usual way to make this pattern is to have one shuttle for the fine and another for the coarse weft, and change them either by hand or with a double box.

To make this pattern with one shuttle, the same apparatus that has been explained for making the cord in No. 61, will do for making the tape in this pattern, by putting in 4 shots of No. 80s in one shed, then changing the shed and putting in other 4 shots, and repeating this for 12 times, which will be equal to 12 shots of coarse weft, because 4 ply of 80s are equal to 2 ply of 40s.

After this, the wypers are allowed to work two inches of plain cloth to form the body of the check, and that will complete the pattern. It will be apparent that this plan of making tape checks is more suitable for small patterns than large ones.

For keeping the shed open for the purpose of throwing in more shots than one, some parties do it differently from the method just explained. One of the plans is to draw the small pulley out from under the wyper, and, by doing so, it is not acted upon by the wyper to form the shed, while the other is locked down to hold the shed open. Another way, is to have a spiral spring placed between one of the treadles and the heddles, this spring to be sufficiently strong to form the shed when the other treadle is not locked, and when it is locked to keep the shed open. The spring will yield to the action of the wyper. Another way, is to have both wypers loose on the shaft, and a clutch for each wyper, which can be made to gear with them, when their actions are required for the shedding.

There is another machine for working heddle leaves, known in the trade by the name, "dobie," which some manufacturers use in preference to those plans just described. This machine is very well got up, and is one of those which will work almost any kind of pattern that can be made with heddles. It is placed in the same position on the loom as the skeleton jacquard machine; and as it is just another modification of the jacquard machine, no further notice of it is required in this place.

CHAPTER VIII.

CALCULATIONS, TABLES, &c.

COSTING GOODS.

The meaning of costing is to find, by calculation, what money it will cost the manufacturer to make a given piece of cloth. It is very important that the person whose charge it is to rate the goods should have some uniform method to keep by, because, changing from one system to another, they are apt to forget some item in their calculation; therefore, before making any further remarks about the costing of goods, we will give a few specimens of rating. The prices affixed are nominal, as the specimens given are merely to show the principle of rating goods.

Rating for 50 yards of a 36 inch 12^{00} shirting, with 14 shots.

	Lbs.	Rate.	Pence.
Length, 50 yards,			
Width, 36 inches,			
Splits, 1265,			
Ends, 2530,			
Warp No. 32's, 165 hanks,	5⅛	£0 1 3	77½
Weft No. 32's, 192½ hanks,	6	0 1 2	84
Warping,			2
Dressing,			5
Weaving,			25
Charges,			20
Total cost,			214½
Discount, 5 per cent.,			10¼
Cost per yard 4½d.,			225¼
To sell at 4¾d. per yard, 5 per cent. off,			

It is better, when rating goods, to put down the amount in pence, as in the specimen given, and also to add, as in this case, the shrinkage and waste into the number of hanks of both warp and weft.

In the above rating the whole cost, with 5 per cent. added, is 225¼ pence, which when divided by 50 (the length of the piece), shows the price to be 4½d. per yard.

Rating for a 12^{00} tape check with 11 shots.

Length, 50 yards,
Breadth, $32\frac{1}{2}$ inches,
Splits, 1024 for fine, 96 for coarse, = 1120,
Ends, 2048, No. 70's, 430, No. 50, = 2478,

	Lbs.	Rate.			Pence.
Warp No. 70's, 130 hanks,	1.85	£0	2	3	$50\frac{1}{4}$
Warp No. 50's, 28 hanks,	.56	0	1	6	10
Weft No. 90's, 120 hanks,	1.33	0	2	2	$34\frac{3}{4}$
Weft No. 40's, 2 ply, 20 hanks,	.50	0	1	3	$7\frac{1}{2}$
Dressing,					$3\frac{1}{2}$
Weaving,					22
Charges,					20
Total cost,					148
Discount,					8
Cost per yard, 3.12 per yard,					156
To sell at 14s. per piece,					

In the above fabric there is 430 ends of No. 50's warp for the tape, and 12 tapes in the breadth of the web, giving 34 ends for each tape, and 22 ends for selvage yarn. There are 8 splits occupied for each tape, with 4 ends in each split, except the two outside splits, they having 5 ends in each, to form a cord or finish at the edges of the tape; this makes up the 34 ends for each tape.

Rating for a blue and white check.

	Lbs.	Rate.			Pence.
Reed, 100°,					
Shots, 12,					
Length, 72 yards,					
Breadth, 38 inches,					
Splits, 1065,					
Ends, 1062 for blue, 1068 for white, = 2130,					
Warp 24's for blue, 102 hanks,	4.25	£0	1	0	51
Warp 20's for white, 102 hanks,	5.10	0	0	11	56½
Weft 20's for blue, 123 hanks,	6.15	0	0	10	61½
Weft 16's for white, 123 hanks,	7.68	0	0	9½	73½
Bleaching half of the warp and weft,	12.78	0	0	1	13
Dyeing,	10.40	0	0	5	52½
Winding 11⅓ spindles, warp at 1d. 13⅝ weft, 1½d.,					32
Warping,					5
Dressing,					9
Weaving,					115
Charges,					24
Total cost nett,					493
Price per yard, 6.84,					
Selling price per yard, 7½d.					

The above rating is made out on the supposition that the web is to be woven in the hand-loom, the web being dressed and prepared in the same manner as for the power-loom. The white warp is rather less than 56½ pence, also the white weft is less than 73½, but the manufacturer takes the benefit of the fractions.

FORM FOR RATING BOOK.

	Lbs.	Rate.	Pence.
Date,			
Reed,			
Shots,			
Length,			
Breadth,			
Splits,			
Ends or runners,			
Warp, cotton, hanks,			
Warp, silk, hanks,			
Warp, lace yarn, hanks,			
Weft, cotton, hanks,			
Weft, silk, hanks,			
Whip,			
Bleaching,			
Dyeing,			
Winding, spindles,			
Warping,			
Dressing,			
Drawing or twisting,			
Weaving,			
Finishing,			
Charges,			
Total cost,			
Price per piece,			
Price per yard,			

The above is considered one of the best forms, as it will answer for most kinds of work; and the manufacturer, by having the rating-book ruled and printed according to this form, or any other he may think better, will save himself a considerable amount of trouble. A blank space should be left at the bottom of each page for remarks.

ONCOST OR CHARGES.

Before the charges can be properly ascertained for any piece of goods, it is necessary to know what may be called the rent of the loom, also the sum that is required for furnishings, &c., and this will entirely depend upon the nature of the cloth to be woven.

For some power-loom factories, where common light cloth is to be woven, the whole outlay for buildings, boilers, engines, gearing, winding, warping, and dressing machines; looms, water, steam, and gas pipes, along with warehouse furniture, will not be more than £21 per loom, supposing the factory to be as large as will contain 500 looms, as the smaller the factory is it will cost the more per loom.

For weaving some kinds of goods, the outlay per loom is as high as £80, before cloth can be made. However, we will take the outlay at £30 per loom for a data, to show how the oncost expenses, or charges are found; what that £30 is made up of will be shown in another place.

In a mill with 500 looms, the following sums affixed to the different articles, have been found in practice to be nearly correct, taking an average of a few years. This statement, except the first seven items, and two or three others, was given to the writer some years ago, by a manager in the power-loom trade, who has had long experience in the management of power-loom factories; but every manufacturer will require to find out the exact sum for himself, which can be easily done at the end of six or twelve months. The amounts given in this place are for one year.

STATEMENT OF EXPENSES FOR ONE YEAR.

500 looms at the rate of £30 each is £15,000.

1—Interest on £15,000 at 5 per cent., - -	£750	0 0
2—Depreciation for one year, - - - -	750	0 0
3—Insurance on Mill and Stock, - - -	270	0 0
4—Feu duty, poor and police rates, &c., say -	240	0 0
5—For gas, nett, - - - - - -	114	8 10
6—Water for boilers, &c., - - - -	95	0 0
7—Manager's salary, - - - - -	180	0 0
	£2399	8 10
8—Fuel, 1245 waggons, at 4s. 6d., - -	280	2 6
9—Reed-maker's account for one year, - -	65	10 0
10—Heddles, - - - - - - -	133	0 0
11—Rods, heddles, shafts, and shuttles, - -	57	8 0
12—Castings, iron, and work done out, - -	279	0 0
13—Ironmongery, - - - - - -	33	0 0
14—Brushes, - - - - - - -	24	16 6
15—Tinsmith's account, - - - - -	19	0 0
16—Rope-spinner's account for pace cord, &c., -	22	0 0
17—Shuttle cords, - - - - - -	146	0 0
18—Oil, Tallow, and Soap, - - - -	280	0 0
19—Heddle paint, - - - - - -	6	12 0
20—Wood, - - - - - - -	27	0 0
Carried forward, - - -	£3772	17 10

		£	s.	d.
	Brought forward,	3772	17	10
21—	Shuttle drivers,	25	10	0
22—	File-cutter,	6	5	0
23—	Cooperage,	3	8	0
24—	Leather,	56	0	0
25—	Glazier's account,	11	10	0
26—	Slater's account,	4	7	0
27—	Plumber's account,	3	14	0
28—	Stationery,	27	15	0
29—	Doctor's Expenses,	5	0	0
30—	Incidental expenses,	69	11	0
		£3985	17	10

To the above list must be added the following sums for wages.

		£	s.	d.
31—	1 Watchman for night, 15s. per week,	39	0	0
32—	1 Gate-keeper, 10s. per week,	26	0	0
33—	2 Sweepers for cleaning, &c., 7s. 6d.,	39	0	0
34—	1 Engineman, 24s. per week,	62	8	0
35—	For porterage,	32	0	0
36—	Blacksmith and Mechanics' wages,	176	16	0
37—	Wages for warehouse hands,	109	0	0
38—	Dressing-master, 30s. per week,	78	0	0
39—	Twisting-master, 20s. per week,	52	0	0
40—	Cleaning flues, boilers, &c.,	6	0	0
41—	Rent for town warehouse, and taxes,	90	0	0
42—	Salesman, clerk, and porters' wages,	270	0	0
43—	Postage stamps, and other expenses,	10	0	0
		£5086	1	10

After taking off the holidays, fastdays, &c., not more than 300 working days can be calculated upon for one year; so the sum, £5086 1s. 10d., divided by 300, and the product by 500 (the number of looms), will give the charge for one loom per day.

EXAMPLE.

£5086 1 10
     20
———————
101721
    12
———————
300)1220662(4068
1200
———————
 2066
 1800
———————
  2662
  2400
———————
   262

Say 4069
500)4069(8⅛
    4000
———————
     69
      8
———————
    552

This calculation shows that the expense for one loom per day to be eight pence and one eighth, which gives four shillings and three farthings per week; and suppose that one loom will produce three pieces of cloth per week, the charges for one piece will be one shilling and four pence farthing. To this will require to be added, any wages that are not put down specially in the rating, such as the tenter's wages, which is not shown in the form given for the rating-book.

The foregoing statement and observations have been made more for the guidance of new beginners than for those already in the trade, for every manufacturer who takes the trouble to look into his accounts at the end of the year, soon finds out what the oncost charges are. And it will be apparent, that if the production can be increased from three pieces per week, to four or five, the charge upon one piece will be considerably less. And it may be remarked, that the desire to make a loom to produce as much as possible in a given time, has been the great stimulant for the many improvements that have been made in power-looms of late. When it is taken into consideration how these improvements are taken advantage of, by people putting up new works, the reader will not be surprised at the item, No. 2, which is £750 per annum, being put down in the statement, for the fact is, that even 5 per cent. does not compensate, in many instances, for the depreciation that takes place in the machinery used for weaving by power; and it would be better for those in the trade, if they can manage it at all, to throw out their old machinery, and put in new whenever it is proven that the new is better, either for quantity or quality; for if they do not they are sure to be cut out of the trade by the parties who have got the improved machinery, as they are enabled to undersell them in the market, and have a profit too. However, this will be shown more clearly in another place.

MANUFACTURERS', WARPERS', AND BEAMERS' TABLES.

The annexed tables are to show the quantity of yarn contained in any given web. The use of them will be apparent to the beamer, warper, and manufacturer, as they will save time in calculation. The first column to the left hand side of each page are splits. The figures in the second column represent the porters contained in the number of splits on the same line. The first row of figures on the top of the page are ells; and the second row are yards. The body of the pages shows the number of spindles, hanks, and parts of a hank. Examples are given at the end of the tables, how they can be applied by the warper, beamer, &c.

Ells.		$\frac{4}{5}$	$1\frac{3}{5}$	$2\frac{2}{5}$	$3\frac{1}{5}$	4	$4\frac{4}{5}$
Yards.		1	2	3	4	5	6
Splits.	Porters.	Sp. Hk.	Sp. Hk.	Sp. Hk.	Sp. Hk.	Sp. Hk.	Sp. Hk.
2	$\frac{1}{10}$						
4	$\frac{1}{5}$						
5	$\frac{1}{4}$						
10	$\frac{1}{2}$				$\frac{1}{7}$	$\frac{1}{7}$	$\frac{1}{7}$
20	1		$\frac{1}{7}$	$\frac{1}{7}$	$\frac{1}{7}$	$\frac{2}{7}$	$\frac{2}{7}$
30	$1\frac{1}{2}$		$\frac{1}{7}$	$\frac{1}{7}$	$\frac{2}{7}$	$\frac{2}{7}$	$\frac{3}{7}$
40	2	$\frac{1}{7}$	$\frac{1}{7}$	$\frac{2}{7}$	$\frac{3}{7}$	$\frac{3}{7}$	$\frac{4}{7}$
50	$2\frac{1}{2}$	$\frac{1}{7}$	$\frac{2}{7}$	$\frac{2}{7}$	$\frac{3}{7}$	$\frac{4}{7}$	$\frac{5}{7}$
60	3	$\frac{1}{7}$	$\frac{2}{7}$	$\frac{3}{7}$	$\frac{4}{7}$	$\frac{5}{7}$	$\frac{6}{7}$
70	$3\frac{1}{2}$	$\frac{1}{7}$	$\frac{2}{7}$	$\frac{3}{7}$	$\frac{4}{7}$	$\frac{6}{7}$	1
80	4	$\frac{1}{7}$	$\frac{3}{7}$	$\frac{4}{7}$	$\frac{5}{7}$	1	$1\frac{1}{7}$
90	$4\frac{1}{2}$	$\frac{1}{7}$	$\frac{3}{7}$	$\frac{4}{7}$	$\frac{6}{7}$	1	$1\frac{2}{7}$
100	5	$\frac{2}{7}$	$\frac{3}{7}$	$\frac{5}{7}$	1	$1\frac{1}{7}$	$1\frac{3}{7}$
200	10	$\frac{3}{7}$	1	$1\frac{3}{7}$	$1\frac{6}{7}$	$2\frac{3}{7}$	$2\frac{6}{7}$
300	15	$\frac{5}{7}$	$1\frac{3}{7}$	$2\frac{1}{7}$	$2\frac{6}{7}$	$3\frac{4}{7}$	$4\frac{2}{7}$
400	20	1	$1\frac{6}{7}$	$2\frac{6}{7}$	$3\frac{6}{7}$	$4\frac{5}{7}$	$5\frac{5}{7}$
500	25	$1\frac{1}{7}$	$2\frac{3}{7}$	$3\frac{4}{7}$	$4\frac{5}{7}$	6	$7\frac{1}{7}$
600	30	$1\frac{3}{7}$	$2\frac{6}{7}$	$4\frac{2}{7}$	$5\frac{5}{7}$	$7\frac{1}{7}$	$8\frac{4}{7}$
700	35	$1\frac{5}{7}$	$3\frac{3}{7}$	5	$6\frac{5}{7}$	$8\frac{3}{7}$	10
800	40	$1\frac{6}{7}$	$3\frac{6}{7}$	$5\frac{5}{7}$	$7\frac{4}{7}$	$9\frac{4}{7}$	$11\frac{3}{7}$
900	45	$2\frac{1}{7}$	$4\frac{3}{7}$	$6\frac{3}{7}$	$8\frac{4}{7}$	$10\frac{5}{7}$	$12\frac{6}{7}$
1000	50	$2\frac{3}{7}$	$4\frac{5}{7}$	$7\frac{1}{7}$	$9\frac{4}{7}$	$11\frac{6}{7}$	$14\frac{2}{7}$
2000	100	4	$9\frac{4}{7}$	$14\frac{2}{7}$	1 1	1 $5\frac{5}{7}$	1 $10\frac{4}{7}$
3000	150	$7\frac{1}{7}$	$14\frac{2}{7}$	1 $3\frac{3}{7}$	1 $10\frac{4}{7}$	1 $17\frac{5}{7}$	2 $6\frac{6}{7}$
4000	200	$9\frac{4}{7}$	1 1	1 $10\frac{4}{7}$	2 $2\frac{1}{7}$	2 $11\frac{4}{7}$	3 $3\frac{1}{7}$

Ells.		5 3/5		6 2/5		7 1/5		8		8 4/5		9 3/5	
Yards.		7		8		9		10		11		12	
Splits.	Porters.	Sp.	Hk.	Sp.	Hk.	Sp.	Hk.	Sp.	Hk.	Sp.	Hk.	Sp.	Hk.
2	1/10												
4	1/5				1/7		1/7		1/7		1/7		1/7
5	1/4		1/7		1/7		1/7		1/7		1/7		1/7
10	1/2		1/7		1/7		1/7		2/7		2/7		2/7
20	1		2/7		3/7		3/7		3/7		3/7		4/7
30	1 1/2		3/7		4/7		4/7		5/7		5/7		6/7
40	2		5/7		5/7		6/7		1		1 1/7		1 1/7
50	2 1/2		6/7		1		1		1 1/7		1 2/7		1 3/7
60	3		1		1 1/7		1 2/7		1 3/7		1 4/7		1 5/7
70	3 1/2		1 1/7		1 2/7		1 3/7		1 5/7		1 6/7		2
80	4		1 2/7		1 4/7		1 5/7		1 6/7		2		2 2/7
90	4 1/2		1 3/7		1 5/7		1 6/7		2 1/7		2 2/7		2 4/7
100	5		1 5/7		1 6/7		2 1/7		2 3/7		2 5/7		2 6/7
200	10		3 2/7		3 6/7		4 2/7		4 5/7		5 1/7		5 5/7
300	15		5		5 5/7		6 3/7		7 1/7		7 6/7		8 4/7
400	20		6 5/7		7 4/7		8 4/7		9 4/7		10 1/7		11 3/7
500	25		8 2/7		9 4/7		10 5/7		11 6/7		13		14 2/7
600	30		10		11 3/7		12 6/7		14 2/7		15 5/7		17 1/7
700	35		11 5/7		13 2/7		15		16 5/7	1	2/7	1	2
800	40		13 2/7		15 2/7		17 1/7	1	1	1	2 6/7	1	4 6/7
900	45		15		17 1/7	1	1 2/7	1	3 3/7	1	5 4/7	1	7 5/7
1000	50		16 5/7	1	1	1	3 3/7	1	5 6/7	1	7 1/7	1	10 4/7
2000	100	1	15 2/7	2	2 1/7	2	6 6/7	2	11 4/7	2	16 2/7	3	3 1/7
3000	150	2	14	3	3 1/7	3	10 2/7	3	17 3/7	4	6 4/7	4	13 5/7
4000	200	3	12 5/7	4	4 1/7	4	13 5/7	5	5 2/7	5	14 5/7	6	6 2/7

Ells.		$10\frac{2}{5}$		$11\frac{1}{5}$		12		$12\frac{4}{5}$		$13\frac{3}{5}$		$14\frac{2}{5}$	
Yards.		13		14		15		16		17		18	
Splits.	Porters.	Sp.	Hk.	Sp.	Hk.	Sp.	Hk.	Sp.	Hk.	Sp.	Hk.	Sp.	Hk.
2	$\frac{1}{10}$												
4	$\frac{1}{5}$		$\frac{1}{7}$		$\frac{1}{7}$		$\frac{1}{7}$		$\frac{1}{7}$		$\frac{2}{7}$		$\frac{2}{7}$
5	$\frac{1}{4}$		$\frac{1}{7}$		$\frac{1}{7}$		$\frac{1}{7}$		$\frac{1}{7}$		$\frac{2}{7}$		$\frac{2}{7}$
10	$\frac{1}{2}$		$\frac{2}{7}$		$\frac{3}{7}$		$\frac{3}{7}$		$\frac{3}{7}$		$\frac{3}{7}$		$\frac{3}{7}$
20	1		$\frac{4}{7}$		$\frac{4}{7}$		$\frac{5}{7}$		$\frac{5}{7}$		$\frac{5}{7}$		$\frac{5}{7}$
30	$1\frac{1}{2}$		$\frac{6}{7}$	1		1		$1\frac{1}{7}$		$1\frac{1}{7}$		$1\frac{2}{7}$	
40	2		$1\frac{2}{7}$		$1\frac{3}{7}$		$1\frac{3}{7}$		$1\frac{4}{7}$		$1\frac{5}{7}$		$1\frac{5}{7}$
50	$2\frac{1}{2}$		$1\frac{4}{7}$		$1\frac{5}{7}$		$1\frac{5}{7}$		$1\frac{6}{7}$		2		$2\frac{1}{7}$
60	3		$1\frac{6}{7}$		2		$2\frac{1}{7}$		$2\frac{2}{7}$		$2\frac{3}{7}$		$2\frac{4}{7}$
70	$3\frac{1}{2}$		$2\frac{1}{7}$		$2\frac{3}{7}$		$2\frac{4}{7}$		$2\frac{5}{7}$		$2\frac{6}{7}$		3
80	4		$2\frac{3}{7}$		$2\frac{4}{7}$		$2\frac{6}{7}$		3		$3\frac{1}{7}$		$3\frac{3}{7}$
90	$4\frac{1}{2}$		$2\frac{5}{7}$		3		$3\frac{1}{7}$		$3\frac{3}{7}$		$3\frac{4}{7}$		$3\frac{6}{7}$
100	5		$3\frac{1}{7}$		$3\frac{3}{7}$		$3\frac{4}{7}$		$3\frac{6}{7}$		$4\frac{1}{7}$		$4\frac{2}{7}$
200	10		$6\frac{1}{7}$		$6\frac{3}{7}$		$7\frac{1}{7}$		$7\frac{3}{7}$		8		$8\frac{4}{7}$
300	15		$9\frac{2}{7}$		10		$10\frac{5}{7}$		$11\frac{3}{7}$		$12\frac{1}{7}$		$12\frac{6}{7}$
400	20		$12\frac{3}{7}$		$13\frac{3}{7}$		$14\frac{2}{7}$		$15\frac{2}{7}$		$16\frac{2}{7}$		$17\frac{1}{7}$
500	25		$15\frac{3}{7}$		$16\frac{4}{7}$		$17\frac{6}{7}$	1	1	1	$2\frac{1}{7}$	1	$3\frac{3}{7}$
600	30	1	$\frac{4}{7}$	1	2	1	$3\frac{3}{7}$	1	$4\frac{6}{7}$	1	$6\frac{2}{7}$	1	$7\frac{5}{7}$
700	35	1	$3\frac{5}{7}$	1	$5\frac{3}{7}$	1	7	1	$8\frac{5}{7}$	1	$10\frac{3}{7}$	1	12
800	40	1	$6\frac{4}{7}$	1	$8\frac{4}{7}$	1	$10\frac{4}{7}$	1	$12\frac{3}{7}$	1	$14\frac{3}{7}$	1	$16\frac{3}{7}$
900	45	1	$9\frac{6}{7}$	1	12	1	$14\frac{1}{7}$	1	$16\frac{2}{7}$	2	$\frac{3}{7}$	2	$2\frac{4}{7}$
1000	50	1	13	1	$15\frac{3}{7}$	1	$17\frac{5}{7}$	2	$2\frac{1}{7}$	2	$4\frac{3}{7}$	2	$6\frac{5}{7}$
2000	100	3	$7\frac{6}{7}$	3	$12\frac{3}{7}$	3	$17\frac{3}{7}$	4	$2\frac{1}{7}$	4	$8\frac{6}{7}$	4	$13\frac{3}{7}$
3000	150	5	$2\frac{6}{7}$	5	10	5	$17\frac{1}{7}$	6	$6\frac{3}{7}$	6	$13\frac{3}{7}$	7	$2\frac{4}{7}$
4000	200	6	$15\frac{6}{7}$	7	$7\frac{4}{7}$	7	$16\frac{6}{7}$	8	$8\frac{3}{7}$	8	$17\frac{6}{7}$	9	$9\frac{3}{7}$

BEAMERS' TABLES.

Ells.		$15\frac{1}{5}$		16		$16\frac{4}{5}$		$17\frac{3}{5}$		$18\frac{2}{5}$		$19\frac{1}{5}$	
Yards.		19		20		21		22		23		24	
Splits.	Porters.	Sp.	Hk.	Sp.	Hk.	Sp.	Hk.	Sp.	Hk.	Sp.	Hk.	Sp.	Hk.
2	$\frac{1}{10}$												
4	$\frac{1}{5}$		$\frac{2}{7}$		$\frac{1}{7}$		$\frac{1}{7}$		$\frac{1}{7}$		$\frac{1}{7}$		$\frac{1}{7}$
5	$\frac{1}{4}$		$\frac{2}{7}$		$\frac{2}{7}$		$\frac{2}{7}$		$\frac{2}{7}$		$\frac{2}{7}$		$\frac{2}{7}$
10	$\frac{1}{2}$		$\frac{3}{7}$		$\frac{3}{7}$		$\frac{3}{7}$		$\frac{4}{7}$		$\frac{4}{7}$		$\frac{4}{7}$
20	1		$\frac{6}{7}$	1		1		$1\frac{1}{7}$		$1\frac{1}{7}$		$1\frac{1}{7}$	
30	$1\frac{1}{2}$	$1\frac{2}{7}$		$1\frac{3}{7}$		$1\frac{3}{7}$		$1\frac{4}{7}$		$1\frac{4}{7}$		$1\frac{5}{7}$	
40	2	$1\frac{6}{7}$		$1\frac{6}{7}$		2		$2\frac{1}{7}$		$2\frac{1}{7}$		$2\frac{2}{7}$	
50	$2\frac{1}{2}$	$2\frac{1}{7}$		$2\frac{3}{7}$		$2\frac{4}{7}$		$2\frac{5}{7}$		$2\frac{5}{7}$		$2\frac{6}{7}$	
60	3	$2\frac{5}{7}$		$2\frac{6}{7}$		3		$3\frac{1}{7}$		$3\frac{2}{7}$		$3\frac{3}{7}$	
70	$3\frac{1}{2}$	$3\frac{1}{7}$		$3\frac{2}{7}$		$3\frac{3}{7}$		4		$3\frac{5}{7}$		4	
80	4	$3\frac{4}{7}$		$3\frac{6}{7}$		4		$4\frac{2}{7}$		$4\frac{3}{7}$		$4\frac{4}{7}$	
90	$4\frac{1}{2}$	4		$4\frac{2}{7}$		$4\frac{3}{7}$		$4\frac{5}{7}$		$4\frac{6}{7}$		$5\frac{1}{7}$	
100	5	$4\frac{4}{7}$		$4\frac{5}{7}$		5		$5\frac{2}{7}$		$5\frac{3}{7}$		$5\frac{5}{7}$	
200	10	9		$9\frac{4}{7}$		10		$10\frac{4}{7}$		11		$11\frac{3}{7}$	
300	15	$13\frac{4}{7}$		$14\frac{2}{7}$		15		$15\frac{5}{7}$		$16\frac{3}{7}$		$17\frac{1}{7}$	
400	20	1	$\frac{1}{7}$	1	1	1	2	1	3	1	$3\frac{6}{7}$	1	$4\frac{6}{7}$
500	25	1	$4\frac{4}{7}$	1	$5\frac{6}{7}$	1	7	1	$8\frac{1}{7}$	1	$9\frac{3}{7}$	1	$10\frac{4}{7}$
600	30	1	$9\frac{1}{7}$	1	$10\frac{4}{7}$	1	12	1	$13\frac{3}{7}$	1	$14\frac{6}{7}$	1	$16\frac{2}{7}$
700	35	1	$13\frac{5}{7}$	1	$15\frac{2}{7}$	1	17	2	$\frac{4}{7}$	2	$2\frac{3}{7}$	2	4
800	40	2	$\frac{1}{7}$	2	$2\frac{1}{7}$	2	4	2	$5\frac{6}{7}$	2	$7\frac{6}{7}$	2	$9\frac{5}{7}$
900	45	2	$4\frac{5}{7}$	2	$6\frac{6}{7}$	2	9	2	$11\frac{1}{7}$	2	$13\frac{2}{7}$	2	$15\frac{3}{7}$
1000	50	2	$9\frac{2}{7}$	2	$11\frac{4}{7}$	2	14	2	$16\frac{3}{7}$	3	$\frac{4}{7}$	3	$3\frac{1}{7}$
2000	100	5	$\frac{3}{7}$	5	$5\frac{2}{7}$	5	10	5	$14\frac{5}{7}$	6	$1\frac{3}{7}$	6	$6\frac{2}{7}$
3000	150	7	$9\frac{5}{7}$	7	$16\frac{6}{7}$	8	6	8	$13\frac{1}{7}$	9	$2\frac{3}{7}$	9	$9\frac{3}{7}$
4000	200	10	1	10	$10\frac{3}{7}$	11	2	11	$11\frac{4}{7}$	12	3	12	$12\frac{4}{7}$

Ells.		20	$20\frac{4}{5}$	$21\frac{3}{5}$	$22\frac{2}{5}$	$23\frac{1}{5}$	24
Yards.		25	26	27	28	29	30
Splits.	Porters.	Sp. Hk.	Sp. Hk.	Sp. Hk.	Sp. Hk.	Sp. Hk.	Sp. Hk.
2	$\frac{1}{10}$						
4	$\frac{1}{5}$	$\frac{2}{7}$	$\frac{2}{7}$	$\frac{2}{7}$	$\frac{2}{7}$	$\frac{2}{7}$	$\frac{2}{7}$
5	$\frac{1}{4}$	$\frac{2}{7}$	$\frac{2}{7}$	$\frac{2}{7}$	$\frac{2}{7}$	$\frac{2}{7}$	$\frac{2}{7}$
10	$\frac{1}{2}$	$\frac{4}{7}$	$\frac{4}{7}$	$\frac{4}{7}$	$\frac{5}{7}$	$\frac{5}{7}$	$\frac{5}{7}$
20	1	$1\frac{2}{7}$	$1\frac{2}{7}$	$1\frac{3}{7}$	$1\frac{3}{7}$	$1\frac{3}{7}$	$1\frac{3}{7}$
30	$1\frac{1}{2}$	$1\frac{5}{7}$	$1\frac{6}{7}$	$1\frac{6}{7}$	2	2	$2\frac{1}{7}$
40	2	$2\frac{3}{7}$	$2\frac{3}{7}$	$2\frac{4}{7}$	$2\frac{5}{7}$	$2\frac{5}{7}$	$2\frac{6}{7}$
50	$2\frac{1}{2}$	3	$3\frac{1}{7}$	$3\frac{2}{7}$	$3\frac{3}{7}$	$3\frac{3}{7}$	$3\frac{4}{7}$
60	3	$3\frac{4}{7}$	$3\frac{5}{7}$	$3\frac{6}{7}$	4	$4\frac{1}{7}$	$4\frac{2}{7}$
70	$3\frac{1}{2}$	$4\frac{1}{7}$	$4\frac{2}{7}$	$4\frac{3}{7}$	$4\frac{5}{7}$	$4\frac{5}{7}$	5
80	4	$4\frac{6}{7}$	5	$5\frac{1}{7}$	$5\frac{3}{7}$	$5\frac{4}{7}$	$5\frac{5}{7}$
90	$4\frac{1}{2}$	$5\frac{3}{7}$	$5\frac{4}{7}$	$5\frac{5}{7}$	6	$6\frac{1}{7}$	$6\frac{3}{7}$
100	5	6	$6\frac{1}{7}$	$6\frac{3}{7}$	$6\frac{5}{7}$	$6\frac{6}{7}$	$7\frac{1}{7}$
200	10	12	$12\frac{3}{7}$	$12\frac{6}{7}$	$13\frac{3}{7}$	$13\frac{6}{7}$	$14\frac{2}{7}$
300	15	$17\frac{6}{7}$	1 $\frac{4}{7}$	1 $1\frac{3}{7}$	1 2	1 $2\frac{4}{7}$	1 $3\frac{3}{7}$
400	20	1 $5\frac{6}{7}$	1 $6\frac{5}{7}$	1 $7\frac{5}{7}$	1 $8\frac{5}{7}$	1 $9\frac{4}{7}$	1 $10\frac{4}{7}$
500	25	1 $11\frac{5}{7}$	1 13	1 $14\frac{1}{7}$	1 $15\frac{2}{7}$	1 $16\frac{4}{7}$	1 $17\frac{5}{7}$
600	30	1 $17\frac{5}{7}$	2 $1\frac{1}{7}$	2 $2\frac{4}{7}$	2 4	2 $5\frac{3}{7}$	2 $6\frac{6}{7}$
700	35	2 $5\frac{5}{7}$	2 $7\frac{2}{7}$	2 9	2 $10\frac{5}{7}$	2 $12\frac{3}{7}$	2 14
800	40	2 $11\frac{4}{7}$	2 $13\frac{4}{7}$	2 $15\frac{3}{7}$	2 $17\frac{2}{7}$	3 $1\frac{2}{7}$	3 $3\frac{1}{7}$
900	45	2 $17\frac{4}{7}$	3 $1\frac{5}{7}$	3 $4\frac{2}{7}$	3 6	3 $8\frac{1}{7}$	3 $10\frac{2}{7}$
1000	50	3 $5\frac{4}{7}$	3 $7\frac{6}{7}$	3 $10\frac{2}{7}$	3 $12\frac{5}{7}$	3 15	3 $17\frac{3}{7}$
2000	100	6 10	6 $15\frac{5}{7}$	7 $2\frac{4}{7}$	7 $7\frac{3}{7}$	7 $11\frac{1}{7}$	7 $16\frac{6}{7}$
3000	150	9 $16\frac{4}{7}$	10 $5\frac{5}{7}$	10 $12\frac{6}{7}$	11 2	11 $9\frac{1}{7}$	11 $16\frac{2}{7}$
4000	200	13 $4\frac{5}{7}$	13 $13\frac{4}{7}$	14 $5\frac{1}{7}$	14 $14\frac{5}{7}$	15 $6\frac{1}{7}$	15 $15\frac{5}{7}$

Ells.		24 4/5		25 3/5		26 2/5		27 1/5		28		28 4/5	
Yards.		31		32		33		34		35		36	
Splits.	Porters.	Sp.	Hk.	Sp.	Hk.	Sp.	Hk.	Sp.	Hk.	Sp.	Hk	Sp.	Hk.
2	1/10												
4	1/5		2/7		2/7		2/7		2/7		2/7		2/7
5	1/4		2/7		2/7		2/7		2/7		3/7		3/7
10	1/2		5/7		5/7		5/7		6/7		6/7		6/7
20	1		1 3/7		1 4/7		1 4/7		1 4/7		1 5/7		1 6/7
30	1 1/2		2 1/7		2 2/7		2 2/7		2 3/7		2 4/7		2 4/7
40	2		3		3		3 1/7		3 2/7		3 3/7		3 3/7
50	2 1/2		3 5/7		3 6/7		3 6/7		4		4 1/7		4 2/7
60	3		4 3/7		4 4/7		4 5/7		4 6/7		5		5 1/7
70	3 1/2		5 1/7		5 2/7		5 3/7		5 5/7		5 6/7		6
80	4		5 6/7		6 1/7		6 2/7		6 3/7		6 5/7		6 6/7
90	4 1/2		6 4/7		6 6/7		7		7 2/7		7 3/7		7 5/7
100	5		7 3/7		7 4/7		7 6/7		8 1/7		8 2/7		8 4/7
200	10		14 5/7		15 2/7		15 5/7		16 1/7		16 5/7		17 1/7
300	15	1	4 1/7	1	4 6/7	1	5 4/7	1	6 2/7	1	7	1	7 5/7
400	20	1	10 6/7	1	12 3/7	1	13 3/7	1	14 3/7	1	15 2/7	1	16 2/7
500	25	2	6/7	2	2 1/7	2	3 2/7	2	4 3/7	2	5 5/7	2	6 6/7
600	30	2	8 2/7	2	9 5/7	2	11 1/7	2	12 4/7	2	14	2	15 3/7
700	35	2	15 5/7	2	17 2/7	3	1	3	2 5/7	3	4 2/7	3	6
800	40	3	5	3	7	3	8 6/7	3	10 5/7	3	12 5/7	3	14 4/7
900	45	3	12 3/7	3	14 4/7	3	16 5/7	4	6/7	4	3	4	5 1/7
1000	50	4	1 6/7	4	4 1/7	4	6 4/7	4	9	4	11 2/7	4	13 5/7
2000	100	8	3 4/7	8	8 3/7	8	13 1/7	8	17 6/7	9	4 4/7	9	7 3/7
3000	150	12	5 3/7	12	12 4/7	13	1 5/7	13	8 6/7	13	16	14	5 1/7
4000	200	16	7 2/7	16	16 5/7	17	8 2/7	17	17 6/7	18	9 2/7	19	6/7

Ells.		$29\frac{3}{5}$		$30\frac{2}{5}$		$31\frac{1}{5}$		32		$32\frac{4}{5}$		$33\frac{3}{5}$	
Yards.		37		38		39		40		41		42	
Splits.	Porters.	Sp.	Hk.	Sp.	Hk.	Sp.	Hk.	Sp.	Hk.	Sp.	Hk.	Sp.	Hk.
2	$\frac{1}{10}$												
4	$\frac{1}{5}$		$\frac{2}{7}$		$\frac{3}{7}$		$\frac{3}{7}$		$\frac{3}{7}$		$\frac{3}{7}$		$\frac{3}{7}$
5	$\frac{1}{4}$		$\frac{3}{7}$		$\frac{3}{7}$		$\frac{3}{7}$		$\frac{3}{7}$		$\frac{3}{7}$		$\frac{3}{7}$
10	$\frac{1}{2}$		$\frac{6}{7}$		$\frac{6}{7}$		$\frac{6}{7}$		1		$1\frac{1}{7}$		$1\frac{1}{7}$
20	1		$1\frac{5}{7}$		$1\frac{6}{7}$		$1\frac{6}{7}$		$1\frac{6}{7}$		$1\frac{6}{7}$		2
30	$1\frac{1}{2}$		$2\frac{4}{7}$		$2\frac{5}{7}$		$2\frac{5}{7}$		$2\frac{6}{7}$		$2\frac{6}{7}$		3
40	2		$3\frac{4}{7}$		$3\frac{4}{7}$		$3\frac{5}{7}$		$3\frac{6}{7}$		4		4
50	$2\frac{1}{2}$		$4\frac{3}{7}$		$4\frac{4}{7}$		$4\frac{4}{7}$		$4\frac{5}{7}$		$4\frac{6}{7}$		5
60	3		$5\frac{2}{7}$		$5\frac{3}{7}$		$5\frac{4}{7}$		$5\frac{5}{7}$		$5\frac{6}{7}$		6
70	$3\frac{1}{2}$		$6\frac{1}{7}$		$6\frac{2}{7}$		$6\frac{3}{7}$		$6\frac{5}{7}$		$6\frac{6}{7}$		7
80	4		7		$7\frac{2}{7}$		$7\frac{3}{7}$		$7\frac{4}{7}$		$7\frac{5}{7}$		8
90	$4\frac{1}{2}$		$7\frac{6}{7}$		$8\frac{1}{7}$		$8\frac{2}{7}$		$8\frac{4}{7}$		$8\frac{5}{7}$		9
100	5		$8\frac{6}{7}$		9		$9\frac{2}{7}$		$9\frac{4}{7}$		$9\frac{6}{7}$		10
200	10		$17\frac{4}{7}$	1	$\frac{1}{7}$	1	$\frac{4}{7}$	1	1	1	$1\frac{3}{7}$	1	2
300	15	1	$8\frac{3}{7}$	1	$9\frac{1}{7}$	1	$9\frac{6}{7}$	1	$10\frac{4}{7}$	1	$11\frac{2}{7}$	1	12
400	20	1	$17\frac{2}{7}$	2	$\frac{1}{7}$	2	$1\frac{1}{7}$	2	$2\frac{1}{7}$	2	$3\frac{6}{7}$	2	4
500	25	2	8	2	$9\frac{2}{7}$	2	$10\frac{4}{7}$	2	$11\frac{4}{7}$	2	$12\frac{5}{7}$	2	14
600	30	2	$16\frac{6}{7}$	3	$\frac{2}{7}$	3	$1\frac{5}{7}$	3	$3\frac{1}{7}$	3	$4\frac{4}{7}$	3	6
700	35	3	$7\frac{5}{7}$	3	$9\frac{2}{7}$	3	11	3	$12\frac{4}{7}$	3	$14\frac{2}{7}$	3	16
800	40	3	$16\frac{3}{7}$	4	$\frac{3}{7}$	4	$2\frac{2}{7}$	4	$4\frac{1}{7}$	4	6	4	8
900	45	4	$7\frac{2}{7}$	4	$9\frac{3}{7}$	4	$11\frac{4}{7}$	4	$13\frac{5}{7}$	4	$15\frac{6}{7}$	5	0
1000	50	4	$16\frac{1}{7}$	5	$\frac{3}{7}$	5	$2\frac{6}{7}$	5	$5\frac{2}{7}$	5	$7\frac{4}{7}$	5	10
2000	100	9	$14\frac{2}{7}$	10	1	10	$5\frac{5}{7}$	10	$10\frac{3}{7}$	10	$15\frac{2}{7}$	11	2
3000	150	14	$12\frac{2}{7}$	15	$1\frac{3}{7}$	15	$8\frac{4}{7}$	15	$15\frac{5}{7}$	16	$4\frac{6}{7}$	16	12
4000	200	19	$10\frac{4}{7}$	20	$1\frac{6}{7}$	20	$11\frac{3}{7}$	21	3	21	$12\frac{4}{7}$	22	4

BEAMERS' TABLES.

Ells.		$34\frac{2}{5}$		$35\frac{1}{5}$		36		$36\frac{4}{5}$		$37\frac{3}{5}$		$38\frac{2}{5}$	
Yards.		43		44		45		46		47		48	
Splits.	Porters.	Sp.	Hk.	Sp.	Hk.	Sp.	Hk.	Sp.	Hk.	Sp.	Hk.	Sp.	Hk.
2	$\frac{1}{10}$												
4	$\frac{1}{5}$		$\frac{3}{7}$		$\frac{3}{7}$		$\frac{3}{7}$		$\frac{3}{7}$		$\frac{3}{7}$		$\frac{4}{7}$
5	$\frac{1}{4}$		$\frac{3}{7}$		$\frac{3}{7}$		$\frac{3}{7}$		$\frac{3}{7}$		$\frac{4}{7}$		$\frac{4}{7}$
10	$\frac{1}{2}$		1		$1\frac{1}{7}$		$1\frac{1}{7}$		$1\frac{1}{7}$		$1\frac{1}{7}$		$1\frac{1}{7}$
20	1		2		2		$2\frac{1}{7}$		$2\frac{1}{7}$		$2\frac{1}{7}$		$2\frac{2}{7}$
30	$1\frac{1}{2}$		3		$3\frac{1}{7}$		$3\frac{1}{7}$		$3\frac{2}{7}$		$3\frac{2}{7}$		$3\frac{2}{7}$
40	2		$4\frac{1}{7}$		$4\frac{2}{7}$		$4\frac{2}{7}$		$4\frac{3}{7}$		$4\frac{3}{7}$		$4\frac{4}{7}$
50	$2\frac{1}{2}$		5		$5\frac{1}{7}$		$5\frac{2}{7}$		$5\frac{3}{7}$		$5\frac{4}{7}$		$5\frac{4}{7}$
60	3		$6\frac{1}{7}$		$6\frac{2}{7}$		$6\frac{3}{7}$		$6\frac{4}{7}$		$6\frac{5}{7}$		$6\frac{6}{7}$
70	$3\frac{1}{2}$		$7\frac{1}{7}$		$7\frac{3}{7}$		$7\frac{4}{7}$		$7\frac{5}{7}$		$7\frac{6}{7}$		8
80	4		$8\frac{1}{7}$		$8\frac{2}{7}$		$8\frac{4}{7}$		$8\frac{5}{7}$		$8\frac{6}{7}$		$9\frac{1}{7}$
90	$4\frac{1}{2}$		$9\frac{1}{7}$		$9\frac{2}{7}$		$9\frac{4}{7}$		$9\frac{5}{7}$		10		$10\frac{2}{7}$
100	5		$10\frac{2}{7}$		$10\frac{4}{7}$		$10\frac{5}{7}$		11		$11\frac{1}{7}$		$11\frac{3}{7}$
200	10	1	$2\frac{3}{7}$	1	$2\frac{6}{7}$	1	$3\frac{2}{7}$	1	$3\frac{6}{7}$	1	$4\frac{2}{7}$	1	$4\frac{6}{7}$
300	15	1	$12\frac{5}{7}$	1	$13\frac{3}{7}$	1	$14\frac{1}{7}$	1	$14\frac{6}{7}$	1	$15\frac{4}{7}$	1	$16\frac{2}{7}$
400	20	2	5	2	$5\frac{6}{7}$	2	$6\frac{6}{7}$	2	$7\frac{6}{7}$	2	$8\frac{5}{7}$	2	$9\frac{5}{7}$
500	25	2	$15\frac{1}{7}$	2	$16\frac{2}{7}$	2	$17\frac{4}{7}$	3	$\frac{5}{7}$	3	$1\frac{6}{7}$	3	$3\frac{1}{7}$
600	30	3	$7\frac{3}{7}$	3	$8\frac{6}{7}$	3	$10\frac{2}{7}$	3	$11\frac{5}{7}$	3	$13\frac{1}{7}$	3	$14\frac{4}{7}$
700	35	3	$17\frac{5}{7}$	4	$1\frac{2}{7}$	4	3	4	$4\frac{5}{7}$	4	$6\frac{2}{7}$	4	8
800	40	4	$9\frac{6}{7}$	4	$11\frac{5}{7}$	4	$13\frac{5}{7}$	4	$15\frac{4}{7}$	4	$17\frac{3}{7}$	5	$1\frac{3}{7}$
900	45	5	$2\frac{1}{7}$	5	$4\frac{2}{7}$	5	$6\frac{3}{7}$	5	$8\frac{4}{7}$	5	$10\frac{5}{7}$	5	$12\frac{6}{7}$
1000	50	5	$12\frac{3}{7}$	5	$14\frac{4}{7}$	5	$17\frac{5}{7}$	6	$1\frac{4}{7}$	6	$3\frac{6}{7}$	6	$6\frac{2}{7}$
2000	100	11	$6\frac{5}{7}$	11	$11\frac{3}{7}$	11	$16\frac{2}{7}$	12	3	12	$7\frac{5}{7}$	12	$12\frac{4}{7}$
3000	150	17	$1\frac{1}{7}$	17	$8\frac{2}{7}$	17	$15\frac{3}{7}$	18	$4\frac{4}{7}$	18	$11\frac{5}{7}$	19	$\frac{6}{7}$
4000	200	22	$13\frac{4}{7}$	23	5	23	$14\frac{4}{7}$	24	6	24	$16\frac{4}{7}$	25	7

Ells.		$39\tfrac{1}{5}$	40	$40\tfrac{4}{5}$	$41\tfrac{3}{5}$	$42\tfrac{2}{5}$	$43\tfrac{1}{5}$
Yards.		49	50	51	52	53	54
Splits.	Porters.	Sp. Hk.	Sp. Hk.	Sp. Hk.	Sp. Hk.	Sp. Hk.	Sp. Hk.
2	$\tfrac{1}{10}$						
4	$\tfrac{1}{5}$	$\tfrac{3}{7}$	$\tfrac{3}{7}$	$\tfrac{3}{7}$	$\tfrac{3}{7}$	$\tfrac{3}{7}$	$\tfrac{3}{7}$
5	$\tfrac{1}{4}$	$\tfrac{4}{7}$	$\tfrac{4}{7}$	$\tfrac{4}{7}$	$\tfrac{4}{7}$	$\tfrac{4}{7}$	$\tfrac{4}{7}$
10	$\tfrac{1}{2}$	$1\tfrac{1}{7}$	$1\tfrac{1}{7}$	$1\tfrac{1}{7}$	$1\tfrac{1}{7}$	$1\tfrac{1}{7}$	$1\tfrac{2}{7}$
20	1	$2\tfrac{3}{7}$	$2\tfrac{3}{7}$	$2\tfrac{3}{7}$	$2\tfrac{4}{7}$	$2\tfrac{4}{7}$	$2\tfrac{4}{7}$
30	$1\tfrac{1}{2}$	$3\tfrac{3}{7}$	$3\tfrac{4}{7}$	$3\tfrac{4}{7}$	$3\tfrac{5}{7}$	$3\tfrac{5}{7}$	$3\tfrac{6}{7}$
40	2	$4\tfrac{5}{7}$	$4\tfrac{5}{7}$	$4\tfrac{6}{7}$	$4\tfrac{6}{7}$	5	$5\tfrac{1}{7}$
50	$2\tfrac{1}{2}$	$5\tfrac{5}{7}$	6	$6\tfrac{1}{7}$	$6\tfrac{2}{7}$	$6\tfrac{3}{7}$	$6\tfrac{3}{7}$
60	3	7	$7\tfrac{1}{7}$	$7\tfrac{2}{7}$	$7\tfrac{3}{7}$	$7\tfrac{4}{7}$	$7\tfrac{5}{7}$
70	$3\tfrac{1}{2}$	$8\tfrac{1}{7}$	$8\tfrac{2}{7}$	$8\tfrac{3}{7}$	$8\tfrac{4}{7}$	$8\tfrac{5}{7}$	9
80	4	$9\tfrac{2}{7}$	$9\tfrac{4}{7}$	$9\tfrac{5}{7}$	10	$10\tfrac{1}{7}$	$10\tfrac{2}{7}$
90	$4\tfrac{1}{2}$	$10\tfrac{3}{7}$	$10\tfrac{5}{7}$	$10\tfrac{6}{7}$	$11\tfrac{1}{7}$	$11\tfrac{2}{7}$	$11\tfrac{4}{7}$
100	5	$11\tfrac{5}{7}$	$11\tfrac{6}{7}$	$12\tfrac{1}{7}$	$12\tfrac{2}{7}$	$12\tfrac{4}{7}$	$12\tfrac{6}{7}$
200	10	1 $5\tfrac{3}{7}$	1 $5\tfrac{6}{7}$	1 $6\tfrac{1}{7}$	1 $6\tfrac{5}{7}$	1 $7\tfrac{2}{7}$	1 $7\tfrac{5}{7}$
300	15	1 17	1 $17\tfrac{5}{7}$	2 $\tfrac{3}{7}$	2 $1\tfrac{1}{7}$	2 $1\tfrac{6}{7}$	2 $2\tfrac{3}{7}$
400	20	2 $10\tfrac{5}{7}$	2 $11\tfrac{4}{7}$	2 $12\tfrac{4}{7}$	2 $13\tfrac{3}{7}$	2 $14\tfrac{1}{7}$	2 $15\tfrac{3}{7}$
500	25	3 $4\tfrac{3}{7}$	3 $5\tfrac{4}{7}$	3 $6\tfrac{3}{7}$	3 $7\tfrac{6}{7}$	3 $9\tfrac{1}{7}$	3 $10\tfrac{2}{7}$
600	30	3 16	3 $17\tfrac{3}{7}$	4 $\tfrac{6}{7}$	4 $2\tfrac{2}{7}$	4 $3\tfrac{5}{7}$	4 $5\tfrac{1}{7}$
700	35	4 $9\tfrac{3}{7}$	4 $11\tfrac{2}{7}$	4 13	4 $14\tfrac{4}{7}$	4 $16\tfrac{1}{7}$	5 0
800	40	5 $3\tfrac{2}{7}$	5 $5\tfrac{2}{7}$	5 $7\tfrac{1}{7}$	5 9	5 11	5 $12\tfrac{6}{7}$
900	45	5 15	5 $17\tfrac{1}{7}$	6 $1\tfrac{2}{7}$	6 $3\tfrac{3}{7}$	6 $5\tfrac{4}{7}$	6 $7\tfrac{5}{7}$
1000	50	6 $8\tfrac{5}{7}$	6 11	6 $13\tfrac{3}{7}$	6 $15\tfrac{5}{7}$	7 $\tfrac{1}{7}$	7 $2\tfrac{4}{7}$
2000	100	12 $17\tfrac{3}{7}$	13 $4\tfrac{1}{7}$	13 $8\tfrac{6}{7}$	13 $18\tfrac{1}{7}$	14 $\tfrac{3}{7}$	14 $5\tfrac{1}{7}$
3000	150	19 8	19 $15\tfrac{1}{7}$	20 $4\tfrac{3}{7}$	20 $11\tfrac{4}{7}$	21 $\tfrac{4}{7}$	21 $7\tfrac{5}{7}$
4000	200	25 $16\tfrac{4}{7}$	26 $8\tfrac{1}{7}$	26 $17\tfrac{5}{7}$	27 $9\tfrac{1}{7}$	28 $\tfrac{4}{7}$	28 $10\tfrac{3}{7}$

BEAMERS' TABLES.

Ells.		44	$44\frac{4}{5}$	$45\frac{3}{5}$	$46\frac{2}{5}$	$47\frac{1}{5}$	48
Yards.		55	56	57	58	59	60
Splits.	Porters.	Sp. Hk.	Sp. Hk.	Sp. Hk.	Sp. Hk.	Sp. Hk.	Sp. Hk.
2	$\frac{1}{10}$						
4	$\frac{1}{5}$	$\frac{3}{7}$	$\frac{3}{7}$	$\frac{3}{7}$	$\frac{4}{7}$	$\frac{4}{7}$	$\frac{4}{7}$
5	$\frac{1}{4}$	$\frac{4}{7}$	$\frac{4}{7}$	$\frac{4}{7}$	$\frac{4}{7}$	$\frac{5}{7}$	$\frac{5}{7}$
10	$\frac{1}{2}$	$1\frac{2}{7}$	$1\frac{2}{7}$	$1\frac{2}{7}$	$1\frac{2}{7}$	$1\frac{2}{7}$	$1\frac{3}{7}$
20	1	$2\frac{5}{7}$	$2\frac{5}{7}$	$2\frac{5}{7}$	$2\frac{6}{7}$	$2\frac{6}{7}$	$2\frac{6}{7}$
30	$1\frac{1}{2}$	$3\frac{6}{7}$	4	4	$4\frac{1}{7}$	$4\frac{1}{7}$	$4\frac{2}{7}$
40	2	$5\frac{1}{7}$	$5\frac{2}{7}$	$5\frac{3}{7}$	$5\frac{3}{7}$	$5\frac{4}{7}$	$5\frac{5}{7}$
50	$2\frac{1}{2}$	$6\frac{3}{7}$	$6\frac{5}{7}$	$6\frac{6}{7}$	7	7	$7\frac{1}{7}$
60	3	$7\frac{6}{7}$	8	$8\frac{1}{7}$	$8\frac{2}{7}$	$8\frac{3}{7}$	$8\frac{4}{7}$
70	$3\frac{1}{2}$	$9\frac{1}{7}$	$9\frac{2}{7}$	$9\frac{3}{7}$	$9\frac{4}{7}$	$9\frac{5}{7}$	10
80	4	$10\frac{4}{7}$	$10\frac{5}{7}$	$10\frac{6}{7}$	$11\frac{1}{7}$	$11\frac{2}{7}$	$11\frac{3}{7}$
90	$4\frac{1}{2}$	$11\frac{5}{7}$	12	$12\frac{1}{7}$	$12\frac{3}{7}$	$12\frac{4}{7}$	$12\frac{6}{7}$
100	5	13	$13\frac{2}{7}$	$13\frac{4}{7}$	$13\frac{5}{7}$	14	$14\frac{2}{7}$
200	10	1 $4\frac{1}{7}$	1 $8\frac{5}{7}$	1 $9\frac{1}{7}$	1 $9\frac{4}{7}$	1 $10\frac{1}{7}$	1 $10\frac{4}{7}$
300	15	2 $3\frac{2}{7}$	2 4	2 $4\frac{5}{7}$	2 $5\frac{3}{7}$	2 $6\frac{1}{7}$	2 $6\frac{6}{7}$
400	20	2 $16\frac{2}{7}$	2 $17\frac{2}{7}$	3 $\frac{2}{7}$	3 $1\frac{1}{7}$	3 $2\frac{1}{7}$	3 $3\frac{1}{7}$
500	25	3 $11\frac{3}{7}$	3 $12\frac{5}{7}$	3 $13\frac{6}{7}$	3 15	3 $16\frac{2}{7}$	3 $17\frac{3}{7}$
600	30	4 $6\frac{4}{7}$	4 8	4 $9\frac{3}{7}$	4 $10\frac{6}{7}$	4 $12\frac{2}{7}$	4 $13\frac{3}{7}$
700	35	5 $1\frac{5}{7}$	5 $3\frac{2}{7}$	5 5	5 $6\frac{4}{7}$	5 $8\frac{2}{7}$	5 10
800	40	5 $14\frac{5}{7}$	5 $16\frac{5}{7}$	6 $\frac{4}{7}$	6 $2\frac{3}{7}$	6 $4\frac{3}{7}$	6 $6\frac{2}{7}$
900	45	6 $9\frac{6}{7}$	6 12	6 $14\frac{1}{7}$	6 $16\frac{2}{7}$	7 $\frac{3}{7}$	7 $2\frac{4}{7}$
1000	50	7 $4\frac{6}{7}$	7 $7\frac{2}{7}$	7 $9\frac{5}{7}$	7 12	7 $14\frac{3}{7}$	7 $16\frac{6}{7}$
2000	100	14 $9\frac{6}{7}$	14 $14\frac{5}{7}$	15 $1\frac{6}{7}$	15 $6\frac{1}{7}$	15 11	15 $15\frac{5}{7}$
3000	150	21 $14\frac{6}{7}$	22 4	22 $11\frac{1}{7}$	23 $\frac{2}{7}$	23 $7\frac{3}{7}$	23 $14\frac{4}{7}$
4000	200	29 $1\frac{5}{7}$	29 $11\frac{3}{7}$	30 $2\frac{6}{7}$	30 $12\frac{3}{7}$	31 $3\frac{6}{7}$	31 $13\frac{3}{7}$

Ells.		$48\frac{4}{5}$	$49\frac{3}{5}$	$50\frac{2}{5}$	$51\frac{1}{5}$	52	$52\frac{4}{5}$
Yards.		61	62	63	64	65	66
Splits.	Porters.	Sp. Hk.	Sp. Hk.	Sp. Hk.	Sp. Hk.	Sp. Hk.	Sp. Hk.
2	$\frac{1}{10}$						
4	1	$\frac{4}{7}$	$\frac{4}{7}$	$\frac{4}{7}$	$\frac{4}{7}$	$\frac{4}{7}$	$\frac{4}{7}$
5	$1\frac{1}{4}$	$\frac{5}{7}$	$\frac{5}{7}$	$\frac{5}{7}$	$\frac{5}{7}$	$\frac{5}{7}$	$\frac{5}{7}$
10	$\frac{1}{2}$	$1\frac{3}{7}$	$1\frac{3}{7}$	$1\frac{3}{7}$	$1\frac{4}{7}$	$1\frac{4}{7}$	$1\frac{4}{7}$
20	1	$2\frac{6}{7}$	3	3	3	$3\frac{1}{7}$	$3\frac{1}{7}$
30	$1\frac{1}{2}$	$4\frac{2}{7}$	$4\frac{3}{7}$	$4\frac{3}{7}$	$4\frac{4}{7}$	$4\frac{4}{7}$	$4\frac{5}{7}$
40	2	$5\frac{6}{7}$	$5\frac{6}{7}$	6	$6\frac{1}{7}$	$6\frac{1}{7}$	$6\frac{2}{7}$
50	$2\frac{1}{2}$	$7\frac{2}{7}$	$7\frac{3}{7}$	$7\frac{3}{7}$	$7\frac{4}{7}$	$7\frac{5}{7}$	$7\frac{6}{7}$
60	3	$8\frac{5}{7}$	$8\frac{6}{7}$	9	$9\frac{1}{7}$	$9\frac{2}{7}$	$9\frac{3}{7}$
70	$3\frac{1}{2}$	$10\frac{1}{7}$	$10\frac{2}{7}$	$10\frac{3}{7}$	$10\frac{5}{7}$	$10\frac{6}{7}$	11
80	4	$11\frac{4}{7}$	$11\frac{6}{7}$	12	$12\frac{1}{7}$	$12\frac{2}{7}$	$12\frac{4}{7}$
90	$4\frac{1}{2}$	13	$13\frac{2}{7}$	$13\frac{3}{7}$	$13\frac{5}{7}$	$13\frac{6}{7}$	$14\frac{1}{7}$
100	5	$14\frac{4}{7}$	$14\frac{5}{7}$	15	$15\frac{2}{7}$	$15\frac{3}{7}$	$15\frac{5}{7}$
200	10	1 11	1 $11\frac{4}{7}$	1 12	1 $12\frac{3}{7}$	1 13	1 $13\frac{3}{7}$
300	15	2 $7\frac{4}{7}$	2 $8\frac{2}{7}$	2 9	2 $9\frac{5}{7}$	2 $10\frac{3}{7}$	2 $11\frac{1}{7}$
400	20	3 $4\frac{1}{7}$	3 5	3 6	3 7	3 $7\frac{6}{7}$	3 $8\frac{6}{7}$
500	25	4 $\frac{3}{7}$	4 $1\frac{6}{7}$	4 3	4 $4\frac{1}{7}$	4 $5\frac{3}{7}$	4 $6\frac{4}{7}$
600	30	4 $15\frac{1}{7}$	4 $16\frac{4}{7}$	5 0	5 $1\frac{3}{7}$	5 $2\frac{6}{7}$	5 $4\frac{2}{7}$
700	35	5 $11\frac{5}{7}$	5 $13\frac{2}{7}$	5 15	5 $16\frac{5}{7}$	6 $\frac{2}{7}$	6 2
800	40	6 $8\frac{1}{7}$	6 $10\frac{1}{7}$	6 12	6 $13\frac{6}{7}$	6 $15\frac{6}{7}$	6 $17\frac{5}{7}$
900	45	7 $4\frac{5}{7}$	7 $6\frac{6}{7}$	7 9	7 $11\frac{1}{7}$	7 $13\frac{3}{7}$	7 $15\frac{3}{7}$
1000	50	8 $1\frac{2}{7}$	8 $3\frac{4}{7}$	8 6	8 $8\frac{3}{7}$	8 $10\frac{3}{7}$	8 $13\frac{1}{7}$
2000	100	16 $2\frac{3}{7}$	16 $7\frac{2}{7}$	16 12	16 $16\frac{5}{7}$	17 $3\frac{4}{7}$	17 $8\frac{2}{7}$
3000	150	24 $3\frac{5}{7}$	24 $10\frac{6}{7}$	25 0	25 $7\frac{1}{7}$	25 $14\frac{2}{7}$	26 $3\frac{3}{7}$
4000	200	32 5	32 $14\frac{3}{7}$	33 $6\frac{4}{7}$	34 $5\frac{1}{7}$	34 7	34 $16\frac{4}{7}$

BEAMERS' TABLES.

Ells.		$53\frac{3}{5}$	$54\frac{2}{5}$	$55\frac{1}{5}$	56	$56\frac{4}{5}$	$57\frac{3}{5}$
Yards.		67	68	69	70	71	72
Splits.	Porters.	Sp. Hk.	Sp. Hk.	Sp. Hk.	Sp. Hk.	Sp. Hk.	Sp. Hk.
2	$\frac{1}{10}$						
4	$\frac{1}{5}$	$\frac{4}{7}$	$\frac{5}{7}$	$\frac{5}{7}$	$\frac{5}{7}$	$\frac{6}{7}$	$\frac{5}{7}$
5	$\frac{1}{4}$	$\frac{6}{7}$	$\frac{6}{7}$	$\frac{6}{7}$	$\frac{6}{7}$	$\frac{6}{7}$	$\frac{6}{7}$
10	$\frac{1}{2}$	$1\frac{4}{7}$	$1\frac{4}{7}$	$1\frac{4}{7}$	$1\frac{5}{7}$	$1\frac{5}{7}$	$1\frac{5}{7}$
20	1	$3\frac{1}{7}$	$3\frac{2}{7}$	$3\frac{2}{7}$	$3\frac{2}{7}$	$3\frac{3}{7}$	$3\frac{3}{7}$
30	$1\frac{1}{2}$	$4\frac{6}{7}$	$4\frac{6}{7}$	$4\frac{6}{7}$	5	5	6
40	2	$6\frac{3}{7}$	$6\frac{3}{7}$	$6\frac{4}{7}$	$6\frac{5}{7}$	$6\frac{6}{7}$	$6\frac{6}{7}$
50	$2\frac{1}{2}$	8	$8\frac{1}{7}$	$8\frac{1}{7}$	$8\frac{2}{7}$	$8\frac{3}{7}$	$8\frac{4}{7}$
60	3	$9\frac{5}{7}$	$9\frac{5}{7}$	$9\frac{6}{7}$	10	$10\frac{1}{7}$	$10\frac{2}{7}$
70	$3\frac{1}{2}$	$11\frac{1}{7}$	$11\frac{2}{7}$	$11\frac{3}{7}$	$11\frac{5}{7}$	$11\frac{6}{7}$	12
80	4	$12\frac{5}{7}$	13	$13\frac{1}{7}$	$13\frac{3}{7}$	$13\frac{3}{7}$	$13\frac{5}{7}$
90	$4\frac{1}{2}$	$14\frac{2}{7}$	$14\frac{4}{7}$	$14\frac{5}{7}$	15	$15\frac{1}{7}$	$15\frac{5}{7}$
100	5	16	$16\frac{1}{7}$	$16\frac{3}{7}$	$16\frac{5}{7}$	17	$17\frac{1}{7}$
200	10	1 $13\frac{6}{7}$	1 $14\frac{3}{7}$	1 $14\frac{6}{7}$	1 $15\frac{2}{7}$	1 $15\frac{5}{7}$	1 $16\frac{2}{7}$
300	15	2 $11\frac{6}{7}$	2 $12\frac{4}{7}$	2 $13\frac{2}{7}$	2 14	2 $14\frac{5}{7}$	2 $15\frac{3}{7}$
400	20	3 $9\frac{6}{7}$	3 $10\frac{5}{7}$	3 $11\frac{5}{7}$	3 $12\frac{5}{7}$	3 $13\frac{4}{7}$	3 $14\frac{4}{7}$
500	25	4 $7\frac{5}{7}$	4 9	4 $10\frac{1}{7}$	4 $11\frac{2}{7}$	4 $12\frac{3}{7}$	4 $13\frac{5}{7}$
600	30	5 $5\frac{5}{7}$	5 $7\frac{1}{7}$	5 $8\frac{4}{7}$	5 10	5 $11\frac{4}{7}$	5 $12\frac{6}{7}$
700	35	6 $3\frac{5}{7}$	6 $5\frac{2}{7}$	6 7	6 $8\frac{5}{7}$	6 $10\frac{3}{7}$	6 12
800	40	7 $1\frac{4}{7}$	7 $3\frac{4}{7}$	7 $5\frac{3}{7}$	7 $7\frac{2}{7}$	7 $9\frac{1}{7}$	7 $11\frac{1}{7}$
900	45	7 $17\frac{4}{7}$	8 $1\frac{5}{7}$	8 $3\frac{6}{7}$	8 6	8 $8\frac{1}{7}$	8 $10\frac{2}{7}$
1000	50	8 $15\frac{4}{7}$	8 $17\frac{6}{7}$	9 $2\frac{2}{7}$	9 $4\frac{5}{7}$	9 7	9 $9\frac{2}{7}$
2000	100	17 13	17 $17\frac{6}{7}$	18 $4\frac{4}{7}$	18 $9\frac{2}{7}$	18 14	19 $\frac{6}{7}$
3000	150	26 $10\frac{4}{7}$	26 $17\frac{5}{7}$	27 $6\frac{6}{7}$	27 14	28 $3\frac{1}{7}$	28 $10\frac{2}{7}$
4000	200	35 $8\frac{1}{7}$	35 $17\frac{4}{7}$	36 $9\frac{1}{7}$	37 0	37 $9\frac{2}{7}$	38 $1\frac{4}{7}$

Ells.		$58\frac{2}{5}$		$59\frac{1}{5}$		60		$60\frac{4}{5}$		$61\frac{3}{5}$		$62\frac{2}{5}$	
Yards.		73		74		75		76		77		78	
Splits.	Porters.	Sp.	Hk.	Sp.	Hk.	Sp.	Hk.	Sp.	Hk.	Sp.	Hk.	Sp.	Hk.
2	$\frac{1}{10}$												
4	$\frac{1}{5}$		$\frac{5}{7}$		$\frac{5}{7}$		$\frac{5}{7}$		$\frac{5}{7}$		$\frac{5}{7}$		$\frac{5}{7}$
5	$\frac{1}{4}$		$\frac{6}{7}$		$\frac{6}{7}$		$\frac{6}{7}$		$\frac{6}{7}$		1		1
10	$\frac{1}{2}$		$1\frac{5}{7}$		$1\frac{6}{7}$		$1\frac{6}{7}$		$1\frac{6}{7}$		$1\frac{6}{7}$		$1\frac{6}{7}$
20	1		$3\frac{3}{7}$		$3\frac{3}{7}$		$3\frac{4}{7}$		$3\frac{4}{7}$		$3\frac{4}{7}$		$3\frac{5}{7}$
30	$1\frac{1}{2}$		$5\frac{1}{7}$		$5\frac{2}{7}$		$5\frac{2}{7}$		$5\frac{3}{7}$		$5\frac{3}{7}$		$5\frac{4}{7}$
40	2		7		$7\frac{1}{7}$		$7\frac{1}{7}$		$7\frac{2}{7}$		$7\frac{3}{7}$		$7\frac{3}{7}$
50	$2\frac{1}{2}$		$8\frac{4}{7}$		$8\frac{5}{7}$		$8\frac{6}{7}$		9		$9\frac{1}{7}$		$9\frac{2}{7}$
60	3		$10\frac{3}{7}$		$10\frac{4}{7}$		$10\frac{5}{7}$		$10\frac{6}{7}$		11		$11\frac{1}{7}$
70	$3\frac{1}{2}$		$12\frac{1}{7}$		$12\frac{3}{7}$		$12\frac{4}{7}$		$12\frac{5}{7}$		$12\frac{6}{7}$		13
80	4		$13\frac{6}{7}$		14		$14\frac{2}{7}$		$14\frac{3}{7}$		$14\frac{4}{7}$		$14\frac{6}{7}$
90	$4\frac{1}{2}$		$15\frac{4}{7}$		$15\frac{6}{7}$		16		$16\frac{2}{7}$		$16\frac{3}{7}$		$16\frac{5}{7}$
100	5		$17\frac{3}{7}$		$17\frac{5}{7}$		$17\frac{6}{7}$	1	$\frac{1}{7}$	1	$\frac{3}{7}$	1	$\frac{4}{7}$
200	10	1	$16\frac{5}{7}$	1	$17\frac{1}{7}$	1	$17\frac{5}{7}$	2	$\frac{1}{7}$	2	$\frac{4}{7}$	2	$1\frac{1}{7}$
300	15	2	$16\frac{1}{7}$	2	$16\frac{6}{7}$	2	$17\frac{4}{7}$	3	$\frac{2}{7}$	3	1	3	$1\frac{5}{7}$
400	20	3	$15\frac{3}{7}$	3	$16\frac{3}{7}$	3	$17\frac{3}{7}$	4	$\frac{3}{7}$	4	$1\frac{2}{7}$	4	$2\frac{2}{7}$
500	25	4	$14\frac{6}{7}$	4	16	4	$17\frac{2}{7}$	5	$\frac{3}{7}$	5	$1\frac{4}{7}$	5	$2\frac{6}{7}$
600	30	5	$14\frac{2}{7}$	5	$15\frac{5}{7}$	5	$17\frac{1}{7}$	6	$\frac{4}{7}$	6	2	6	$3\frac{3}{7}$
700	35	6	$13\frac{4}{7}$	6	$15\frac{3}{7}$	6	17	7	$\frac{4}{7}$	7	$2\frac{2}{7}$	7	4
800	40	7	13	7	$14\frac{6}{7}$	7	$16\frac{6}{7}$	8	$\frac{5}{7}$	8	$2\frac{4}{7}$	8	$4\frac{4}{7}$
900	45	8	$12\frac{2}{7}$	8	$14\frac{4}{7}$	8	$16\frac{5}{7}$	9	$\frac{6}{7}$	9	3	9	$5\frac{1}{7}$
1000	50	9	$11\frac{6}{7}$	9	$14\frac{1}{7}$	9	$16\frac{4}{7}$	10	1	10	$3\frac{3}{7}$	10	$5\frac{5}{7}$
2000	100	19	$5\frac{4}{7}$	19	$10\frac{2}{7}$	19	$15\frac{1}{7}$	20	$1\frac{6}{7}$	20	$6\frac{4}{7}$	20	$11\frac{3}{7}$
3000	150	28	$17\frac{3}{7}$	29	$6\frac{4}{7}$	29	$13\frac{4}{7}$	30	$2\frac{5}{7}$	30	10	30	$17\frac{1}{7}$
4000	200	38	$11\frac{2}{7}$	39	$2\frac{5}{7}$	39	$12\frac{2}{7}$	40	$3\frac{5}{7}$	40	$13\frac{2}{7}$	41	$4\frac{6}{7}$

BEAMERS' TABLES.

Ells.		$63\frac{1}{5}$		64		$64\frac{4}{5}$		$65\frac{3}{5}$		$66\frac{2}{5}$		$67\frac{1}{5}$	
Yards.		79		80		81		82		83		84	
Splits.	Porters.	Sp.	Hk.	Sp.	Hk.	Sp.	Hk.	Sp.	Hk.	Sp.	Hk	Sp.	Hk.
2	$\frac{1}{10}$												
4	$\frac{1}{5}$		$\frac{5}{7}$		$\frac{5}{7}$		$\frac{5}{7}$		$\frac{5}{7}$		$\frac{4}{7}$		$\frac{4}{7}$
5	$\frac{1}{4}$		1		1		1		1		1		1
10	$\frac{1}{2}$		$1\frac{6}{7}$		$1\frac{6}{7}$		$1\frac{9}{7}$		$1\frac{6}{7}$		$1\frac{6}{7}$		2
20	1		$3\frac{5}{7}$		$3\frac{6}{7}$		$3\frac{6}{7}$		4		4		4
30	$1\frac{1}{2}$		$5\frac{5}{7}$		$5\frac{5}{7}$		$5\frac{5}{7}$		$5\frac{6}{7}$		6		6
40	2		$7\frac{4}{7}$		$7\frac{4}{7}$		$7\frac{5}{7}$		$7\frac{5}{7}$		$7\frac{6}{7}$		8
50	$2\frac{1}{2}$		$9\frac{3}{7}$		$9\frac{4}{7}$		$9\frac{5}{7}$		$9\frac{6}{7}$		$9\frac{6}{7}$		10
60	3		$11\frac{3}{7}$		$11\frac{3}{7}$		$11\frac{4}{7}$		$11\frac{5}{7}$		$11\frac{6}{7}$		12
70	$3\frac{1}{2}$		$13\frac{1}{7}$		$13\frac{2}{7}$		$13\frac{3}{7}$		$13\frac{4}{7}$		$13\frac{5}{7}$		14
80	4		15		$15\frac{2}{7}$		$15\frac{3}{7}$		$15\frac{4}{7}$		$15\frac{6}{7}$		16
90	$4\frac{1}{2}$		$16\frac{6}{7}$		$17\frac{1}{7}$		$17\frac{2}{7}$		$17\frac{4}{7}$		$17\frac{5}{7}$	1	0
100	5	1	$\frac{6}{7}$	1	1	1	$1\frac{2}{7}$	1	$1\frac{3}{7}$	1	$1\frac{5}{7}$	1	2
200	10	2	$1\frac{4}{7}$	2	$2\frac{1}{7}$	2	$2\frac{4}{7}$	2	3	2	$3\frac{4}{7}$	2	4
300	15	3	$2\frac{3}{7}$	3	$3\frac{1}{7}$	3	$3\frac{6}{7}$	3	$4\frac{4}{7}$	3	$5\frac{2}{7}$	3	6
400	20	4	$3\frac{2}{7}$	4	$4\frac{1}{7}$	4	$5\frac{1}{7}$	4	6	4	7	4	8
500	25	5	4	5	$5\frac{2}{7}$	5	$6\frac{3}{7}$	5	$7\frac{4}{7}$	5	$8\frac{6}{7}$	5	10
600	30	6	$4\frac{6}{7}$	6	$6\frac{2}{7}$	6	$7\frac{5}{7}$	6	$9\frac{1}{7}$	6	$10\frac{4}{7}$	6	12
700	35	7	$5\frac{5}{7}$	7	$7\frac{2}{7}$	7	9	7	$10\frac{5}{7}$	7	$12\frac{2}{7}$	7	14
800	40	8	$6\frac{3}{7}$	8	$8\frac{2}{7}$	8	$10\frac{2}{7}$	8	$12\frac{1}{7}$	8	$14\frac{1}{7}$	8	16
900	45	9	$7\frac{2}{7}$	9	$9\frac{2}{7}$	9	$11\frac{4}{7}$	9	$13\frac{5}{7}$	9	$15\frac{6}{7}$	10	0
1000	50	10	$8\frac{1}{7}$	10	$10\frac{3}{7}$	10	$12\frac{6}{7}$	10	$15\frac{1}{7}$	10	$17\frac{4}{7}$	11	2
2000	100	20	$16\frac{1}{7}$	21	3	21	$7\frac{5}{7}$	21	$12\frac{3}{7}$	21	$17\frac{2}{7}$	22	4
3000	150	31	$6\frac{2}{7}$	31	$13\frac{2}{7}$	32	$2\frac{4}{7}$	32	$9\frac{4}{7}$	32	$16\frac{6}{7}$	33	6
4000	200	41	$14\frac{2}{7}$	42	$5\frac{6}{7}$	42	$15\frac{3}{7}$	43	$6\frac{6}{7}$	43	$16\frac{2}{7}$	44	8

322   MANUFACTURERS', WARPERS', AND

Ells.		68	68$\frac{4}{5}$	69$\frac{3}{5}$	70$\frac{2}{5}$	71$\frac{1}{5}$	72
Yards.		85	86	87	88	89	90
Splits.	Porters.	Sp. Hk.	Sp. Hk.	Sp. Hk.	Sp. Hk.	Sp. Hk.	Sp. Hk.
2	$\frac{1}{10}$						
4	$\frac{1}{5}$	$\frac{5}{7}$	$\frac{5}{7}$	$\frac{5}{7}$	$\frac{6}{7}$	$\frac{6}{7}$	$\frac{6}{7}$
5	$\frac{1}{4}$	1	1	1$\frac{1}{7}$	1$\frac{1}{7}$	1$\frac{1}{7}$	1$\frac{1}{7}$
10	$\frac{1}{2}$	2	2	2	2	2	2$\frac{1}{7}$
20	1	4$\frac{1}{7}$	4$\frac{1}{7}$	4$\frac{1}{7}$	4$\frac{2}{7}$	4$\frac{2}{7}$	4$\frac{2}{7}$
30	1$\frac{1}{2}$	6	6$\frac{1}{7}$	6$\frac{1}{7}$	6$\frac{2}{7}$	6$\frac{2}{7}$	6$\frac{3}{7}$
40	2	8	8$\frac{1}{7}$	8$\frac{2}{7}$	8$\frac{2}{7}$	8$\frac{3}{7}$	8$\frac{4}{7}$
50	2$\frac{1}{2}$	10$\frac{1}{7}$	10$\frac{2}{7}$	10$\frac{3}{7}$	10$\frac{4}{7}$	10$\frac{4}{7}$	10$\frac{5}{7}$
60	3	12$\frac{1}{7}$	12$\frac{2}{7}$	12$\frac{3}{7}$	12$\frac{4}{7}$	12$\frac{5}{7}$	12$\frac{6}{7}$
70	3$\frac{1}{2}$	14$\frac{1}{7}$	14$\frac{2}{7}$	14$\frac{3}{7}$	14$\frac{4}{7}$	14$\frac{5}{7}$	15
80	4	16$\frac{2}{7}$	16$\frac{3}{7}$	16$\frac{4}{7}$	16$\frac{6}{7}$	17	17$\frac{1}{7}$
90	4$\frac{1}{2}$	1 $\frac{1}{7}$	1 $\frac{3}{7}$	1 $\frac{4}{7}$	1 $\frac{6}{7}$	1 1	1 1$\frac{2}{7}$
100	5	1 2$\frac{1}{7}$	1 2$\frac{3}{7}$	1 2$\frac{5}{7}$	1 2$\frac{6}{7}$	1 3$\frac{1}{7}$	1 3$\frac{3}{7}$
200	10	2 4$\frac{3}{7}$	2 5	2 5$\frac{3}{7}$	2 5$\frac{6}{7}$	2 6$\frac{3}{7}$	2 6$\frac{6}{7}$
300	15	3 6$\frac{5}{7}$	3 7$\frac{3}{7}$	3 8$\frac{1}{7}$	3 8$\frac{6}{7}$	3 9$\frac{4}{7}$	3 10$\frac{2}{7}$
400	20	4 8$\frac{6}{7}$	4 9$\frac{6}{7}$	4 10$\frac{6}{7}$	4 11$\frac{5}{7}$	4 12$\frac{5}{7}$	4 13$\frac{5}{7}$
500	25	5 11$\frac{1}{7}$	5 12$\frac{3}{7}$	5 13$\frac{4}{7}$	5 14$\frac{5}{7}$	5 16	5 17$\frac{1}{7}$
600	30	6 13$\frac{3}{7}$	6 14$\frac{6}{7}$	6 16$\frac{2}{7}$	6 17$\frac{5}{7}$	7 1$\frac{1}{7}$	7 2$\frac{4}{7}$
700	35	7 15$\frac{4}{7}$	7 17$\frac{2}{7}$	8 1	8 2$\frac{4}{7}$	8 4$\frac{2}{7}$	8 6
800	40	8 17$\frac{6}{7}$	9 1$\frac{6}{7}$	9 3$\frac{5}{7}$	9 5$\frac{4}{7}$	9 7$\frac{4}{7}$	9 9$\frac{3}{7}$
900	45	10 2$\frac{1}{7}$	10 4$\frac{2}{7}$	10 6$\frac{3}{7}$	10 8$\frac{4}{7}$	10 10$\frac{5}{7}$	10 12$\frac{6}{7}$
1000	50	11 4$\frac{2}{7}$	11 6$\frac{5}{7}$	11 9$\frac{1}{7}$	11 11$\frac{3}{7}$	11 13$\frac{6}{7}$	11 16$\frac{2}{7}$
2000	100	22 8$\frac{5}{7}$	22 13$\frac{4}{7}$	23 $\frac{2}{7}$	23 5$\frac{2}{7}$	23 9$\frac{5}{7}$	23 14$\frac{4}{7}$
3000	150	33 13$\frac{1}{7}$	34 2$\frac{2}{7}$	34 9$\frac{3}{7}$	34 16$\frac{4}{7}$	35 5$\frac{4}{7}$	35 12$\frac{6}{7}$
4000	200	44 17$\frac{3}{7}$	45 9	46 $\frac{4}{7}$	46 10	47 1$\frac{4}{7}$	47 11$\frac{1}{7}$

BEAMERS' TABLES.

Ells.		$72\frac{4}{5}$	$73\frac{3}{5}$	$74\frac{2}{5}$	$75\frac{1}{5}$	76	$76\frac{4}{5}$
Yards.		91	92	93	94	95	96
Splits.	Porters.	Sp. Hk.	Sp. Hk.	Sp. Hk.	Sp. Hk.	Sp. Hk.	Sp. Hk.
2	$\frac{1}{10}$						
4	$\frac{1}{5}$						
5	$\frac{1}{4}$	1 $\frac{6}{7}$	1 $\frac{6}{7}$	$1\frac{1}{7}$ $\frac{6}{7}$	$1\frac{1}{7}$ $\frac{6}{7}$	$1\frac{1}{7}$ $\frac{6}{7}$	$1\frac{1}{7}$ $\frac{6}{7}$
10	$\frac{1}{2}$	$2\frac{1}{7}$	$2\frac{1}{7}$	$2\frac{1}{7}$	$2\frac{2}{7}$	$2\frac{2}{7}$	$2\frac{2}{7}$
20	1	$4\frac{2}{7}$	$4\frac{3}{7}$	$4\frac{3}{7}$	$4\frac{3}{7}$	$4\frac{4}{7}$	$4\frac{4}{7}$
30	$1\frac{1}{2}$	$6\frac{3}{7}$	$6\frac{4}{7}$	$6\frac{4}{7}$	$6\frac{5}{7}$	$6\frac{5}{7}$	$6\frac{6}{7}$
40	2	$8\frac{5}{7}$	$8\frac{5}{7}$	$8\frac{6}{7}$	9	9	$9\frac{1}{7}$
50	$2\frac{1}{2}$	$10\frac{6}{7}$	11	11	$11\frac{1}{7}$	$11\frac{2}{7}$	$11\frac{3}{7}$
60	3	13	$13\frac{1}{7}$	$13\frac{2}{7}$	$13\frac{3}{7}$	$13\frac{4}{7}$	$13\frac{5}{7}$
70	$3\frac{1}{2}$	$15\frac{1}{7}$	$15\frac{2}{7}$	$15\frac{3}{7}$	$15\frac{5}{7}$	$15\frac{6}{7}$	16
80	4	$17\frac{2}{7}$	$17\frac{4}{7}$	$17\frac{5}{7}$	$17\frac{6}{7}$	1 $\frac{1}{7}$	1 $\frac{2}{7}$
90	$4\frac{1}{2}$	1 $1\frac{3}{7}$	1 $1\frac{5}{7}$	1 $1\frac{6}{7}$	1 $2\frac{1}{7}$	1 $2\frac{3}{7}$	1 $2\frac{4}{7}$
100	5	1 $3\frac{5}{7}$	1 $3\frac{6}{7}$	1 $4\frac{1}{7}$	1 $4\frac{3}{7}$	1 $4\frac{4}{7}$	1 $4\frac{6}{7}$
200	10	2 $7\frac{2}{7}$	2 $7\frac{6}{7}$	2 $8\frac{2}{7}$	2 $8\frac{5}{7}$	2 $9\frac{2}{7}$	2 $9\frac{5}{7}$
300	15	3 11	3 $11\frac{5}{7}$	3 $12\frac{3}{7}$	3 $13\frac{1}{7}$	3 $13\frac{6}{7}$	3 $14\frac{4}{7}$
400	20	4 $14\frac{4}{7}$	4 $15\frac{4}{7}$	4 $16\frac{4}{7}$	4 $17\frac{4}{7}$	5 $\frac{3}{7}$	5 $1\frac{3}{7}$
500	25	6 $\frac{2}{7}$	6 $1\frac{4}{7}$	6 $2\frac{5}{7}$	6 $3\frac{6}{7}$	6 $5\frac{1}{7}$	6 $6\frac{2}{7}$
600	30	7 4	7 $5\frac{3}{7}$	7 $6\frac{6}{7}$	7 $8\frac{2}{7}$	7 $9\frac{5}{7}$	7 $11\frac{1}{7}$
700	35	8 $7\frac{5}{7}$	8 $9\frac{2}{7}$	8 11	8 $12\frac{5}{7}$	8 $14\frac{2}{7}$	8 16
800	40	9 $11\frac{2}{7}$	9 $13\frac{2}{7}$	9 $15\frac{1}{7}$	9 17	10 1	10 $2\frac{6}{7}$
900	45	10 15	10 $17\frac{1}{7}$	11 $1\frac{2}{7}$	11 $3\frac{3}{7}$	11 $5\frac{4}{7}$	11 $7\frac{5}{7}$
1000	50	12 $\frac{5}{7}$	12 3	12 $5\frac{3}{7}$	12 $7\frac{6}{7}$	12 $10\frac{1}{7}$	12 $12\frac{4}{7}$
2000	100	24 $1\frac{2}{7}$	24 $6\frac{1}{7}$	24 $10\frac{6}{7}$	24 $15\frac{4}{7}$	25 $2\frac{3}{7}$	25 $7\frac{1}{7}$
3000	150	36 2	36 $9\frac{1}{7}$	36 $16\frac{2}{7}$	37 $5\frac{3}{7}$	37 $12\frac{4}{7}$	38 $1\frac{6}{7}$
4000	200	48 $2\frac{5}{7}$	48 $12\frac{1}{7}$	49 $3\frac{5}{7}$	49 $13\frac{2}{7}$	50 $4\frac{6}{7}$	50 $14\frac{3}{7}$

324   MANUFACTURERS', WARPERS', AND

Ells.		$77\frac{3}{5}$	$78\frac{2}{5}$	$79\frac{1}{5}$	80	$80\frac{4}{5}$	$81\frac{3}{5}$
Yards.		97	98	99	100	101	102
Splits.	Porters.	Sp. Hk.	Sp. Hk.	Sp. Hk.	Sp. Hk.	Sp. Hk.	Sp. Hk.
2	$\frac{1}{10}$						
4	$\frac{1}{5}$	$\frac{6}{7}$	1	1	1	1	1
5	$\frac{1}{4}$	$1\frac{1}{7}$	$1\frac{1}{7}$	$1\frac{1}{7}$	$1\frac{1}{7}$	$1\frac{1}{7}$	$1\frac{1}{7}$
10	$\frac{1}{2}$	$2\frac{3}{7}$	$2\frac{3}{7}$	$2\frac{3}{7}$	$2\frac{3}{7}$	$2\frac{3}{7}$	$2\frac{3}{7}$
20	1	$4\frac{4}{7}$	$4\frac{5}{7}$	$4\frac{5}{7}$	$4\frac{5}{7}$	$4\frac{5}{7}$	$4\frac{6}{7}$
30	$1\frac{1}{2}$	$6\frac{6}{7}$	7	7	$7\frac{1}{7}$	$7\frac{1}{7}$	$7\frac{2}{7}$
40	2	$9\frac{2}{7}$	$9\frac{2}{7}$	$9\frac{3}{7}$	$9\frac{4}{7}$	$9\frac{5}{7}$	$9\frac{5}{7}$
50	$2\frac{1}{2}$	$11\frac{4}{7}$	$11\frac{5}{7}$	$11\frac{5}{7}$	$11\frac{6}{7}$	12	$12\frac{1}{7}$
60	3	$13\frac{6}{7}$	14	$14\frac{1}{7}$	$14\frac{2}{7}$	$14\frac{3}{7}$	$14\frac{4}{7}$
70	$3\frac{1}{2}$	$16\frac{1}{7}$	$16\frac{2}{7}$	$16\frac{3}{7}$	$16\frac{5}{7}$	$16\frac{5}{7}$	17
80	4	1 $\frac{3}{7}$	1 $\frac{5}{7}$	1 $\frac{6}{7}$	1 1	1 $1\frac{1}{7}$	1 $1\frac{3}{7}$
90	$4\frac{1}{2}$	1 $2\frac{5}{7}$	1 3	1 $3\frac{1}{7}$	1 $3\frac{3}{7}$	1 $3\frac{4}{7}$	1 $3\frac{6}{7}$
100	5	1 $5\frac{1}{7}$	1 $5\frac{2}{7}$	1 $5\frac{4}{7}$	1 $5\frac{6}{7}$	1 6	1 $6\frac{2}{7}$
200	10	2 $10\frac{1}{7}$	2 $10\frac{5}{7}$	2 $11\frac{1}{7}$	2 $11\frac{4}{7}$	2 12	2 $12\frac{4}{7}$
300	15	3 $15\frac{2}{7}$	3 16	3 $16\frac{5}{7}$	3 $17\frac{3}{7}$	4 $\frac{1}{7}$	4 $\frac{6}{7}$
400	20	5 $2\frac{3}{7}$	5 $3\frac{2}{7}$	5 $4\frac{2}{7}$	5 $5\frac{2}{7}$	5 $6\frac{1}{7}$	5 $7\frac{1}{7}$
500	25	6 $7\frac{3}{7}$	6 $8\frac{3}{7}$	6 $9\frac{6}{7}$	6 11	6 $12\frac{1}{7}$	6 $13\frac{3}{7}$
600	30	7 $12\frac{4}{7}$	7 14	7 $15\frac{3}{7}$	7 $16\frac{6}{7}$	8 $\frac{2}{7}$	8 $1\frac{5}{7}$
700	35	8 $17\frac{5}{7}$	9 $1\frac{2}{7}$	9 3	9 $4\frac{5}{7}$	9 $6\frac{2}{7}$	9 8
800	40	10 $4\frac{5}{7}$	10 $6\frac{5}{7}$	10 $8\frac{4}{7}$	10 $10\frac{3}{7}$	10 $12\frac{2}{7}$	10 $14\frac{2}{7}$
900	45	11 $9\frac{6}{7}$	11 12	11 $14\frac{1}{7}$	11 $16\frac{2}{7}$	12 $\frac{3}{7}$	12 $2\frac{4}{7}$
1000	50	12 15	12 $17\frac{2}{7}$	13 $1\frac{5}{7}$	13 $4\frac{1}{7}$	13 $6\frac{3}{7}$	13 $8\frac{6}{7}$
2000	100	25 $11\frac{6}{7}$	25 $16\frac{5}{7}$	26 $3\frac{3}{7}$	26 $8\frac{1}{7}$	26 $12\frac{6}{7}$	26 $17\frac{5}{7}$
3000	150	38 $8\frac{2}{7}$	38 16	39 $5\frac{1}{7}$	39 $12\frac{2}{7}$	40 $1\frac{3}{7}$	40 $8\frac{4}{7}$
4000	200	51 $5\frac{6}{7}$	51 $15\frac{2}{7}$	52 $6\frac{6}{7}$	52 $16\frac{3}{7}$	53 $7\frac{5}{7}$	53 $17\frac{3}{7}$

BEAMERS' TABLES.

Ells.		$82\frac{2}{5}$	$83\frac{1}{5}$	84	$84\frac{4}{5}$	$85\frac{3}{5}$	$86\frac{2}{5}$
Yards.		103	104	105	106	107	108
Splits.	Porters.	Sp. Hk.	Sp. Hk.	Sp. Hk.	Sp. Hk.	Sp. Hk	Sp. Hk.
2	$\frac{1}{10}$						
4	$\frac{1}{5}$	1	1	1	1	1	$1\frac{1}{7}$
5	$\frac{1}{4}$	$1\frac{1}{7}$	$1\frac{1}{7}$	$1\frac{1}{7}$	$1\frac{1}{7}$	$1\frac{2}{7}$	$1\frac{2}{7}$
10	$\frac{1}{2}$	$2\frac{3}{7}$	$2\frac{4}{7}$	$2\frac{4}{7}$	$2\frac{4}{7}$	$2\frac{4}{7}$	$2\frac{4}{7}$
20	1	$4\frac{6}{7}$	$4\frac{6}{7}$	5	5	5	$5\frac{1}{7}$
30	$1\frac{1}{2}$	$7\frac{2}{7}$	$7\frac{3}{7}$	$7\frac{3}{7}$	$7\frac{4}{7}$	$7\frac{4}{7}$	$7\frac{5}{7}$
40	2	$9\frac{6}{7}$	10	10	$10\frac{1}{7}$	$10\frac{2}{7}$	$10\frac{2}{7}$
50	$2\frac{1}{2}$	$12\frac{1}{7}$	$12\frac{2}{7}$	$12\frac{3}{7}$	$12\frac{4}{7}$	$12\frac{5}{7}$	$12\frac{6}{7}$
60	3	$14\frac{6}{7}$	$14\frac{6}{7}$	15	$15\frac{1}{7}$	$15\frac{3}{7}$	$15\frac{3}{7}$
70	$3\frac{1}{2}$	$17\frac{1}{7}$	$17\frac{3}{7}$	$17\frac{4}{7}$	$17\frac{5}{7}$	$17\frac{6}{7}$	1 0
80	4	1 $1\frac{4}{7}$	1 $1\frac{5}{7}$	1 2	1 $2\frac{1}{7}$	1 $2\frac{2}{7}$	1 $2\frac{4}{7}$
90	$4\frac{1}{2}$	1 4	1 $4\frac{2}{7}$	1 $4\frac{3}{7}$	1 $4\frac{5}{7}$	1 $4\frac{6}{7}$	1 $5\frac{1}{7}$
100	5	1 $6\frac{4}{7}$	1 $6\frac{5}{7}$	1 7	1 $7\frac{2}{7}$	1 $7\frac{3}{7}$	1 $7\frac{5}{7}$
200	10	2 13	2 $13\frac{3}{7}$	2 14	2 $14\frac{3}{7}$	2 $14\frac{6}{7}$	2 $15\frac{3}{7}$
300	15	4 $1\frac{4}{7}$	4 $2\frac{2}{7}$	4 3	4 $3\frac{5}{7}$	4 $4\frac{3}{7}$	4 $5\frac{1}{7}$
400	20	5 $8\frac{1}{7}$	5 9	5 10	5 11	5 $11\frac{6}{7}$	5 $12\frac{6}{7}$
500	25	6 $14\frac{4}{7}$	6 $15\frac{5}{7}$	6 17	7 $\frac{1}{7}$	7 $1\frac{3}{7}$	7 $2\frac{4}{7}$
600	30	8 $3\frac{1}{7}$	8 $4\frac{4}{7}$	8 6	8 $7\frac{3}{7}$	8 $8\frac{6}{7}$	8 $10\frac{2}{7}$
700	35	9 $9\frac{5}{7}$	9 $11\frac{2}{7}$	9 13	9 $14\frac{5}{7}$	9 $16\frac{2}{7}$	10 0
800	40	10 $16\frac{1}{7}$	10 18	11 2	11 $3\frac{6}{7}$	11 $5\frac{5}{7}$	11 $7\frac{5}{7}$
900	45	12 $4\frac{4}{7}$	12 $6\frac{6}{7}$	12 9	12 $11\frac{1}{7}$	12 $13\frac{4}{7}$	12 $15\frac{3}{7}$
1000	50	13 $11\frac{2}{7}$	13 $13\frac{4}{7}$	13 16	14 $\frac{3}{7}$	14 $2\frac{4}{7}$	14 $5\frac{1}{7}$
2000	100	27 $4\frac{4}{7}$	27 $9\frac{1}{7}$	27 14	28 $\frac{5}{7}$	28 $5\frac{3}{7}$	28 $10\frac{2}{7}$
3000	150	40 $15\frac{5}{7}$	41 $4\frac{6}{7}$	41 12	42 $1\frac{1}{7}$	42 $8\frac{2}{7}$	42 $12\frac{3}{7}$
4000	200	54 9	55 $\frac{2}{7}$	55 10	56 $1\frac{4}{7}$	56 11	57 $2\frac{4}{7}$

Ells.		$87\frac{1}{5}$		88		$88\frac{4}{5}$		$89\frac{3}{5}$		$90\frac{2}{5}$		$91\frac{1}{5}$	
Yards.		109		110		111		112		113		114	
Splits.	Porters.	Sp.	Hk.	Sp.	Hk.	Sp.	Hk.	Sp.	Hk.	Sp.	Hk.	Sp.	Hk.
2	$\frac{1}{10}$												
4	$\frac{1}{5}$		$1\frac{1}{7}$		$1\frac{1}{7}$		$1\frac{1}{7}$		$1\frac{1}{7}$		$1\frac{1}{7}$		$1\frac{1}{7}$
5	$\frac{1}{4}$		$1\frac{2}{7}$		$1\frac{2}{7}$		$1\frac{2}{7}$		$1\frac{2}{7}$		$1\frac{2}{7}$		$1\frac{2}{7}$
10	$\frac{1}{2}$		$2\frac{4}{7}$		$2\frac{5}{7}$		$2\frac{5}{7}$		$2\frac{5}{7}$		$2\frac{5}{7}$		$2\frac{6}{7}$
20	1		$5\frac{1}{7}$		$5\frac{1}{7}$		$5\frac{1}{7}$		$5\frac{3}{7}$		$5\frac{3}{7}$		$5\frac{3}{7}$
30	$1\frac{1}{2}$		$7\frac{5}{7}$		$7\frac{6}{7}$		$7\frac{6}{7}$		8		8		$8\frac{1}{7}$
40	2		$10\frac{3}{7}$		$10\frac{4}{7}$		$10\frac{5}{7}$		$10\frac{5}{7}$		$10\frac{6}{7}$		11
50	$2\frac{1}{2}$		$12\frac{6}{7}$		13		$13\frac{1}{7}$		$13\frac{2}{7}$		$13\frac{3}{7}$		$13\frac{3}{7}$
60	3		$15\frac{4}{7}$		$15\frac{5}{7}$		$15\frac{6}{7}$		16		$16\frac{1}{7}$		$16\frac{2}{7}$
70	$3\frac{1}{2}$	1	$\frac{1}{7}$	1	$\frac{1}{7}$	1	$\frac{3}{7}$	1	$\frac{3}{7}$	1	$\frac{4}{7}$	1	$\frac{6}{7}$
80	4	1	$2\frac{5}{7}$	1	$2\frac{6}{7}$	1	3	1	$3\frac{2}{7}$	1	$3\frac{3}{7}$	1	$3\frac{4}{7}$
90	$4\frac{1}{2}$	1	$5\frac{2}{7}$	1	$5\frac{4}{7}$	1	$5\frac{5}{7}$	1	6	1	$6\frac{1}{7}$	1	$6\frac{3}{7}$
100	5	1	8	1	$8\frac{1}{7}$	1	$8\frac{3}{7}$	1	$8\frac{4}{7}$	1	$8\frac{6}{7}$	1	$9\frac{1}{7}$
200	10	2	$15\frac{6}{7}$	2	$16\frac{2}{7}$	2	$16\frac{5}{7}$	2	$17\frac{2}{7}$	2	$17\frac{5}{7}$	3	$\frac{1}{7}$
300	15	4	$5\frac{6}{7}$	4	$6\frac{4}{7}$	4	$7\frac{2}{7}$	4	8	4	$8\frac{4}{7}$	4	$9\frac{3}{7}$
400	20	5	$13\frac{6}{7}$	5	$14\frac{5}{7}$	5	$15\frac{5}{7}$	5	$16\frac{4}{7}$	5	$17\frac{4}{7}$	6	1
500	25	7	$3\frac{3}{7}$	7	$4\frac{6}{7}$	7	6	7	$7\frac{2}{7}$	7	$8\frac{3}{7}$	7	9
600	30	8	$11\frac{5}{7}$	8	$13\frac{1}{7}$	8	$14\frac{4}{7}$	8	16	8	$17\frac{3}{7}$	9	$\frac{6}{7}$
700	35	10	$1\frac{5}{7}$	10	$3\frac{2}{7}$	10	5	10	$6\frac{4}{7}$	10	$8\frac{2}{7}$	10	10
800	40	11	$9\frac{4}{7}$	11	$11\frac{3}{7}$	11	$13\frac{2}{7}$	11	$15\frac{2}{7}$	11	$17\frac{1}{7}$	12	$\frac{1}{7}$
900	45	12	$17\frac{4}{7}$	13	$1\frac{5}{7}$	13	$3\frac{6}{7}$	13	6	13	$8\frac{1}{7}$	13	$10\frac{3}{7}$
1000	50	14	$7\frac{4}{7}$	14	$9\frac{6}{7}$	14	$12\frac{2}{7}$	14	$14\frac{4}{7}$	14	17	15	$1\frac{3}{7}$
2000	100	28	15	29	$1\frac{4}{7}$	29	$6\frac{3}{7}$	29	$11\frac{2}{7}$	29	16	30	$2\frac{5}{7}$
3000	150	43	$4\frac{4}{7}$	43	$11\frac{5}{7}$	44	$\frac{4}{7}$	44	8	44	$15\frac{1}{7}$	45	$4\frac{2}{7}$
4000	200	57	$12\frac{1}{7}$	58	$3\frac{4}{7}$	58	$18\frac{1}{7}$	59	$4\frac{4}{7}$	59	$14\frac{1}{7}$	60	$5\frac{4}{7}$

Ells.		92		92 4/5		93 3/5		94 2/5		95 3/5		96	
Yards.		115		116		117		118		119		120	
Splits.	Porters.	Sp.	Hk.	Sp.	Hk.	Sp.	Hk.	Sp.	Hk.	Sp.	Hk.	Sp.	Hk.
2	1/10												
4	1/5		1 1/7		1 1/7		1 1/7		1 1/7		1 1/7		1 1/7
5	1/4		1 2/7		1 2/7		1 3/7		1 3/7		1 3/7		1 3/7
10	1/2		2 6/7		2 6/7		2 6/7		2 6/7		2 6/7		2 6/7
20	1		5 3/7		5 3/7		5 3/7		5 4/7		5 4/7		5 5/7
30	1 1/2		8 1/7		8 2/7		8 2/7		8 3/7		8 3/7		8 4/7
40	2		11		11		11 1/7		11 1/7		11 2/7		11 2/7
50	2 1/2		13 4/7		13 5/7		13 6/7		14		14		14 2/7
60	3		16 3/7		16 4/7		16 5/7		16 6/7		17		17 1/7
70	3 1/2	1	1 1/7	1	1 2/7	1	1 3/7	1	1 4/7	1	1 5/7	1	2
80	4	1	3 6/7	1	4	1	4 1/7	1	4 3/7	1	4 4/7	1	4 6/7
90	4 1/2	1	6 4/7	1	6 6/7	1	7	1	7 2/7	1	7 3/7	1	7 5/7
100	5	1	9 2/7	1	9 4/7	1	9 5/7	1	10	1	10 2/7	1	10 4/7
200	10	3	5/7	3	1 1/7	3	1 4/7	3	2 1/7	3	2 4/7	3	3 1/7
300	15	4	10 1/7	4	10 6/7	4	11 4/7	4	12 2/7	4	13	4	13 5/7
400	20	6	1 3/7	6	2 3/7	6	3 3/7	6	4 2/7	6	5 2/7	6	6 2/7
500	25	7	10 6/7	7	12	7	13 1/7	7	14 3/7	7	15 4/7	7	16 6/7
600	30	9	2 2/7	9	3 5/7	9	5 1/7	9	6 4/7	9	8	9	9 3/7
700	35	10	11 4/7	10	13 2/7	10	15	10	16 4/7	11	2/7	11	2
800	40	12	3	12	4 6/7	12	6 5/7	12	8 5/7	12	10 1/7	12	12 4/7
900	45	13	12 3/7	13	14 4/7	13	16 5/7	14	6/7	14	3	14	4 1/7
1000	50	15	3 4/7	15	6 1/7	15	8 4/7	15	10 6/7	15	13 2/7	15	17 5/7
2000	100	30	7 1/7	30	12 2/7	30	17	31	3 6/7	31	8 5/7	31	13 2/7
3000	150	45	11 3/7	46	4/7	46	7 5/7	46	14 6/7	47	4	47	9 1/7
4000	200	60	15 1/7	61	6 5/7	61	16 2/7	62	7 4/7	62	17 3/7	63	8 6/7

Ells.		$96\frac{4}{5}$	$97\frac{3}{5}$	$98\frac{2}{5}$	$99\frac{1}{5}$	100	$100\frac{4}{5}$
Yards.		121	122	123	124	125	126
Splits.	Porters.	Sp. Hk.	Sp. Hk.	Sp. Hk.	Sp. Hk.	Sp. Hk.	Sp. Hk.
2	$\frac{1}{10}$						
4	$\frac{1}{5}$	$1\frac{1}{7}$	$1\frac{1}{7}$	$1\frac{1}{7}$	$1\frac{1}{7}$	$1\frac{1}{7}$	$1\frac{1}{7}$
5	$\frac{1}{4}$	$1\frac{3}{7}$	$1\frac{3}{7}$	$1\frac{3}{7}$	$1\frac{3}{7}$	$1\frac{3}{7}$	$1\frac{3}{7}$
10	$\frac{1}{2}$	$2\frac{6}{7}$	$2\frac{6}{7}$	$2\frac{6}{7}$	3	3	3
20	1	$5\frac{5}{7}$	$5\frac{6}{7}$	$5\frac{6}{7}$	$5\frac{6}{7}$	6	6
30	$1\frac{1}{2}$	$8\frac{4}{7}$	$8\frac{5}{7}$	$8\frac{5}{7}$	$8\frac{5}{7}$	$8\frac{6}{7}$	9
40	2	$11\frac{4}{7}$	$11\frac{4}{7}$	$11\frac{5}{7}$	$11\frac{6}{7}$	$11\frac{6}{7}$	12
50	$2\frac{1}{2}$	$14\frac{3}{7}$	$14\frac{4}{7}$	$14\frac{4}{7}$	$14\frac{5}{7}$	$14\frac{6}{7}$	15
60	3	$17\frac{2}{7}$	$17\frac{3}{7}$	$17\frac{4}{7}$	$17\frac{5}{7}$	$17\frac{6}{7}$	1 0
70	$3\frac{1}{2}$	1 $2\frac{1}{7}$	1 $2\frac{2}{7}$	1 $2\frac{3}{7}$	1 $2\frac{5}{7}$	1 3	1 3
80	4	1 5	1 $5\frac{1}{7}$	1 $5\frac{3}{7}$	1 $5\frac{4}{7}$	1 $5\frac{5}{7}$	1 6
90	$4\frac{1}{2}$	1 $7\frac{6}{7}$	1 $8\frac{1}{7}$	1 $8\frac{3}{7}$	1 $8\frac{4}{7}$	1 $8\frac{5}{7}$	1 9
100	5	1 $10\frac{6}{7}$	1 11	1 $11\frac{2}{7}$	1 $11\frac{3}{7}$	1 $11\frac{5}{7}$	1 12
200	10	3 $3\frac{4}{7}$	3 4	3 $4\frac{4}{7}$	3 5	3 $5\frac{3}{7}$	3 6
300	15	4 $14\frac{3}{7}$	4 $15\frac{1}{7}$	4 $15\frac{6}{7}$	4 $16\frac{4}{7}$	4 $17\frac{4}{7}$	5 0
400	20	6 $7\frac{1}{7}$	6 $8\frac{1}{7}$	6 $9\frac{1}{7}$	6 10	6 11	6 12
500	25	8 0	8 $1\frac{1}{7}$	8 $2\frac{3}{7}$	8 $3\frac{4}{7}$	8 $4\frac{5}{7}$	8 6
600	30	9 $10\frac{6}{7}$	9 $12\frac{3}{7}$	9 $13\frac{5}{7}$	9 $15\frac{1}{7}$	9 $16\frac{4}{7}$	10 0
700	35	11 $3\frac{4}{7}$	11 $5\frac{2}{7}$	11 7	11 $8\frac{4}{7}$	11 $10\frac{2}{7}$	11 12
800	40	12 $14\frac{3}{7}$	12 $16\frac{2}{7}$	13 $\frac{2}{7}$	13 $2\frac{1}{7}$	13 4	13 6
900	45	14 $7\frac{2}{7}$	14 $9\frac{2}{7}$	14 $11\frac{4}{7}$	14 $13\frac{4}{7}$	14 $15\frac{6}{7}$	15 0
1000	50	16 0	16 $2\frac{3}{7}$	16 $4\frac{6}{7}$	16 $7\frac{1}{7}$	16 $9\frac{4}{7}$	16 12
2000	100	32 $1\frac{1}{7}$	32 $4\frac{6}{7}$	32 $9\frac{6}{7}$	32 $14\frac{3}{7}$	33 $1\frac{1}{7}$	33 6
3000	150	48 $\frac{3}{7}$	48 $7\frac{3}{7}$	48 $14\frac{4}{7}$	49 $3\frac{5}{7}$	49 $10\frac{6}{7}$	50 0
4000	200	64 $\frac{3}{7}$	64 $9\frac{6}{7}$	65 $1\frac{3}{7}$	65 $10\frac{6}{7}$	66 $2\frac{3}{7}$	66 12

Ells.		$101\frac{3}{5}$	$102\frac{2}{5}$	$103\frac{1}{5}$	104	$104\frac{4}{5}$	$105\frac{3}{5}$
Yards.		127	128	129	130	131	132
Splits.	Porters.	Sp. Hk.	Sp. Hk.	Sp. Hk.	Sp. Hk.	Sp. Hk.	Sp. Hk.
2	$\frac{1}{10}$						
4	$\frac{1}{5}$	$1\frac{3}{7}$	$1\frac{3}{7}$	$1\frac{3}{7}$	$1\frac{3}{7}$	$1\frac{3}{7}$	$1\frac{3}{7}$
5	$\frac{1}{4}$	$1\frac{4}{7}$	$1\frac{4}{7}$	$1\frac{4}{7}$	$1\frac{4}{7}$	$1\frac{4}{7}$	$1\frac{4}{7}$
10	$\frac{1}{2}$	3	3	3	$3\frac{1}{7}$	$3\frac{1}{7}$	$3\frac{1}{7}$
20	1	6	$6\frac{1}{7}$	$6\frac{1}{7}$	$6\frac{1}{7}$	$6\frac{1}{7}$	$6\frac{2}{7}$
30	$1\frac{1}{2}$	9	$9\frac{1}{7}$	$9\frac{1}{7}$	$9\frac{2}{7}$	$9\frac{2}{7}$	$9\frac{2}{7}$
40	2	12	$12\frac{1}{7}$	$12\frac{2}{7}$	$12\frac{2}{7}$	$12\frac{3}{7}$	$12\frac{4}{7}$
50	$2\frac{1}{2}$	$15\frac{1}{7}$	$15\frac{1}{7}$	$15\frac{3}{7}$	$15\frac{4}{7}$	$15\frac{4}{7}$	$15\frac{5}{7}$
60	3	1 $\frac{1}{7}$	1 $\frac{2}{7}$	1 $\frac{3}{7}$	1 $\frac{4}{7}$	1 $\frac{4}{7}$	1 $\frac{6}{7}$
70	$3\frac{1}{2}$	1 $3\frac{1}{7}$	1 $3\frac{3}{7}$	1 $3\frac{3}{7}$	1 $3\frac{5}{7}$	1 $3\frac{6}{7}$	1 4
80	4	1 $6\frac{1}{7}$	1 $6\frac{2}{7}$	1 $6\frac{4}{7}$	1 $6\frac{5}{7}$	1 $6\frac{6}{7}$	1 $7\frac{1}{7}$
90	$4\frac{1}{2}$	1 $9\frac{1}{7}$	1 $9\frac{3}{7}$	1 $9\frac{4}{7}$	1 $9\frac{6}{7}$	1 10	1 $10\frac{2}{7}$
100	5	1 $12\frac{1}{7}$	1 $12\frac{3}{7}$	1 $12\frac{5}{7}$	1 13	1 $13\frac{1}{7}$	1 $13\frac{3}{7}$
200	10	3 $6\frac{3}{7}$	3 $6\frac{6}{7}$	3 $7\frac{3}{7}$	3 $7\frac{6}{7}$	3 $8\frac{3}{7}$	3 $8\frac{6}{7}$
300	15	5 $\frac{5}{7}$	5 $1\frac{3}{7}$	5 $2\frac{1}{7}$	5 $2\frac{6}{7}$	5 $3\frac{4}{7}$	5 $4\frac{2}{7}$
400	20	6 13	6 $13\frac{6}{7}$	6 $14\frac{6}{7}$	6 $15\frac{6}{7}$	6 $16\frac{5}{7}$	6 $17\frac{5}{7}$
500	25	8 $7\frac{1}{7}$	8 $8\frac{3}{7}$	8 $9\frac{4}{7}$	8 $10\frac{5}{7}$	8 $11\frac{6}{7}$	8 $13\frac{1}{7}$
600	30	10 $1\frac{3}{7}$	10 $2\frac{6}{7}$	10 $4\frac{2}{7}$	10 $5\frac{5}{7}$	10 $7\frac{1}{7}$	10 $8\frac{4}{7}$
700	35	11 $13\frac{1}{7}$	11 $15\frac{5}{7}$	11 17	12 $\frac{5}{7}$	12 $2\frac{3}{7}$	12 4
800	40	13 $7\frac{6}{7}$	13 $9\frac{5}{7}$	13 $11\frac{5}{7}$	13 $13\frac{4}{7}$	13 $15\frac{3}{7}$	13 $17\frac{3}{7}$
900	45	15 $2\frac{1}{7}$	15 $4\frac{4}{7}$	15 $6\frac{3}{7}$	15 $8\frac{4}{7}$	15 $10\frac{5}{7}$	15 $12\frac{6}{7}$
1000	50	16 $14\frac{3}{7}$	16 $16\frac{5}{7}$	17 $1\frac{1}{7}$	17 $3\frac{3}{7}$	17 $5\frac{6}{7}$	17 $8\frac{3}{7}$
2000	100	33 $10\frac{6}{7}$	33 $15\frac{3}{7}$	34 $2\frac{2}{7}$	34 7	34 $11\frac{5}{7}$	34 $16\frac{3}{7}$
3000	150	50 $11\frac{1}{7}$	50 $14\frac{2}{7}$	51 $3\frac{3}{7}$	51 $10\frac{4}{7}$	51 $17\frac{4}{7}$	52 $6\frac{5}{7}$
4000	200	67 $3\frac{1}{7}$	67 13	68 $4\frac{1}{7}$	68 $14\frac{1}{7}$	69 $5\frac{1}{7}$	69 $15\frac{1}{7}$

Ells.		$106\frac{2}{5}$		$107\frac{1}{5}$		108		$108\frac{4}{5}$		$109\frac{3}{5}$		$110\frac{2}{5}$	
Yards.		133		134		135		136		137		138	
Splits.	Porters.	Sp.	Hk.	Sp.	Hk.	Sp.	Hk.	Sp.	Hk.	Sp.	Hk.	Sp.	Hk.
2	$\frac{1}{10}$												
4	$\frac{1}{5}$		$1\frac{2}{7}$		$1\frac{2}{7}$		$1\frac{2}{7}$		$1\frac{2}{7}$		$1\frac{2}{7}$		$1\frac{2}{7}$
5	$\frac{1}{4}$		$1\frac{4}{7}$		$1\frac{4}{7}$		$1\frac{4}{7}$		$1\frac{4}{7}$		$1\frac{4}{7}$		$1\frac{4}{7}$
10	$\frac{1}{2}$		$3\frac{1}{7}$		$3\frac{2}{7}$		$3\frac{2}{7}$		$3\frac{2}{7}$		$3\frac{2}{7}$		$3\frac{2}{7}$
20	1		$6\frac{2}{7}$		$6\frac{2}{7}$		$6\frac{3}{7}$		$6\frac{3}{7}$		$6\frac{3}{7}$		$6\frac{4}{7}$
30	$1\frac{1}{2}$		$9\frac{3}{7}$		$9\frac{4}{7}$		$9\frac{4}{7}$		$9\frac{4}{7}$		$9\frac{5}{7}$		$9\frac{6}{7}$
40	2		$12\frac{5}{7}$		$12\frac{6}{7}$		$12\frac{6}{7}$		13		$13\frac{1}{7}$		$13\frac{1}{7}$
50	$2\frac{1}{2}$		$15\frac{6}{7}$		$15\frac{6}{7}$		16		$16\frac{1}{7}$		$16\frac{2}{7}$		$16\frac{3}{7}$
60	3	1	1	1	$1\frac{1}{7}$	1	$1\frac{2}{7}$	1	$1\frac{3}{7}$	1	$1\frac{3}{7}$	1	$1\frac{4}{7}$
70	$3\frac{1}{2}$	1	$4\frac{1}{7}$	1	$4\frac{2}{7}$	1	$4\frac{3}{7}$	1	$4\frac{5}{7}$	1	$4\frac{6}{7}$	1	5
80	4	1	$7\frac{2}{7}$	1	$7\frac{3}{7}$	1	$7\frac{5}{7}$	1	$7\frac{6}{7}$	1	8	1	$8\frac{2}{7}$
90	$4\frac{1}{2}$	1	$10\frac{3}{7}$	1	$10\frac{5}{7}$	1	$10\frac{6}{7}$	1	$11\frac{1}{7}$	1	$11\frac{2}{7}$	1	$11\frac{4}{7}$
100	5	1	$13\frac{4}{7}$	1	$13\frac{5}{7}$	1	$14\frac{1}{7}$	1	$14\frac{3}{7}$	1	$14\frac{4}{7}$	1	$14\frac{6}{7}$
200	10	3	$9\frac{3}{7}$	3	$9\frac{5}{7}$	3	$10\frac{2}{7}$	3	$10\frac{5}{7}$	3	$11\frac{1}{7}$	3	$11\frac{4}{7}$
300	15	5	5	5	$5\frac{4}{7}$	5	$6\frac{3}{7}$	5	$7\frac{1}{7}$	5	$7\frac{6}{7}$	5	$8\frac{4}{7}$
400	20	7	$\frac{5}{7}$	7	$1\frac{4}{7}$	7	$2\frac{4}{7}$	7	$3\frac{4}{7}$	7	$4\frac{3}{7}$	7	$5\frac{3}{7}$
500	25	8	$14\frac{2}{7}$	8	$15\frac{3}{7}$	8	$16\frac{5}{7}$	8	$17\frac{6}{7}$	9	1	9	$2\frac{2}{7}$
600	30	10	10	10	$11\frac{3}{7}$	10	$12\frac{6}{7}$	10	$14\frac{2}{7}$	10	$15\frac{5}{7}$	10	$17\frac{1}{7}$
700	35	12	$5\frac{5}{7}$	12	$7\frac{2}{7}$	12	9	12	$10\frac{5}{7}$	12	$12\frac{3}{7}$	12	14
800	40	14	$1\frac{4}{7}$	14	$3\frac{1}{7}$	14	$5\frac{1}{7}$	14	7	14	$8\frac{6}{7}$	14	$10\frac{6}{7}$
900	45	15	14	15	$17\frac{1}{7}$	16	$1\frac{2}{7}$	16	$3\frac{2}{7}$	16	$5\frac{4}{7}$	16	$7\frac{4}{7}$
1000	50	17	$10\frac{5}{7}$	17	13	17	$15\frac{3}{7}$	17	$17\frac{6}{7}$	18	$2\frac{1}{7}$	18	$4\frac{3}{7}$
2000	100	35	$3\frac{2}{7}$	35	8	35	$12\frac{4}{7}$	35	$17\frac{4}{7}$	36	$4\frac{2}{7}$	36	$9\frac{1}{7}$
3000	150	52	14	53	$3\frac{1}{7}$	53	$10\frac{2}{7}$	53	$17\frac{3}{7}$	54	$6\frac{4}{7}$	54	$13\frac{5}{7}$
4000	200	70	$6\frac{5}{7}$	70	$16\frac{1}{7}$	71	$7\frac{5}{7}$	71	$17\frac{2}{7}$	72	$8\frac{4}{7}$	73	$\frac{2}{7}$

BEAMERS' TABLES.

Ells.		$111\frac{1}{5}$	112	$112\frac{4}{5}$	$113\frac{3}{5}$	$114\frac{2}{5}$	$115\frac{1}{5}$
Yards.		139	140	141	142	143	144
Splits.	Porters.	Sp. Hk.	Sp. Hk.	Sp. Hk.	Sp. Hk.	Sp. Hk.	Sp. Hk.
2	$\frac{1}{10}$						
4	$\frac{1}{5}$	$1\frac{3}{7}$	$1\frac{3}{7}$	$1\frac{3}{7}$	$1\frac{3}{7}$	$1\frac{3}{7}$	$1\frac{3}{7}$
5	$\frac{1}{4}$	$1\frac{4}{7}$	$1\frac{4}{7}$	$1\frac{4}{7}$	$1\frac{4}{7}$	$1\frac{4}{7}$	$1\frac{4}{7}$
10	$\frac{1}{2}$	$3\frac{2}{7}$	$3\frac{4}{7}$	$3\frac{4}{7}$	$3\frac{4}{7}$	$3\frac{4}{7}$	$3\frac{4}{7}$
20	1	$6\frac{4}{7}$	$6\frac{4}{7}$	$6\frac{4}{7}$	$6\frac{5}{7}$	$6\frac{5}{7}$	$6\frac{5}{7}$
30	$1\frac{1}{2}$	$9\frac{6}{7}$	10	10	$10\frac{1}{7}$	$10\frac{2}{7}$	$10\frac{2}{7}$
40	2	$13\frac{3}{7}$	$13\frac{3}{7}$	$13\frac{4}{7}$	$13\frac{5}{7}$	$13\frac{5}{7}$	$13\frac{6}{7}$
50	$2\frac{1}{2}$	$16\frac{5}{7}$	$16\frac{4}{7}$	$16\frac{6}{7}$	$16\frac{6}{7}$	$16\frac{6}{7}$	17
60	3	1 2	1 2	1 $2\frac{1}{7}$	1 $2\frac{2}{7}$	1 $2\frac{3}{7}$	1 $2\frac{4}{7}$
70	$3\frac{1}{2}$	1 $5\frac{1}{7}$	1 $5\frac{2}{7}$	1 $5\frac{3}{7}$	1 $5\frac{4}{7}$	1 $5\frac{5}{7}$	1 6
80	4	1 $8\frac{3}{7}$	1 $8\frac{4}{7}$	1 $8\frac{5}{7}$	1 9	1 $9\frac{1}{7}$	1 $9\frac{2}{7}$
90	$4\frac{1}{2}$	1 $11\frac{5}{7}$	1 12	1 $12\frac{1}{7}$	1 $12\frac{2}{7}$	1 $12\frac{4}{7}$	1 $12\frac{6}{7}$
100	5	1 $15\frac{1}{7}$	1 $15\frac{2}{7}$	1 $15\frac{4}{7}$	1 $15\frac{5}{7}$	1 16	1 $16\frac{2}{7}$
200	10	3 $12\frac{1}{7}$	3 $12\frac{4}{7}$	3 13	3 $13\frac{4}{7}$	3 14	3 $14\frac{3}{7}$
300	15	5 $9\frac{2}{7}$	5 10	5 $10\frac{4}{7}$	5 $11\frac{3}{7}$	5 $12\frac{1}{7}$	5 $12\frac{6}{7}$
400	20	7 $6\frac{3}{7}$	7 $7\frac{4}{7}$	7 $8\frac{4}{7}$	7 $9\frac{1}{7}$	7 $10\frac{2}{7}$	7 $11\frac{1}{7}$
500	25	9 $3\frac{3}{7}$	9 $4\frac{4}{7}$	9 $5\frac{5}{7}$	9 7	9 $8\frac{1}{7}$	9 $9\frac{2}{7}$
600	30	11 $\frac{4}{7}$	11 2	11 $3\frac{3}{7}$	11 $4\frac{6}{7}$	11 $6\frac{2}{7}$	11 $7\frac{5}{7}$
700	35	12 $15\frac{4}{7}$	12 $17\frac{2}{7}$	13 1	13 $2\frac{4}{7}$	13 $4\frac{2}{7}$	13 6
800	40	14 $12\frac{4}{7}$	14 $14\frac{4}{7}$	14 $16\frac{3}{7}$	15 $\frac{3}{7}$	15 $2\frac{2}{7}$	15 $4\frac{1}{7}$
900	45	16 $9\frac{4}{7}$	16 12	16 $14\frac{1}{7}$	16 $16\frac{2}{7}$	17 $\frac{3}{7}$	17 $2\frac{4}{7}$
1000	50	18 7	18 $9\frac{2}{7}$	18 $11\frac{5}{7}$	18 14	18 $16\frac{3}{7}$	19 $\frac{5}{7}$
2000	100	36 $13\frac{6}{7}$	37 $\frac{4}{7}$	37 $5\frac{4}{7}$	37 10	37 $14\frac{6}{7}$	38 $1\frac{4}{7}$
3000	150	55 $2\frac{6}{7}$	55 10	55 $17\frac{1}{7}$	56 $6\frac{2}{7}$	56 $13\frac{3}{7}$	57 $2\frac{4}{7}$
4000	200	73 $9\frac{6}{7}$	74 $1\frac{4}{7}$	74 $10\frac{4}{7}$	75 $2\frac{3}{7}$	75 $11\frac{5}{7}$	76 $3\frac{3}{7}$

Ells.		116		$116\frac{4}{5}$		$117\frac{3}{5}$		$118\frac{2}{5}$		$119\frac{1}{5}$		120	
Yards.		145		146		147		148		149		150	
Splits.	Porters.	Sp.	Hk.	Sp.	Hk.	Sp.	Hk.	Sp.	Hk.	Sp.	Hk.	Sp.	Hk.
2	$\frac{1}{10}$												
4	$\frac{1}{5}$		$1\frac{3}{7}$		$1\frac{3}{7}$		$1\frac{3}{7}$		$1\frac{3}{7}$		$1\frac{3}{7}$		$1\frac{3}{7}$
5	$\frac{1}{4}$		$1\frac{4}{7}$		$1\frac{4}{7}$		$1\frac{5}{7}$		$1\frac{5}{7}$		$1\frac{5}{7}$		$1\frac{5}{7}$
10	$\frac{1}{2}$		$3\frac{4}{7}$		$3\frac{4}{7}$		$3\frac{4}{7}$		$3\frac{4}{7}$		$3\frac{4}{7}$		$3\frac{5}{7}$
20	1		$6\frac{6}{7}$		$6\frac{6}{7}$		$6\frac{6}{7}$		7		7		$7\frac{1}{7}$
30	$1\frac{1}{2}$		$10\frac{4}{7}$		$10\frac{3}{7}$		$10\frac{3}{7}$		$10\frac{4}{7}$		$10\frac{4}{7}$		$10\frac{5}{7}$
40	2		$13\frac{6}{7}$		14		$14\frac{1}{7}$		$14\frac{1}{7}$		$14\frac{2}{7}$		$14\frac{2}{7}$
50	$2\frac{1}{2}$		$17\frac{1}{7}$		$17\frac{2}{7}$		$17\frac{3}{7}$		$17\frac{4}{7}$		$17\frac{5}{7}$		$17\frac{6}{7}$
60	3	1	$2\frac{5}{7}$	1	$2\frac{6}{7}$	1	3	1	$3\frac{1}{7}$	1	$3\frac{2}{7}$	1	$3\frac{3}{7}$
70	$3\frac{1}{2}$	1	$6\frac{1}{7}$	1	$6\frac{2}{7}$	1	$6\frac{3}{7}$	1	$6\frac{4}{7}$	1	$6\frac{5}{7}$	1	7
80	4	1	$9\frac{4}{7}$	1	$9\frac{5}{7}$	1	$9\frac{6}{7}$	1	$10\frac{1}{7}$	1	$10\frac{3}{7}$	1	$10\frac{4}{7}$
90	$4\frac{1}{2}$	1	13	1	$13\frac{3}{7}$	1	$13\frac{3}{7}$	1	$13\frac{5}{7}$	1	$13\frac{6}{7}$	1	$14\frac{1}{7}$
100	5	1	$16\frac{3}{7}$	1	$16\frac{5}{7}$	1	17	1	$17\frac{2}{7}$	1	$17\frac{3}{7}$	1	$17\frac{5}{7}$
200	10	3	15	3	$15\frac{3}{7}$	3	$15\frac{6}{7}$	3	$16\frac{3}{7}$	3	$16\frac{6}{7}$	3	$17\frac{3}{7}$
300	15	5	$13\frac{4}{7}$	5	$14\frac{2}{7}$	5	15	5	$15\frac{5}{7}$	5	$16\frac{3}{7}$	5	$17\frac{1}{7}$
400	20	7	12	7	13	7	14	7	$14\frac{6}{7}$	7	$15\frac{6}{7}$	7	$16\frac{6}{7}$
500	25	9	$10\frac{4}{7}$	9	$11\frac{5}{7}$	9	$12\frac{6}{7}$	9	$14\frac{1}{7}$	9	$15\frac{2}{7}$	9	$16\frac{4}{7}$
600	30	11	$9\frac{1}{7}$	11	$10\frac{4}{7}$	11	12	11	$13\frac{3}{7}$	11	$14\frac{6}{7}$	11	$16\frac{2}{7}$
700	35	13	$7\frac{5}{7}$	13	$9\frac{3}{7}$	13	11	13	$12\frac{4}{7}$	13	$14\frac{2}{7}$	13	16
800	40	15	$6\frac{1}{7}$	15	8	15	$9\frac{6}{7}$	15	$11\frac{6}{7}$	15	$13\frac{5}{7}$	15	$15\frac{5}{7}$
900	45	17	$4\frac{5}{7}$	17	$6\frac{6}{7}$	17	9	17	$11\frac{1}{7}$	17	$13\frac{3}{7}$	17	$15\frac{3}{7}$
1000	50	19	$3\frac{1}{7}$	19	$5\frac{4}{7}$	19	8	19	$10\frac{3}{7}$	19	$12\frac{6}{7}$	19	$15\frac{1}{7}$
2000	100	38	$6\frac{3}{7}$	38	$11\frac{1}{7}$	38	$15\frac{6}{7}$	39	$2\frac{5}{7}$	39	$7\frac{3}{7}$	39	$12\frac{2}{7}$
3000	150	57	$9\frac{4}{7}$	57	$16\frac{6}{7}$	58	6	58	$13\frac{1}{7}$	59	$2\frac{2}{7}$	59	$9\frac{3}{7}$
4000	200	76	$12\frac{6}{7}$	77	$4\frac{3}{7}$	77	14	78	$5\frac{3}{7}$	78	15	79	$6\frac{4}{7}$

BEAMERS' TABLES.

Ells.		$120\frac{2}{5}$	$121\frac{3}{5}$	$122\frac{2}{5}$	$123\frac{1}{5}$	124	$124\frac{4}{5}$
Yards.		151	152	153	154	155	156
Splits.	Porters.	Sp. Hk.	Sp. Hk.	Sp. Hk.	Sp. Hk.	Sp. Hk.	Sp. Hk.
2	$\frac{1}{10}$						
4	$\frac{1}{5}$	$1\frac{3}{7}$	$1\frac{3}{7}$	$1\frac{3}{7}$	$1\frac{3}{7}$	$1\frac{3}{7}$	$1\frac{3}{7}$
5	$\frac{1}{4}$	$1\frac{5}{7}$	$1\frac{5}{7}$	$1\frac{5}{7}$	$1\frac{5}{7}$	$1\frac{5}{7}$	$1\frac{5}{7}$
10	$\frac{1}{2}$	$3\frac{4}{7}$	$3\frac{4}{7}$	$3\frac{4}{7}$	$3\frac{5}{7}$	$3\frac{5}{7}$	$3\frac{5}{7}$
20	1	$7\frac{1}{7}$	$7\frac{2}{7}$	$7\frac{2}{7}$	$7\frac{2}{7}$	$7\frac{3}{7}$	$7\frac{3}{7}$
30	$1\frac{1}{2}$	$10\frac{6}{7}$	11	11	11	11	$11\frac{1}{7}$
40	2	$14\frac{3}{7}$	$14\frac{3}{7}$	$14\frac{4}{7}$	$14\frac{5}{7}$	$14\frac{5}{7}$	$14\frac{6}{7}$
50	$2\frac{1}{2}$	1 0	1 $\frac{1}{7}$	1 $\frac{1}{7}$	1 $\frac{2}{7}$	1 $\frac{3}{7}$	1 $\frac{4}{7}$
60	3	1 $3\frac{4}{7}$	1 $3\frac{5}{7}$	1 $3\frac{6}{7}$	1 4	1 $4\frac{1}{7}$	1 $4\frac{2}{7}$
70	$3\frac{1}{2}$	1 $7\frac{1}{7}$	1 $7\frac{2}{7}$	1 $7\frac{3}{7}$	1 $7\frac{5}{7}$	1 $7\frac{6}{7}$	1 8
80	4	1 $10\frac{5}{7}$	1 11	1 $11\frac{1}{7}$	1 $11\frac{2}{7}$	1 $11\frac{4}{7}$	1 $11\frac{5}{7}$
90	$4\frac{1}{2}$	1 $14\frac{3}{7}$	1 $14\frac{4}{7}$	1 $14\frac{5}{7}$	1 15	1 $15\frac{1}{7}$	1 $15\frac{3}{7}$
100	5	1 $17\frac{6}{7}$	2 $\frac{1}{7}$	2 $\frac{3}{7}$	2 $\frac{4}{7}$	2 $\frac{6}{7}$	2 $1\frac{1}{7}$
200	10	3 $17\frac{6}{7}$	4 $\frac{2}{7}$	4 $\frac{6}{7}$	4 $1\frac{2}{7}$	4 $1\frac{5}{7}$	4 $2\frac{2}{7}$
300	15	5 $17\frac{6}{7}$	6 $\frac{4}{7}$	6 $1\frac{2}{7}$	6 2	6 $2\frac{5}{7}$	6 $3\frac{3}{7}$
400	20	7 $17\frac{5}{7}$	8 $\frac{5}{7}$	8 $1\frac{5}{7}$	8 $2\frac{4}{7}$	8 $3\frac{4}{7}$	8 $4\frac{4}{7}$
500	25	9 $17\frac{5}{7}$	10 $\frac{6}{7}$	10 $2\frac{1}{7}$	10 $3\frac{2}{7}$	10 $4\frac{3}{7}$	10 $5\frac{5}{7}$
600	30	11 $17\frac{5}{7}$	12 $1\frac{2}{7}$	12 $2\frac{4}{7}$	12 4	12 $5\frac{3}{7}$	12 $6\frac{6}{7}$
700	35	13 $17\frac{4}{7}$	14 $1\frac{2}{7}$	14 3	14 $4\frac{4}{7}$	14 $6\frac{2}{7}$	14 $7\frac{6}{7}$
800	40	15 $17\frac{4}{7}$	16 $1\frac{3}{7}$	16 $3\frac{3}{7}$	16 $5\frac{2}{7}$	16 $7\frac{1}{7}$	16 $9\frac{1}{7}$
900	45	17 $17\frac{4}{7}$	18 $1\frac{5}{7}$	18 $3\frac{6}{7}$	18 6	18 $8\frac{1}{7}$	18 11
1000	50	19 $17\frac{4}{7}$	20 $1\frac{6}{7}$	20 $4\frac{2}{7}$	20 $6\frac{4}{7}$	20 9	20 $11\frac{3}{7}$
2000	100	39 17	40 $3\frac{5}{7}$	40 $8\frac{4}{7}$	40 $13\frac{2}{7}$	41 0	41 $4\frac{5}{7}$
3000	150	59 $16\frac{4}{7}$	60 $5\frac{5}{7}$	60 $12\frac{6}{7}$	61 2	61 $9\frac{1}{7}$	61 $16\frac{2}{7}$
4000	200	79 16	80 $7\frac{4}{7}$	80 $17\frac{1}{7}$	81 $8\frac{4}{7}$	82 $\frac{1}{7}$	82 $9\frac{5}{7}$

Ells.		$125\frac{3}{5}$		$126\frac{2}{5}$		$127\frac{1}{5}$		128		$128\frac{4}{5}$		$129\frac{3}{5}$	
Yards.		157		158		159		160		161		162	
Splits.	Porters.	Sp.	Hk.	Sp.	Hk.	Sp.	Hk.	Sp.	Hk.	Sp.	Hk.	Sp.	Hk.
2	$\frac{1}{10}$												
4	$\frac{1}{5}$		$1\frac{3}{7}$		$1\frac{4}{7}$		$1\frac{4}{7}$		$1\frac{4}{7}$		$1\frac{4}{7}$		$1\frac{4}{7}$
5	$\frac{1}{4}$		$1\frac{6}{7}$		$1\frac{6}{7}$		$1\frac{6}{7}$		$1\frac{6}{7}$		$1\frac{6}{7}$		$1\frac{6}{7}$
10	$\frac{1}{2}$		$3\frac{5}{7}$		$3\frac{5}{7}$		$3\frac{5}{7}$		$3\frac{6}{7}$		$3\frac{6}{7}$		$3\frac{6}{7}$
20	1		$7\frac{3}{7}$		$7\frac{4}{7}$		$7\frac{4}{7}$		$7\frac{4}{7}$		$7\frac{4}{7}$		$7\frac{5}{7}$
30	$1\frac{1}{2}$		$11\frac{1}{7}$		$11\frac{2}{7}$		$11\frac{2}{7}$		$11\frac{3}{7}$		$11\frac{3}{7}$		$11\frac{3}{7}$
40	2		$14\frac{6}{7}$		15		$15\frac{1}{7}$		$15\frac{2}{7}$		$15\frac{3}{7}$		$15\frac{3}{7}$
50	$2\frac{1}{2}$	1	$\frac{5}{7}$	1	$\frac{6}{7}$	1	$\frac{6}{7}$	1	1	1	$1\frac{1}{7}$	1	$1\frac{2}{7}$
60	3	1	$4\frac{3}{7}$	1	$4\frac{4}{7}$	1	$4\frac{5}{7}$	1	$4\frac{6}{7}$	1	5	1	$5\frac{1}{7}$
70	$3\frac{1}{2}$	1	$8\frac{1}{7}$	1	$8\frac{2}{7}$	1	$8\frac{3}{7}$	1	$8\frac{5}{7}$	1	$8\frac{6}{7}$	1	9
80	4	1	$11\frac{6}{7}$	1	12	1	$12\frac{1}{7}$	1	$12\frac{3}{7}$	1	$12\frac{4}{7}$	1	$12\frac{5}{7}$
90	$4\frac{1}{2}$	1	$15\frac{4}{7}$	1	$15\frac{6}{7}$	1	16	1	$16\frac{2}{7}$	1	$16\frac{4}{7}$	1	$16\frac{5}{7}$
100	5	2	$1\frac{3}{7}$	2	$1\frac{4}{7}$	2	$1\frac{5}{7}$	2	$2\frac{1}{7}$	2	$2\frac{3}{7}$	2	$2\frac{4}{7}$
200	10	4	$2\frac{5}{7}$	4	$3\frac{1}{7}$	4	$3\frac{5}{7}$	4	$4\frac{1}{7}$	4	$4\frac{4}{7}$	4	$5\frac{1}{7}$
300	15	6	$4\frac{1}{7}$	6	$4\frac{6}{7}$	6	$5\frac{4}{7}$	6	$6\frac{2}{7}$	6	7	6	$7\frac{4}{7}$
400	20	8	$5\frac{3}{7}$	8	$6\frac{3}{7}$	8	$7\frac{3}{7}$	8	$8\frac{3}{7}$	8	$9\frac{3}{7}$	8	$10\frac{3}{7}$
500	25	10	$6\frac{6}{7}$	10	8	10	$9\frac{2}{7}$	10	$10\frac{3}{7}$	10	$11\frac{4}{7}$	10	$12\frac{5}{7}$
600	30	12	$8\frac{2}{7}$	12	$9\frac{5}{7}$	12	$11\frac{1}{7}$	12	$12\frac{4}{7}$	12	14	12	$15\frac{3}{7}$
700	35	14	$9\frac{4}{7}$	14	$11\frac{2}{7}$	14	13	14	$14\frac{5}{7}$	14	$16\frac{2}{7}$	15	0
800	40	16	11	16	$12\frac{6}{7}$	16	$14\frac{6}{7}$	16	$16\frac{5}{7}$	17	$\frac{4}{7}$	17	$2\frac{4}{7}$
900	45	18	$12\frac{3}{7}$	18	$14\frac{4}{7}$	18	$16\frac{5}{7}$	19	$\frac{6}{7}$	19	3	19	$5\frac{1}{7}$
1000	50	20	$13\frac{4}{7}$	20	$16\frac{1}{7}$	21	$\frac{4}{7}$	21	3	21	$5\frac{2}{7}$	21	$7\frac{5}{7}$
2000	100	41	$9\frac{1}{7}$	41	$14\frac{2}{7}$	42	$1\frac{3}{7}$	42	$5\frac{5}{7}$	42	$10\frac{4}{7}$	42	$15\frac{3}{7}$
3000	150	62	$5\frac{3}{7}$	62	$12\frac{3}{7}$	63	$1\frac{5}{7}$	63	$8\frac{5}{7}$	63	16	64	$5\frac{1}{7}$
4000	200	83	$1\frac{4}{7}$	83	$10\frac{5}{7}$	84	$2\frac{3}{7}$	84	$11\frac{4}{7}$	85	$3\frac{4}{7}$	85	$12\frac{6}{7}$

BEAMERS' TABLES.

Ells.		$130\frac{2}{5}$	$131\frac{1}{5}$	132	$132\frac{4}{5}$	$133\frac{3}{5}$	$134\frac{2}{5}$
Yards.		163	164	165	166	167	168
Splits.	Porters.	Sp. Hk.	Sp. Hk.	Sp. Hk.	Sp. Hk.	Sp. Hk.	Sp. Hk.
2	$\frac{1}{10}$						
4	$\frac{1}{5}$	$1\frac{4}{7}$	$1\frac{4}{7}$	$1\frac{4}{7}$	$1\frac{4}{7}$	$1\frac{4}{7}$	$1\frac{5}{7}$
5	$\frac{1}{4}$	$1\frac{6}{7}$	$1\frac{6}{7}$	$1\frac{6}{7}$	$1\frac{6}{7}$	2	2
10	$\frac{1}{2}$	$3\frac{6}{7}$	4	4	4	4	4
20	1	$7\frac{5}{7}$	$7\frac{5}{7}$	$7\frac{6}{7}$	$7\frac{6}{7}$	$7\frac{6}{7}$	8
30	$1\frac{1}{2}$	$11\frac{4}{7}$	$11\frac{4}{7}$	$11\frac{5}{7}$	$11\frac{6}{7}$	$11\frac{6}{7}$	12
40	2	$15\frac{4}{7}$	$15\frac{5}{7}$	$15\frac{5}{7}$	$15\frac{6}{7}$	16	16
50	$2\frac{1}{2}$	1 $1\frac{3}{7}$	1 $1\frac{3}{7}$	1 $1\frac{4}{7}$	1 $1\frac{5}{7}$	1 $1\frac{6}{7}$	1 2
60	3	1 $5\frac{2}{7}$	1 $5\frac{3}{7}$	1 $5\frac{4}{7}$	1 $5\frac{5}{7}$	1 $5\frac{6}{7}$	1 6
70	$3\frac{1}{2}$	1 $9\frac{1}{7}$	1 $9\frac{3}{7}$	1 $9\frac{4}{7}$	1 $9\frac{5}{7}$	1 $9\frac{6}{7}$	1 10
80	4	1 13	1 $13\frac{1}{7}$	1 $13\frac{3}{7}$	1 $13\frac{4}{7}$	1 $13\frac{5}{7}$	1 14
90	$4\frac{1}{2}$	1 $16\frac{6}{7}$	1 $17\frac{1}{7}$	1 $17\frac{2}{7}$	1 $17\frac{4}{7}$	1 $17\frac{5}{7}$	2 0
100	5	2 $2\frac{6}{7}$	2 3	2 $3\frac{2}{7}$	2 $3\frac{4}{7}$	2 $3\frac{5}{7}$	2 4
200	10	4 $5\frac{4}{7}$	4 6	4 $6\frac{4}{7}$	4 7	4 $7\frac{3}{7}$	4 8
300	15	6 $8\frac{3}{7}$	6 $9\frac{1}{7}$	6 $9\frac{6}{7}$	6 $10\frac{4}{7}$	6 $11\frac{3}{7}$	6 12
400	20	8 $11\frac{2}{7}$	8 $12\frac{1}{7}$	8 $13\frac{1}{7}$	8 $14\frac{1}{7}$	8 15	8 16
500	25	10 14	10 $15\frac{1}{7}$	10 $16\frac{3}{7}$	10 $17\frac{4}{7}$	11 $\frac{4}{7}$	11 2
600	30	12 $16\frac{6}{7}$	13 $\frac{2}{7}$	13 $1\frac{5}{7}$	13 $3\frac{1}{7}$	13 $4\frac{4}{7}$	13 6
700	35	15 $1\frac{5}{7}$	15 $3\frac{2}{7}$	15 5	15 $6\frac{5}{7}$	15 $8\frac{2}{7}$	15 10
800	40	17 $4\frac{3}{7}$	17 $6\frac{2}{7}$	17 $8\frac{2}{7}$	17 $10\frac{1}{7}$	17 12	17 14
900	45	19 $7\frac{2}{7}$	19 $9\frac{2}{7}$	19 $11\frac{4}{7}$	19 $13\frac{5}{7}$	19 $15\frac{6}{7}$	20 0
1000	50	21 $10\frac{1}{7}$	21 $11\frac{3}{7}$	21 $14\frac{6}{7}$	21 17	22 $1\frac{1}{7}$	22 4
2000	100	43 $2\frac{1}{7}$	43 $6\frac{6}{7}$	43 $11\frac{5}{7}$	43 $16\frac{3}{7}$	44 $1\frac{1}{7}$	44 8
3000	150	64 $12\frac{2}{7}$	65 $1\frac{3}{7}$	65 $8\frac{4}{7}$	65 $15\frac{5}{7}$	66 $4\frac{6}{7}$	66 12
4000	200	86 $4\frac{3}{7}$	86 14	87 $5\frac{3}{7}$	87 15	88 $6\frac{1}{7}$	88 16

Ells.		$135\frac{1}{5}$		136		$136\frac{4}{5}$		$137\frac{3}{5}$		$138\frac{2}{5}$		$139\frac{1}{5}$	
Yards.		169		170		171		172		173		174	
Splits.	Porters.	Sp.	Hk.	Sp.	Hk.	Sp.	Hk.	Sp.	Hk.	Sp.	Hk.	Sp.	Hk.
2	$\frac{1}{10}$												
4	$\frac{1}{5}$		$1\frac{5}{7}$		$1\frac{5}{7}$		$1\frac{5}{7}$		$1\frac{5}{7}$		$1\frac{5}{7}$		$1\frac{5}{7}$
5	$\frac{1}{4}$		2		2		2		2		2		2
10	$\frac{1}{2}$		4		$4\frac{4}{7}$		$4\frac{1}{7}$		$4\frac{1}{7}$		$4\frac{1}{7}$		$4\frac{1}{7}$
20	1		8		8		8		$8\frac{1}{7}$		$8\frac{1}{7}$		$8\frac{1}{7}$
30	$1\frac{1}{2}$		12		$12\frac{1}{7}$		$12\frac{1}{7}$		$12\frac{2}{7}$		$12\frac{2}{7}$		$12\frac{3}{7}$
40	2		$16\frac{1}{7}$		$16\frac{2}{7}$		$16\frac{3}{7}$		$16\frac{3}{7}$		$16\frac{4}{7}$		$16\frac{4}{7}$
50	$2\frac{1}{2}$	1	2	1	$2\frac{1}{7}$	1	$2\frac{2}{7}$	1	$2\frac{3}{7}$	1	$2\frac{3}{7}$	1	$2\frac{4}{7}$
60	3	1	$6\frac{1}{7}$	1	$6\frac{2}{7}$	1	$6\frac{3}{7}$	1	$6\frac{4}{7}$	1	$6\frac{5}{7}$	1	$6\frac{6}{7}$
70	$3\frac{1}{2}$	1	$10\frac{1}{7}$	1	$10\frac{3}{7}$	1	$10\frac{4}{7}$	1	$10\frac{5}{7}$	1	$10\frac{6}{7}$	1	11
80	4	1	$14\frac{1}{7}$	1	$14\frac{2}{7}$	1	$14\frac{3}{7}$	1	$14\frac{5}{7}$	1	$14\frac{6}{7}$	1	15
90	$4\frac{1}{2}$	2	$\frac{1}{7}$	2	$\frac{3}{7}$	2	$\frac{4}{7}$	2	$\frac{6}{7}$	2	1	2	$1\frac{2}{7}$
100	5	2	$4\frac{2}{7}$	2	$4\frac{3}{7}$	2	$4\frac{4}{7}$	2	$4\frac{6}{7}$	2	$5\frac{1}{7}$	2	$5\frac{2}{7}$
200	10	4	$8\frac{3}{7}$	4	$8\frac{6}{7}$	4	$9\frac{2}{7}$	4	$9\frac{6}{7}$	4	$10\frac{2}{7}$	4	$10\frac{5}{7}$
300	15	6	$12\frac{5}{7}$	6	$13\frac{3}{7}$	6	$14\frac{1}{7}$	6	$14\frac{6}{7}$	6	$15\frac{4}{7}$	6	$16\frac{2}{7}$
400	20	8	17	8	$17\frac{6}{7}$	9	$\frac{6}{7}$	9	$1\frac{5}{7}$	9	$2\frac{4}{7}$	9	$3\frac{4}{7}$
500	25	11	$3\frac{1}{7}$	11	$4\frac{2}{7}$	11	$5\frac{3}{7}$	11	$6\frac{5}{7}$	11	$7\frac{6}{7}$	11	9
600	30	13	$7\frac{3}{7}$	13	$8\frac{6}{7}$	13	$10\frac{2}{7}$	13	$11\frac{5}{7}$	13	$13\frac{1}{7}$	13	$14\frac{4}{7}$
700	35	15	$11\frac{5}{7}$	15	$13\frac{3}{7}$	15	15	15	$16\frac{4}{7}$	16	$\frac{2}{7}$	16	2
800	40	17	$15\frac{6}{7}$	17	$17\frac{5}{7}$	18	$1\frac{4}{7}$	18	$3\frac{4}{7}$	18	$5\frac{3}{7}$	18	$6\frac{2}{7}$
900	45	20	$2\frac{1}{7}$	20	$4\frac{2}{7}$	20	$6\frac{3}{7}$	20	$8\frac{4}{7}$	20	$10\frac{4}{7}$	20	$12\frac{6}{7}$
1000	50	22	$6\frac{5}{7}$	22	$8\frac{5}{7}$	22	$11\frac{6}{7}$	22	$13\frac{3}{7}$	22	$15\frac{6}{7}$	23	$\frac{2}{7}$
2000	100	44	$12\frac{5}{7}$	44	$17\frac{3}{7}$	45	$4\frac{1}{7}$	45	9	45	$13\frac{5}{7}$	46	$\frac{3}{7}$
3000	150	67	$1\frac{1}{7}$	67	$8\frac{2}{7}$	67	$15\frac{3}{7}$	68	$4\frac{4}{7}$	68	$11\frac{4}{7}$	69	$\frac{5}{7}$
4000	200	89	$7\frac{4}{7}$	89	17	90	$8\frac{4}{7}$	91	0	91	$9\frac{4}{7}$	92	$1\frac{1}{7}$

Ells.		140		$140\frac{4}{5}$		$141\frac{3}{5}$		$142\frac{2}{5}$		$143\frac{1}{5}$		144	
Yards.		175		176		177		178		179		180	
Splits.	Porters.	Sp.	Hk.	Sp.	Hk.	Sp.	Hk.	Sp.	Hk.	Sp.	Hk	Sp.	Hk.
2	$\frac{1}{10}$												
4	$\frac{1}{5}$		$1\frac{5}{7}$		$1\frac{5}{7}$		$1\frac{5}{7}$		$1\frac{5}{7}$		$1\frac{5}{7}$		$1\frac{5}{7}$
5	$\frac{1}{4}$		2		2		$2\frac{1}{7}$		$2\frac{1}{7}$		$2\frac{1}{7}$		$2\frac{1}{7}$
10	$\frac{1}{2}$		$4\frac{1}{7}$		$4\frac{1}{7}$		$4\frac{1}{7}$		$4\frac{1}{7}$		$4\frac{1}{7}$		$4\frac{2}{7}$
20	1		$8\frac{2}{7}$		$8\frac{2}{7}$		$8\frac{2}{7}$		$8\frac{2}{7}$		$8\frac{3}{7}$		$8\frac{4}{7}$
30	$1\frac{1}{2}$		$12\frac{3}{7}$		$12\frac{4}{7}$		$12\frac{4}{7}$		$12\frac{5}{7}$		$12\frac{6}{7}$		$12\frac{6}{7}$
40	2		$16\frac{4}{7}$		$16\frac{5}{7}$		$16\frac{6}{7}$		$16\frac{6}{7}$		17		$17\frac{1}{7}$
50	$2\frac{1}{2}$	1	$2\frac{5}{7}$	1	$2\frac{6}{7}$	1	3	1	$3\frac{1}{7}$	1	$3\frac{2}{7}$	1	$3\frac{3}{7}$
60	3	1	7	1	$7\frac{1}{7}$	1	$7\frac{2}{7}$	1	$7\frac{3}{7}$	1	$7\frac{4}{7}$	1	$7\frac{6}{7}$
70	$3\frac{1}{2}$	1	$11\frac{1}{7}$	1	$11\frac{2}{7}$	1	$11\frac{3}{7}$	1	$11\frac{4}{7}$	1	$11\frac{5}{7}$	1	12
80	4	1	$15\frac{2}{7}$	1	$15\frac{3}{7}$	1	$15\frac{4}{7}$	1	$15\frac{6}{7}$	1	16	1	$16\frac{2}{7}$
90	$4\frac{1}{2}$	2	$1\frac{3}{7}$	2	$1\frac{5}{7}$	2	$1\frac{6}{7}$	2	$2\frac{1}{7}$	2	$2\frac{2}{7}$	2	$2\frac{4}{7}$
100	5	2	$5\frac{4}{7}$	2	$5\frac{6}{7}$	2	$6\frac{1}{7}$	2	$6\frac{2}{7}$	2	$6\frac{4}{7}$	2	$6\frac{6}{7}$
200	10	4	$11\frac{2}{7}$	4	$11\frac{5}{7}$	4	$12\frac{1}{7}$	4	$12\frac{5}{7}$	4	$13\frac{1}{7}$	4	$13\frac{5}{7}$
300	15	6	17	6	$17\frac{5}{7}$	7	$\frac{3}{7}$	7	$1\frac{1}{7}$	7	$1\frac{6}{7}$	7	$2\frac{4}{7}$
400	20	9	$4\frac{4}{7}$	9	$5\frac{4}{7}$	9	$6\frac{4}{7}$	9	$7\frac{3}{7}$	9	$8\frac{3}{7}$	9	$9\frac{3}{7}$
500	25	11	$10\frac{2}{7}$	11	$11\frac{3}{7}$	11	$12\frac{4}{7}$	11	$13\frac{6}{7}$	11	15	11	$16\frac{2}{7}$
600	30	13	16	13	$17\frac{3}{7}$	14	$\frac{6}{7}$	14	$2\frac{2}{7}$	14	$3\frac{5}{7}$	14	$5\frac{1}{7}$
700	35	16	$3\frac{4}{7}$	16	$5\frac{2}{7}$	16	7	16	$8\frac{4}{7}$	16	$10\frac{2}{7}$	16	12
800	40	18	$9\frac{2}{7}$	18	$11\frac{1}{7}$	18	13	18	15	18	$16\frac{6}{7}$	19	$\frac{6}{7}$
900	45	20	15	20	$17\frac{1}{7}$	21	$1\frac{2}{7}$	21	$3\frac{3}{7}$	21	$5\frac{4}{7}$	21	$7\frac{5}{7}$
1000	50	23	$2\frac{4}{7}$	23	5	23	$7\frac{3}{7}$	23	$9\frac{5}{7}$	23	$12\frac{1}{7}$	23	$14\frac{4}{7}$
2000	100	46	$5\frac{2}{7}$	46	10	46	$14\frac{5}{7}$	47	$1\frac{4}{7}$	47	$6\frac{2}{7}$	47	$11\frac{1}{7}$
3000	150	69	8	69	$15\frac{1}{7}$	70	$4\frac{2}{7}$	70	$11\frac{3}{7}$	71	$\frac{4}{7}$	71	$7\frac{5}{7}$
4000	200	92	$10\frac{4}{7}$	93	$2\frac{1}{7}$	93	$11\frac{5}{7}$	94	$3\frac{1}{7}$	94	$12\frac{5}{7}$	95	$4\frac{2}{7}$

Ells.		$144\frac{4}{5}$	$145\frac{3}{5}$	$146\frac{2}{5}$	$147\frac{1}{5}$	148	$148\frac{4}{5}$
Yards.		181	182	183	184	185	186
Splits	Porters	Sp. Hk.	Sp. Hk.	Sp. Hk.	Sp. Hk.	Sp. Hk.	Sp. Hk.
2	$\frac{1}{10}$						
4	$\frac{1}{5}$	$1\frac{5}{7}$	$1\frac{5}{7}$	$1\frac{5}{7}$	$1\frac{5}{7}$	$1\frac{5}{7}$	$1\frac{5}{7}$
5	$\frac{1}{4}$	$2\frac{1}{7}$	$2\frac{1}{7}$	$2\frac{1}{7}$	$2\frac{1}{7}$	$2\frac{1}{7}$	$2\frac{1}{7}$
10	$\frac{1}{2}$	$4\frac{2}{7}$	$4\frac{2}{7}$	$4\frac{2}{7}$	$4\frac{3}{7}$	$4\frac{3}{7}$	$4\frac{3}{7}$
20	1	$8\frac{4}{7}$	$8\frac{5}{7}$	$8\frac{5}{7}$	$8\frac{5}{7}$	$8\frac{6}{7}$	$8\frac{6}{7}$
30	$1\frac{1}{2}$	$12\frac{6}{7}$	13	13	$13\frac{1}{7}$	$13\frac{1}{7}$	$13\frac{2}{7}$
40	2	$17\frac{2}{7}$	$17\frac{2}{7}$	$17\frac{3}{7}$	$17\frac{4}{7}$	$17\frac{4}{7}$	$17\frac{5}{7}$
50	$2\frac{1}{2}$	1 $3\frac{4}{7}$	1 $3\frac{5}{7}$	1 $3\frac{6}{7}$	1 $3\frac{6}{7}$	1 4	1 $4\frac{1}{7}$
60	3	1 $7\frac{6}{7}$	1 8	1 $8\frac{1}{7}$	1 $8\frac{2}{7}$	1 $8\frac{3}{7}$	1 $8\frac{4}{7}$
70	$3\frac{1}{2}$	1 $12\frac{1}{7}$	1 $12\frac{2}{7}$	1 $12\frac{3}{7}$	1 $12\frac{5}{7}$	1 $12\frac{6}{7}$	1 13
80	4	1 $16\frac{3}{7}$	1 $16\frac{4}{7}$	1 $16\frac{5}{7}$	1 17	1 $17\frac{1}{7}$	1 $17\frac{3}{7}$
90	$4\frac{1}{2}$	2 $2\frac{5}{7}$	2 3	2 $3\frac{1}{7}$	2 $3\frac{3}{7}$	2 $3\frac{4}{7}$	2 $3\frac{6}{7}$
100	5	2 $7\frac{1}{7}$	2 $7\frac{2}{7}$	2 $7\frac{4}{7}$	2 $7\frac{5}{7}$	2 8	2 $8\frac{2}{7}$
200	10	4 $14\frac{2}{7}$	4 $14\frac{4}{7}$	4 $15\frac{1}{7}$	4 $15\frac{4}{7}$	4 16	4 $16\frac{4}{7}$
300	15	7 $3\frac{2}{7}$	7 4	7 $4\frac{5}{7}$	7 $5\frac{3}{7}$	7 $6\frac{1}{7}$	7 $6\frac{6}{7}$
400	20	9 $10\frac{2}{7}$	9 $11\frac{2}{7}$	9 $12\frac{2}{7}$	9 $13\frac{1}{7}$	9 $14\frac{1}{7}$	9 $15\frac{1}{7}$
500	25	11 $17\frac{3}{7}$	12 $\frac{4}{7}$	12 $1\frac{6}{7}$	12 3	12 $4\frac{2}{7}$	12 $5\frac{3}{7}$
600	30	14 $6\frac{4}{7}$	14 8	14 $9\frac{3}{7}$	14 $10\frac{6}{7}$	14 $12\frac{2}{7}$	14 $13\frac{5}{7}$
700	35	16 $13\frac{4}{7}$	16 $15\frac{2}{7}$	16 17	17 $\frac{4}{7}$	17 $2\frac{2}{7}$	17 4
800	40	19 $2\frac{5}{7}$	19 $4\frac{4}{7}$	19 $6\frac{4}{7}$	19 $8\frac{3}{7}$	19 $10\frac{2}{7}$	19 $12\frac{2}{7}$
900	45	21 $9\frac{6}{7}$	21 12	21 $14\frac{1}{7}$	21 $16\frac{2}{7}$	22 $\frac{4}{7}$	22 $2\frac{4}{7}$
1000	50	23 $16\frac{6}{7}$	24 $1\frac{2}{7}$	24 $3\frac{6}{7}$	24 6	24 $8\frac{3}{7}$	24 $10\frac{6}{7}$
2000	100	47 $15\frac{6}{7}$	48 $2\frac{4}{7}$	48 $7\frac{3}{7}$	48 $12\frac{1}{7}$	48 $16\frac{6}{7}$	49 $8\frac{5}{7}$
3000	150	71 $14\frac{6}{7}$	72 4	72 $11\frac{1}{7}$	73 $\frac{2}{7}$	73 $7\frac{3}{7}$	73 $14\frac{4}{7}$
4000	200	95 $13\frac{4}{7}$	96 $5\frac{2}{7}$	96 $14\frac{6}{7}$	97 $6\frac{2}{7}$	97 $15\frac{6}{7}$	98 $7\frac{4}{7}$

BEAMERS' TABLES.

Ells.		$149\frac{3}{5}$		$150\frac{2}{5}$		$151\frac{1}{5}$		152		$152\frac{4}{5}$		$153\frac{3}{5}$	
Yards.		187		188		189		190		191		192	
Splits.	Porters	Sp.	Hk.	Sp.	Hk.	Sp.	Hk.	Sp.	Hk.	Sp.	Hk	Sp.	Hk.
2	$\frac{1}{10}$												
4	$\frac{1}{5}$		$1\frac{5}{7}$		$1\frac{6}{7}$		$1\frac{6}{7}$		$1\frac{6}{7}$		$1\frac{6}{7}$		$1\frac{5}{7}$
5	$\frac{1}{4}$		$2\frac{2}{7}$		$2\frac{2}{7}$		$2\frac{2}{7}$		$2\frac{2}{7}$		$2\frac{2}{7}$		$2\frac{2}{7}$
10	$\frac{1}{2}$		$4\frac{3}{7}$		$4\frac{3}{7}$		$4\frac{3}{7}$		$4\frac{4}{7}$		$4\frac{4}{7}$		$4\frac{4}{7}$
20	1		$8\frac{6}{7}$		9		9		9		9		$9\frac{1}{7}$
30	$1\frac{1}{2}$		$13\frac{3}{7}$		$13\frac{3}{7}$		$13\frac{3}{7}$		$13\frac{4}{7}$		$13\frac{4}{7}$		$13\frac{5}{7}$
40	2		$17\frac{6}{7}$		$17\frac{6}{7}$	1	0	1	$\frac{1}{7}$	1	$\frac{2}{7}$	1	$\frac{3}{7}$
50	$2\frac{1}{2}$	1	$4\frac{3}{7}$	1	$4\frac{3}{7}$	1	$4\frac{3}{7}$	1	$4\frac{4}{7}$	1	$4\frac{5}{7}$	1	$4\frac{6}{7}$
60	3	1	$8\frac{6}{7}$	1	$8\frac{6}{7}$	1	9	1	$9\frac{1}{7}$	1	$9\frac{2}{7}$	1	$9\frac{3}{7}$
70	$3\frac{1}{2}$	1	$13\frac{1}{7}$	1	$13\frac{2}{7}$	1	$13\frac{3}{7}$	1	$13\frac{5}{7}$	1	$13\frac{6}{7}$	1	14
80	4	1	$17\frac{5}{7}$	1	$17\frac{6}{7}$	2	0	2	$\frac{2}{7}$	2	$\frac{4}{7}$	2	$\frac{6}{7}$
90	$4\frac{1}{2}$	2	4	2	$4\frac{2}{7}$	2	$4\frac{3}{7}$	2	$4\frac{5}{7}$	2	$4\frac{6}{7}$	2	$5\frac{1}{7}$
100	5	2	$8\frac{3}{7}$	2	$8\frac{5}{7}$	2	9	2	$9\frac{2}{7}$	2	$9\frac{3}{7}$	2	$9\frac{5}{7}$
200	10	4	17	4	$17\frac{4}{7}$	5	0	5	$\frac{3}{7}$	5	$\frac{6}{7}$	5	$1\frac{3}{7}$
300	15	7	$7\frac{4}{7}$	7	$8\frac{2}{7}$	7	9	7	$9\frac{5}{7}$	7	$10\frac{3}{7}$	7	$11\frac{1}{7}$
400	20	9	16	9	17	10	0	10	1	10	$1\frac{6}{7}$	10	$2\frac{6}{7}$
500	25	12	$6\frac{4}{7}$	12	$7\frac{5}{7}$	12	9	12	$10\frac{1}{7}$	12	$11\frac{2}{7}$	12	$12\frac{4}{7}$
600	30	14	$15\frac{1}{7}$	14	$16\frac{4}{7}$	15	0	15	$1\frac{3}{7}$	15	$2\frac{6}{7}$	15	$4\frac{2}{7}$
700	35	17	$5\frac{4}{7}$	17	$7\frac{2}{7}$	17	9	17	$10\frac{5}{7}$	17	$12\frac{2}{7}$	17	14
800	40	19	$14\frac{1}{7}$	19	16	20	0	20	$1\frac{6}{7}$	20	$8\frac{5}{7}$	20	$5\frac{5}{7}$
900	45	22	$4\frac{4}{7}$	22	$6\frac{6}{7}$	22	$8\frac{5}{7}$	22	$11\frac{1}{7}$	22	$13\frac{3}{7}$	22	$15\frac{5}{7}$
1000	50	24	$13\frac{1}{7}$	24	$15\frac{4}{7}$	25	0	25	$2\frac{3}{7}$	25	$4\frac{5}{7}$	25	$7\frac{1}{7}$
2000	100	49	$8\frac{3}{7}$	49	$13\frac{1}{7}$	50	0	50	$4\frac{5}{7}$	50	$9\frac{3}{7}$	50	$14\frac{2}{7}$
3000	150	74	$3\frac{5}{7}$	74	$10\frac{6}{7}$	75	0	75	$7\frac{1}{7}$	75	$14\frac{2}{7}$	76	$3\frac{3}{7}$
4000	200	98	$16\frac{6}{7}$	99	$8\frac{3}{7}$	100	0	100	$9\frac{4}{7}$	101	1	101	$10\frac{4}{7}$

Ells.		$154\frac{2}{5}$		$155\frac{1}{5}$		156		$156\frac{4}{5}$		$157\frac{3}{5}$		$158\frac{2}{5}$	
Yards.		193		194		195		196		197		198	
Splits	Porters	Sp.	Hk.	Sp.	Hk.	Sp.	Hk.	Sp.	Hk.	Sp.	Hk.	Sp.	Hk.
2	$\frac{1}{10}$												
4	$\frac{1}{5}$		$1\frac{6}{7}$		$1\frac{6}{7}$		$1\frac{6}{7}$		$1\frac{6}{7}$		$1\frac{6}{7}$		2
5	$\frac{1}{4}$		$2\frac{2}{7}$		$2\frac{2}{7}$		$2\frac{2}{7}$		$2\frac{2}{7}$		$2\frac{2}{7}$		$2\frac{3}{7}$
10	$\frac{1}{2}$		$4\frac{4}{7}$		$4\frac{5}{7}$		$4\frac{5}{7}$		$4\frac{5}{7}$		$4\frac{5}{7}$		$4\frac{5}{7}$
20	1		$9\frac{1}{7}$		$9\frac{2}{7}$		$9\frac{2}{7}$		$9\frac{2}{7}$		$9\frac{3}{7}$		$9\frac{3}{7}$
30	$1\frac{1}{2}$		$13\frac{5}{7}$		$13\frac{6}{7}$		$13\frac{6}{7}$	14		14			$14\frac{1}{7}$
40	2	1	$\frac{3}{7}$	1	$\frac{4}{7}$	1	$\frac{4}{7}$	1	$\frac{5}{7}$	1	$\frac{6}{7}$	1	$\frac{6}{7}$
50	$2\frac{1}{2}$	1	$4\frac{6}{7}$	1	$5\frac{1}{7}$	1	$5\frac{1}{7}$	1	$5\frac{2}{7}$	1	$5\frac{3}{7}$	1	$5\frac{4}{7}$
60	3	1	$9\frac{4}{7}$	1	$9\frac{5}{7}$	1	$9\frac{6}{7}$	1	10	1	$10\frac{1}{7}$	1	$10\frac{2}{7}$
70	$3\frac{1}{2}$	1	$14\frac{1}{7}$	1	$14\frac{3}{7}$	1	$14\frac{4}{7}$	1	$14\frac{5}{7}$	1	$14\frac{6}{7}$	1	15
80	4	2	$\frac{5}{7}$	2	1	2	$1\frac{1}{7}$	2	$1\frac{2}{7}$	2	$1\frac{4}{7}$	2	$1\frac{5}{7}$
90	$4\frac{1}{2}$	2	$5\frac{2}{7}$	2	$5\frac{4}{7}$	2	$5\frac{5}{7}$	2	6	2	$6\frac{1}{7}$	2	$6\frac{3}{7}$
100	5	2	10	2	$10\frac{2}{7}$	2	$10\frac{3}{7}$	2	$10\frac{5}{7}$	2	11	2	$11\frac{1}{7}$
200	10	5	$1\frac{5}{7}$	5	$2\frac{2}{7}$	5	$2\frac{5}{7}$	5	$3\frac{2}{7}$	5	$3\frac{6}{7}$	5	$4\frac{2}{7}$
300	15	7	$11\frac{5}{7}$	7	$12\frac{4}{7}$	7	$13\frac{2}{7}$	7	14	7	$14\frac{5}{7}$	7	$15\frac{3}{7}$
400	20	10	$3\frac{6}{7}$	10	$4\frac{6}{7}$	10	$5\frac{5}{7}$	10	$6\frac{5}{7}$	10	$7\frac{5}{7}$	10	$8\frac{4}{7}$
500	25	12	$13\frac{5}{7}$	12	15	12	$16\frac{1}{7}$	12	$17\frac{2}{7}$	13	$\frac{4}{7}$	13	$1\frac{5}{7}$
600	30	15	$5\frac{5}{7}$	15	$7\frac{1}{7}$	15	$8\frac{4}{7}$	15	10	15	$11\frac{3}{7}$	15	$12\frac{6}{7}$
700	35	17	$15\frac{5}{7}$	17	$17\frac{3}{7}$	18	1	18	$2\frac{5}{7}$	18	$4\frac{3}{7}$	18	6
800	40	20	$7\frac{5}{7}$	20	$9\frac{4}{7}$	20	$11\frac{3}{7}$	20	$13\frac{2}{7}$	20	$15\frac{2}{7}$	20	$17\frac{1}{7}$
900	45	22	$7\frac{4}{7}$	23	$1\frac{5}{7}$	23	$3\frac{6}{7}$	23	6	23	$8\frac{1}{7}$	23	$10\frac{2}{7}$
1000	50	25	$9\frac{4}{7}$	25	11	25	$14\frac{2}{7}$	25	$16\frac{5}{7}$	26	$1\frac{1}{7}$	26	$3\frac{3}{7}$
2000	100	51	1	51	$5\frac{5}{7}$	51	$10\frac{1}{7}$	51	$14\frac{5}{7}$	52	$2\frac{1}{7}$	52	$6\frac{6}{7}$
3000	150	76	$10\frac{4}{7}$	76	$17\frac{5}{7}$	77	$6\frac{6}{7}$	77	14	78	$3\frac{1}{7}$	78	$10\frac{2}{7}$
4000	200	102	$2\frac{1}{7}$	102	$11\frac{5}{7}$	103	$3\frac{1}{7}$	103	$12\frac{5}{7}$	104	$4\frac{3}{7}$	104	$13\frac{4}{7}$

BEAMERS' TABLES.

Ells.		$159\frac{1}{5}$	160	$160\frac{4}{5}$	$161\frac{3}{5}$	$162\frac{2}{5}$	$163\frac{1}{5}$
Yards.		199	200	201	202	203	204
Splits.	Porters	Sp. Hk.	Sp. Hk.	Sp. Hk.	Sp. Hk.	Sp. Hk	Sp. Hk.
2	$\frac{1}{10}$						
4	$\frac{1}{5}$	2	2	2	2	2	2
5	$\frac{1}{4}$	$2\frac{3}{7}$	$2\frac{3}{7}$	$2\frac{3}{7}$	$2\frac{3}{7}$	$2\frac{3}{7}$	$2\frac{3}{7}$
10	$\frac{1}{2}$	$4\frac{5}{7}$	$4\frac{6}{7}$	$4\frac{6}{7}$	$4\frac{6}{7}$	$4\frac{6}{7}$	5
20	1	$9\frac{3}{7}$	$9\frac{4}{7}$	$9\frac{4}{7}$	$9\frac{5}{7}$	$9\frac{5}{7}$	$9\frac{5}{7}$
30	$1\frac{1}{2}$	$14\frac{1}{7}$	$14\frac{2}{7}$	$14\frac{2}{7}$	$14\frac{3}{7}$	$14\frac{3}{7}$	$14\frac{3}{7}$
40	2	1 1	1 $1\frac{1}{7}$	1 $1\frac{2}{7}$	1 $1\frac{3}{7}$	1 $1\frac{3}{7}$	1 $1\frac{4}{7}$
50	$2\frac{1}{2}$	1 $5\frac{5}{7}$	1 $5\frac{6}{7}$	1 6	1 $6\frac{1}{7}$	1 $6\frac{1}{7}$	1 $6\frac{2}{7}$
60	3	1 $10\frac{3}{7}$	1 $10\frac{4}{7}$	1 $10\frac{5}{7}$	1 $10\frac{6}{7}$	1 11	1 $11\frac{1}{7}$
70	$3\frac{1}{2}$	1 $15\frac{1}{7}$	1 $15\frac{3}{7}$	1 $15\frac{4}{7}$	1 $15\frac{5}{7}$	1 $15\frac{6}{7}$	1 $16\frac{1}{7}$
80	4	2 $1\frac{6}{7}$	2 $2\frac{1}{7}$	2 $2\frac{3}{7}$	2 $2\frac{4}{7}$	2 $2\frac{5}{7}$	2 $2\frac{6}{7}$
90	$4\frac{1}{2}$	2 $6\frac{4}{7}$	2 $6\frac{6}{7}$	2 7	2 $7\frac{2}{7}$	2 $7\frac{3}{7}$	2 $7\frac{5}{7}$
100	5	2 $11\frac{3}{7}$	2 $11\frac{5}{7}$	2 12	2 $12\frac{1}{7}$	2 $12\frac{3}{7}$	2 $12\frac{5}{7}$
200	10	5 $4\frac{3}{7}$	5 $5\frac{3}{7}$	5 $5\frac{5}{7}$	5 $6\frac{2}{7}$	5 $6\frac{5}{7}$	5 $7\frac{1}{7}$
300	15	7 $16\frac{1}{7}$	7 $16\frac{6}{7}$	7 $17\frac{4}{7}$	8 $\frac{2}{7}$	8 1	8 $1\frac{5}{7}$
400	20	10 $9\frac{4}{7}$	10 $10\frac{4}{7}$	10 $11\frac{4}{7}$	10 $12\frac{3}{7}$	10 $13\frac{3}{7}$	10 $14\frac{3}{7}$
500	25	13 $2\frac{6}{7}$	13 $4\frac{1}{7}$	13 $5\frac{3}{7}$	13 $6\frac{3}{7}$	13 $7\frac{4}{7}$	13 $8\frac{4}{7}$
600	30	15 $14\frac{2}{7}$	15 $15\frac{5}{7}$	15 $17\frac{1}{7}$	16 $\frac{4}{7}$	16 2	16 $3\frac{3}{7}$
700	35	18 $7\frac{4}{7}$	18 $9\frac{3}{7}$	18 $11\frac{1}{7}$	18 $12\frac{5}{7}$	18 $14\frac{3}{7}$	18 $16\frac{1}{7}$
800	40	21 1	21 3	21 $4\frac{6}{7}$	21 $6\frac{5}{7}$	21 $8\frac{4}{7}$	21 $4\frac{4}{7}$
900	45	23 $12\frac{3}{7}$	23 $14\frac{4}{7}$	23 $16\frac{5}{7}$	24 $\frac{6}{7}$	24 3	24 $5\frac{1}{7}$
1000	50	26 $5\frac{6}{7}$	26 $8\frac{3}{7}$	26 $10\frac{3}{7}$	26 13	26 $15\frac{3}{7}$	26 $17\frac{6}{7}$
2000	100	52 $11\frac{4}{7}$	52 $16\frac{3}{7}$	53 $3\frac{1}{7}$	53 $7\frac{6}{7}$	53 $12\frac{4}{7}$	53 $15\frac{3}{7}$
3000	150	78 $17\frac{3}{7}$	79 $6\frac{4}{7}$	79 $13\frac{5}{7}$	80 $2\frac{6}{7}$	80 10	80 $17\frac{1}{7}$
4000	200	105 $5\frac{2}{7}$	105 $14\frac{6}{7}$	106 $6\frac{3}{7}$	106 $15\frac{6}{7}$	107 $7\frac{4}{7}$	107 17

When the manufacturer wishes to find, from the foregoing tables, the quantity of warp in a given piece of cloth, it can be done in the following manner:—Suppose the piece 80 yards long, and containing 2000 splits, the quantity of spyndles will be found opposite 2000 splits, and under 80 yards at page 321, to be 21 spyndles, 3 hanks, or in all, 381 hanks (as shown in another table). This 381 is divided by the size of the yarn, say No. 36 to find the weight.

EXAMPLE.

36)381(10 lbs. 9⅓ oz.
36
—
21
16
—
126
21
—
336
324
—
12
—
36

This shows the weight of the warp to be 10 lbs. 9⅓ oz. To this weight the allowances will require to be added, which is thought proper for shrinkage, waste, &c., as these tables are all made out nett, taking the hank as 840 yards, and 18 hanks to the spyndle. Our reason for not making allowance for waste, &c., in the tables, is (as stated before) because no given amount could be fixed upon with any degree of accuracy, it altogether depending upon the quality of the yarn, and the kind of cloth to be woven, what the allowance should be.

The quantity of weft can also be found from the tables. After the warp is ascertained, the weft will be the same quantity as the warp, if the number of shots seen by the glass be the same as the number of warp-threads seen, or what is called in the trade, even and even. Suppose the web to be a 14^{00}, with 14 shots, and the quantity of warp to be 56 spyndles, the quantity of weft will be the same. If the shots be more or less than fourteen, the number of spyndles will be in proportion, more or less; for instance, if there be 13 shots, then there will be one fourteenth less, or 52 spyndles; if 15 shots, one fourteenth more, or 60 spyndles; and so on for any other number of shots.

When the warper or beamer wishes to know the quantity of spyndles, or number of lbs., they can find them in the same manner as shown for the manufacturer; but in general, the number of yards put on the beams by the warpers and beamers are greater than what is given in these tables; however, it is easy to get any number that may be desired. For example, if the beam contains 4000 yards, multiply the 200 yards by 10, or add a cipher to the quantity of spyndles found under 200 yards, and that will be the number of spyndles for 4000 yards.

It has been shown how the number of lbs. can be found when the spyndles are known; and if the weaver, who buys his yarn from the spinner in chains, wishes to ascertain if he has got the size ordered, all he has to do is to look up the length and number of splits in the table that are contained in the chain, and the spyndles will be seen. An example for this is given at page 35, under "Yarn in Chain."

To find the number of ends or splits in any given web, a table has already been published, which shows them at a glance, and it can be had on application from the Publisher of this Work.

RATING TABLES.

The annexed tables have been made out principally for the use of manufacturers in rating goods. They will save time, as the number of hanks can be found for any number of splits (or dents) without calculation. They have been made out for 100 yards, and no allowance is made for waste or shrinkage; for, as stated before, this allowance must altogether depend upon circumstances. If these tables had been made out to answer all the different lengths of cloth that are woven, they would have taken up far too much space, therefore 100 yards have been fixed upon as the most suitable number. The hanks are shown on a line with the splits. By dividing the hanks by the size of the yarn, the manufacturer will find the yarn required in lbs. Suppose we take the number 1500 splits, opposite it is 357 hanks.

RATING TABLES.

Split.	Hk.	Sk.	Split.	Hk.	Sk.	Split.	Hk.	Sk.
½		.83	115	27	2.66	270	64	2. 0
1		1.66	120	28	4. 0	275	65	3.33
2		3.33	125	29	5.33	280	66	4.66
3		5. 0	130	30	6.66	285	67	6. 0
4		6.66	135	32	1. 0	290	69	0.33
5	1	1.33	140	33	2.33	295	70	1.66
6	1	3. 0	145	34	3.66	300	71	3. 0
7	1	4.66	150	35	5. 0	305	72	4.33
8	1	6.33	155	36	6.33	310	73	5.66
9	2	1. 0	160	38	.66	315	75	...
10	2	2.66	165	39	2. 0	320	76	1.33
15	3	4. 0	170	40	3.33	325	77	2.66
20	4	5.33	175	41	4.66	330	78	4. 0
25	5	6.66	180	42	6. 0	335	79	5.33
30	7	1. 0	185	44	.33	340	80	6.66
35	8	2.33	190	45	1.66	345	82	1. 0
40	9	3.66	195	46	3. 0	350	83	2.33
45	10	5. 0	200	47	4.33	355	84	3.66
50	11	6.33	205	48	5.66	360	85	5. 0
55	13	.66	210	50	...	365	86	6.33
60	14	2. 0	215	51	1.33	370	88	0.66
65	15	3.33	220	52	2.66	375	89	2. 0
70	16	4.66	225	53	4. 0	380	90	3.33
75	17	6. 0	230	54	5.33	385	91	4.66
80	19	.33	235	55	6.66	390	92	6. 0
85	20	1.66	240	57	1. 0	395	94	0.33
90	21	3. 0	245	58	2.33	400	95	1.66
95	22	4.33	250	59	3.66	405	96	3. 0
100	23	5.66	255	60	5. 0	410	97	4.33
105	25	...	260	61	6.33	415	98	5.66
110	26	1.33	265	63	0.66	420	100	...

RATING TABLES.

Split.	IIk.	Sk.	Split.	IIk.	Sk.	Split.	IIk.	Sk.
425	101	1.33	580	138	0.66	735	175	...
430	102	2.66	585	139	2. 0	740	176	1.33
435	103	4. 0	590	140	3.33	745	177	2.66
440	104	5.33	595	141	4.66	750	178	4. 0
445	105	6.66	600	142	6. 0	755	179	5.33
450	107	1. 0	605	144	0.33	760	180	6.66
455	108	2.33	610	145	1.66	765	182	1. 0
460	109	3.66	615	146	3. 0	770	183	2.33
465	110	5. 0	620	147	4.33	775	184	3.66
470	111	6.33	625	148	5.66	780	185	5. 0
475	113	0.66	630	150	...	785	186	6.33
480	114	2. 0	635	151	1.33	790	188	0.66
485	115	3.33	640	152	2.66	795	189	2. 0
490	116	4.66	645	153	4. 0	800	190	3.33
495	117	6. 0	650	154	5.33	805	191	4.66
500	119	0.33	655	155	6.66	810	192	6. 0
505	120	1.66	660	157	1. 0	815	194	0.33
510	121	3. 0	665	158	2.33	820	195	1.66
515	122	4.33	670	159	3.66	825	196	3. 0
520	123	5.66	675	160	5. 0	830	197	4.33
525	125	...	680	161	6.33	835	198	5.66
530	126	1.33	685	163	0.66	840	200	...
535	127	2.66	690	164	2. 0	845	201	1.33
540	128	4. 0	695	165	3.33	850	202	2.66
545	129	5.33	700	166	4.66	855	203	4. 0
550	130	6.66	705	167	6. 0	860	204	5.33
555	132	1. 0	710	169	0.33	865	205	6.66
560	133	2.33	715	170	1.66	870	207	1. 0
565	134	3.66	720	171	3. 0	875	208	2.33
570	135	5. 0	725	172	4.33	880	209	3.66
575	136	6.33	730	173	5.66	885	210	5. 0

RATING TABLES.

Split.	Hk.	Sk.	Split.	Hk.	Sk.	Split.	Hk.	Sk.
890	211	6.33	1045	248	5.66	1200	285	5. 0
895	213	0.66	1050	250	...	1205	286	6.33
900	214	2. 0	1055	251	1.33	1210	288	0.66
905	215	3.33	1060	252	2.66	1215	289	2. 0
910	216	4.66	1065	253	4. 0	1220	290	3.33
915	217	6. 0	1070	254	5.33	1225	291	4.66
920	219	0.33	1075	255	6.66	1230	292	6. 0
925	220	1.66	1080	257	1. 0	1235	294	0.33
930	221	3. 0	1085	258	2.33	1240	295	1.66
935	222	4.33	1090	259	3.66	1245	296	3. 0
940	223	5.66	1095	260	5. 0	1250	297	4.33
945	225	...	1100	261	6.33	1255	298	5.66
950	226	1.33	1105	263	0.66	1260	300	...
955	227	2.66	1110	264	2. 0	1265	301	1.33
960	228	4. 0	1115	265	3.33	1270	302	2.66
965	229	5.33	1120	266	4.66	1275	303	4. 0
970	230	6.66	1125	267	6. 0	1280	304	5.33
975	232	1. 0	1130	269	0.33	1285	305	6.66
980	233	2.33	1135	270	1.66	1290	307	1. 0
985	234	3.66	1140	271	3. 0	1295	308	2.33
990	235	5. 0	1145	272	4.33	1300	309	3.66
995	236	6.33	1150	273	5.66	1305	310	5. 0
1000	238	0.66	1155	275	...	1310	311	6.33
1005	239	2. 0	1160	276	1.33	1315	313	0.66
1010	240	3.33	1165	277	2.66	1320	314	2. 0
1015	241	4.66	1170	278	4. 0	1325	315	3.33
1020	242	6. 0	1175	279	5.33	1330	316	4.66
1025	244	0.33	1180	280	6.66	1335	317	6. 0
1030	245	1.66	1185	282	1. 0	1340	319	0.33
1035	246	3. 0	1190	283	2.33	1345	320	1.66
1040	247	4.33	1195	284	3.66	1350	321	3. 0

RATING TABLES.

Split.	Hk.	Sk.	Split.	Hk.	Sk.	Split.	Hk.	Sk.
1355	322	4.33	1510	359	3.66	1665	396	3 .0
1360	323	5.66	1515	360	5. 0	1670	397	4.33
1365	325	...	1520	361	6.33	1675	398	5.66
1370	326	1.33	1525	363	0.66	1680	400	...
1375	327	2.66	1530	364	2. 0	1685	401	1.33
1380	328	4. 0	1535	365	3.33	1690	402	2.66
1385	329	5.33	1540	366	4.66	1695	403	4. 0
1390	330	6.66	1545	367	6. 0	1700	404	5.33
1395	332	1. 0	1550	369	0.33	1705	405	6.66
1400	333	2.33	1555	370	1.66	1710	407	1. 0
1405	334	3.66	1560	371	3. 0	1715	408	2.33
1410	335	5. 0	1565	372	4.33	1720	409	3.66
1415	336	6.33	1570	373	5.66	1725	410	5. 0
1420	338	0.66	1575	375	...	1730	411	6.33
1425	339	2. 0	1580	376	1.33	1735	413	0.66
1430	340	3.33	1585	377	2.66	1740	414	2. 0
1435	341	4.66	1590	378	4. 0	1745	415	3.33
1440	342	6. 0	1595	379	5.33	1750	416	4.66
1445	344	0.33	1600	380	6.66	1755	417	6. 0
1450	345	1.66	1605	382	1. 0	1760	419	0.33
1455	346	3. 0	1610	383	2.33	1765	420	1.66
1460	347	4.33	1615	384	3.66	1770	421	3. 0
1465	348	5.66	1620	385	5. 0	1775	422	4.33
1470	350	...	1625	386	6.33	1780	423	5.66
1475	351	1.33	1630	388	0.66	1785	425	...
1480	352	2.66	1635	389	2. 0	1790	426	1.33
1485	353	4. 0	1640	390	3.33	1795	427	2.66
1490	354	5.33	1645	391	4.66	1800	428	4. 0
1495	355	6.66	1650	392	6. 0	1805	429	5.33
1500	357	1. 0	1655	394	0.33	1810	430	6.66
1505	358	2.33	1660	395	1.66	1815	432	1. 0

RATING TABLES.

Split.	Hk.	Sk.	Split.	Hk.	Sk.	Split.	Hk.	Sk.
1820	433	2.33	1975	470	1.66	2130	507	1. 0
1825	434	3.66	1980	471	3. 0	2135	508	2.33
1830	435	5. 0	1985	472	4.33	2140	509	3.66
1835	436	6.33	1990	473	5.66	2145	510	5. 0
1840	438	0.66	1995	475	...	2150	511	6.33
1845	439	2. 0	2000	476	1.33	2155	513	0.66
1850	440	3.33	2005	477	2.66	2160	514	2. 0
1855	441	4.66	2010	478	4. 0	2165	515	3.33
1860	442	6. 0	2015	479	5.33	2170	516	4.66
1865	444	0.33	2020	480	6.66	2175	517	6. 0
1870	445	1.66	2025	482	1. 0	2180	519	0.33
1875	446	3. 0	2030	483	2.33	2185	520	1.66
1880	447	4.33	2035	484	3.66	2190	521	3. 0
1885	448	5.66	2040	485	5. 0	2195	522	4.33
1890	450	...	2045	486	6.33	2200	523	5.66
1895	451	1.33	2050	488	0.66	2205	525	...
1900	452	2.66	2055	489	2. 0	2210	526	1.33
1905	453	4. 0	2060	490	3.33	2215	527	2.66
1910	454	5.33	2065	491	4.66	2220	528	4. 0
1915	455	6.66	2070	492	6. 0	2225	529	5.33
1920	457	1. 0	2075	494	0.33	2230	530	6.66
1925	458	2.33	2080	495	1.66	2235	532	1. 0
1930	459	3.66	2085	496	3. 0	2240	533	2.33
1935	460	5. 0	2090	497	4.33	2245	534	3.66
1940	461	6.33	2095	498	5.66	2250	535	5. 0
1945	463	0.66	2100	500	...	2255	536	6.33
1950	464	2. 0	2105	501	1.33	2260	538	0.66
1955	465	3.33	2110	502	2.66	2265	539	2. 0
1960	466	4.66	2115	503	4. 0	2270	540	3.33
1965	467	6. 0	2120	504	5.33	2275	541	4.66
1970	469	0.33	2125	505	6.66	2280	542	6. 0

RATING TABLES.

Split.	Hk.	Sk.	Split.	Hk.	Sk.	Split.	Hk.	Sk.
2285	544	0.33	2440	580	6.66	2595	617	6 .0
2290	545	1.66	2445	582	1. 0	2600	619	0.33
2295	546	3. 0	2450	583	2.33	2605	620	1.66
2300	547	4.33	2455	584	3.66	2610	621	3. 0
2305	548	5.66	2460	585	5. 0	2615	622	4.33
2310	550	...	2465	586	6.33	2620	623	5.66
2315	551	1.33	2470	588	0.66	2625	625	...
2320	552	2.66	2475	589	2. 0	2630	626	1.33
2325	553	4. 0	2480	590	3.33	2635	627	2.66
2330	554	5.33	2485	591	4.66	2640	628	4. 0
2335	555	6.66	2490	592	5. 0	2645	629	5.33
2340	557	1. 0	2495	594	0.33	2650	630	6.66
2345	558	2.33	2500	595	1.66	2655	632	1. 0
2350	559	3.66	2505	596	3. 0	2660	633	2.33
2355	560	5. 0	2510	597	4.33	2665	634	3.66
2360	561	6.33	2515	598	5.66	2670	635	5. 0
2365	563	0.66	2520	600	...	2675	636	6.33
2370	564	2. 0	2525	601	1.33	2680	638	0.66
2375	565	3.33	2530	602	2.66	2685	639	2. 0
2380	566	4.66	2535	603	4. 0	2690	640	3.33
2385	567	6. 0	2540	604	5.33	2695	641	4.66
2390	569	0.33	2545	605	6.66	2700	642	6. 0
2395	570	1.66	2550	607	1. 0	2705	644	0.33
2400	571	3. 0	2555	608	2.33	2710	645	1.66
2405	572	4.33	2560	609	3.66	2715	646	3. 0
2410	573	5.66	2565	610	5. 0	2720	647	4.33
2415	575	...	2570	611	6.33	2725	648	5.66
2420	576	1.33	2575	613	0.66	2730	650	...
2425	577	2.66	2580	614	2. 0	2735	651	1.33
2430	578	4. 0	2585	615	3.33	2740	652	2.66
2435	579	5.33	2590	616	4.66	2745	653	4. 0

RATING TABLES.

Split.	Hk.	Sk.	Split.	Hk.	Sk.	Split.	Hk.	Sk.
2750	654	5.33	2905	691	4.66	3060	728	4. 0
2755	655	6.66	2910	692	6. 0	3065	729	5.33
2760	657	1. 0	2915	694	0.33	3070	730	6.66
2765	658	2.33	2920	695	1.66	3075	732	1. 0
2770	659	3.66	2925	696	3. 0	3080	733	2.33
2775	660	5. 0	2930	697	4.33	3085	734	3.66
2780	661	6.33	2935	698	5.66	3090	735	5. 0
2785	663	0.66	2940	700	...	3095	736	6.33
2790	664	2. 0	2945	701	1.33	3100	738	0.66
2795	665	3.33	2950	702	2.66	3105	739	2. 0
2800	666	4.66	2955	703	4. 0	3110	740	3.33
2805	667	6. 0	2960	704	5.33	3115	741	4.66
2810	669	0.33	2965	705	6.66	3120	742	6. 0
2815	670	1.66	2970	707	1. 0	3125	744	0.33
2820	671	3. 0	2975	708	2.33	3130	745	1.66
2825	672	4.33	2980	709	3.66	3135	746	3. 0
2830	673	5.66	2985	710	5. 0	3140	747	4.33
2835	675	...	2990	711	6.33	3145	748	5.66
2840	676	1.33	2995	713	0.66	3150	750	...
2845	677	2.66	3000	714	2. 0	3155	751	1.33
2850	678	4. 0	3005	715	3.33	3160	752	2.66
2855	679	5.33	3010	716	4.66	3165	753	4. 0
2860	680	6.66	3015	717	6. 0	3170	754	5.33
2865	682	1. 0	3020	719	0.33	3175	755	6.66
2870	683	2.33	3025	720	1.66	3180	757	1. 0
2875	684	3.66	3030	721	3. 0	3185	758	2.33
2880	685	5. 0	3035	722	4.33	3190	759	3.66
2885	686	6.33	3040	723	5.66	3195	760	5. 0
2890	688	0.66	3045	725	...	3200	761	6.33
2895	689	2. 0	3050	726	1.33	3205	763	0.66
2900	690	3.33	3055	727	2.66	3210	764	2. 0

RATING TABLES.

Split.	Hk.	Sk.	Split.	Hk.	Sk.	Split.	Hk.	Sk.
3215	765	3.33	3370	802	2.66	3525	839	2. 0
3220	766	4.66	3375	803	4. 0	3530	840	3.33
3225	767	6. 0	3380	804	5.33	3535	841	4.66
3230	769	0.33	3385	805	6.66	3540	842	6. 0
3235	770	1.66	3390	807	1. 0	3545	844	0.33
3240	771	3. 0	3395	808	2.33	3550	845	1.66
3245	772	4.33	3400	809	3.66	3555	846	3. 0
3250	773	5.66	3405	810	5. 0	3560	847	4.33
3255	775	...	3410	811	6.33	3565	848	5.66
3260	776	1.33	3415	813	0.66	3570	850	...
3265	777	2.66	3420	814	2. 0	3575	851	1.33
3270	778	4. 0	3425	815	3.33	3580	852	2.66
3275	779	5.33	3430	816	4.66	3585	853	4. 0
3280	780	6.66	3435	817	6. 0	3590	854	5.33
3285	782	1. 0	3440	819	0.33	3595	855	6.66
3290	783	2.33	3445	820	1.66	3600	857	1. 0
3295	784	3.66	3450	821	3. 0	3605	858	2.33
3300	785	5. 0	3455	822	4.33	3610	859	3.66
3305	786	6.33	3460	823	5.66	3615	860	5. 0
3310	788	0.66	3465	825	...	3620	861	6.33
3315	789	2. 0	3470	826	1.33	3625	863	0.66
3320	790	3.33	3475	827	2.66	3630	864	2. 0
3325	791	4.66	3480	828	4. 0	3635	865	3.33
3330	792	6. 0	3485	829	5.33	3640	866	4.66
3335	794	0.33	3490	830	6.66	3645	867	6. 0
3340	795	1.66	3495	832	1. 0	3650	869	0.33
3345	796	3. 0	3500	833	2.33	3655	870	1.66
3350	797	4.33	3505	834	3.66	3660	871	3. 0
3355	798	5.66	3510	835	5. 0	3665	872	4.33
3360	800	...	3515	836	6.33	3670	873	5.66
3365	801	1.33	3520	838	0.66	3675	875	...

CHAPTER IX.

MISCELLANEOUS REMARKS CONNECTED WITH POWER-LOOM WEAVING.

ERECTING A NEW FACTORY.

Before commencing to build a power-loom factory it is requisite for the projector to make considerable enquiry, to obtain knowledge concerning things that are likely to contribute to the success of the undertaking, such as feu-duty, or ground-rent, situation as to workers; coals, water; the market where the yarn is to be bought, and the cloth sold; the form of the mill; the kind of boilers, engines, gearing, machinery, &c.

There is no doubt but a populous district is the best place for workers, and would be a good situation for a factory, provided there is no other obstacle to make the quantity of workers no object, such as the ground rent, local taxes, water, coals, &c., being so high in price, as to make the work unprofitable; therefore, all the different circumstances must be taken into calculation. The carriage from and to the market where the yarn may be bought, and the cloth sold, is not so expensive an item as it was before steam was taken advantage of for that purpose, and it often happens, that the mills erected in country villages are as profitable as those in the large cities.

When the situation is fixed upon, plans of the whole should be drawn out by some party capable of doing it, under the direction of one who is thoroughly acquainted with power-loom weaving. After the plans are finished, and the quantity of looms ascertained that will be required to fill the work, the cost of the whole can be calculated.

It is at once apparent, that to conduct a factory for power-loom weaving profitably, it must be a certain size; the smallest should not be less than one tenter's charge; but even this is by far too small to do anything like a profitable business. A good size for giving an opportunity for our remarks would be a mill that could contain 720 looms, with the necessary preparation machines, &c.

The most approved form of a weaving factory, is a ground flat or shed, built so as to be suitable for getting the machinery placed to the best advantage, some of the reasons given for the ground flat being preferred over the mill with four or five flats, may be stated here. The loom, when bolted down upon heavy stones, works smoother. The carriage of the beams and yarn are done with less labour. The atmosphere is more favourable in the ground flat for weaving. The workers can be better arranged, and are all under the eye of the manager at the same time.

The following description gives the plans of what is considered a very good mill for 720 ¼ power-looms. The length of the shed inside is 206 feet, and the breadth 160 feet. The looms are placed across the house in eighteen rows, 40 looms in each row; this gives 5 feet for each loom, and 6 feet extra space at the end of the flat, where the beam racks, tenters' benches, &c., are placed. Allowing 8 feet for each loom and passages, the eighteen rows will occupy 144 feet of the breadth of the flat, leaving 16 feet at the one side, and the whole length of the flat for preparation machinery, storeage, &c.

It is of the utmost importance to have the machinery and workers so arranged that no time will be lost in passing the goods from one place to another in the process of manufacturing. By attending to this it will add much to the advantage of the workers, and the profit of the establishment; because a constant communication is always going on between the different parts of the work, and what accelerates the progress of the work by saving time, must be a benefit to all concerned. We will state here what is just now considered the best arrangement, but would advise new beginners, or those intending to put up new works, to visit a number of factories, already in operation, before deciding upon any plan.

A wall is built the whole length of the shed, enclosing the looms from the other machinery, and this portion of the building is made two storeys or flats, which will be 160 feet wide and 206 feet long. A portion of the corner of the ground floor nearest the entrance to the factory is appropriated for the warehouse, with counting-house above, it occupying only a small portion of the second floor. Next to the counting-house is the warp-winders, then the warpers, and then the tape-leg dressers, all in the second floor. When the winders have got the bobbins filled, they are passed to the warpers; and when the warpers have got the beams filled, they are sent on to the dressers; and the dressed webs are lowered down to the under flat, at the opposite end from the warehouse, for the purpose of being drawn into the heddles, or twisted. From this place they pass into the weaving shed.

A portion of the under flat, next to the warehouse, is occupied as a store for furnishings required for the factory, and next to it is the yarn store, then the mechanics' shop, and as stated before, the drawers and twisters are at the end of this under flat. This arrangement of the different places and machinery gives the least possible distance for any of the articles to be carried, which are required in the manufacture of the cloth. The mechanic shop being at or near the centre of the mill, places it in the most convenient part for getting any repairs done to the machinery that may be required; and it is an advantage to the work to get the webs out of the dressing place as soon as they are finished, for the purpose of allowing them to cool before being put into the loom.

Ten or twelve feet from the mill, on this side of it, stands the engine-house and boilers. The furnaces of the boilers face the gate, through which the carts pass with the fuel. Behind the engine-house a small house is built, with two apartments, one is used for oil waste, and the other for a smithy. This completes the buildings, all except the chimney (or stalk), which should be built in some convenient place near to the boilers, and apart from the mill.

STEAM BOILERS.

There are so many different kinds of boilers in use for generating steam, for the purpose of driving the engine and heating the factory, that it is difficult to say which is the best. Some people approve of the vertical kind, which is composed of a series of tubes. Their advocates say they take up less room, and that they generate a given quantity of steam with less fuel than any other, and as the diameter of the tubes are comparatively small, they stand a greater pressure than the common kind, consequently less liable to burst.

Whatever kind of boilers the proprietors adopt, it is advisable to have them made so as they will stand at least a pressure of 100 lbs. to the square inch, and then they may be wrought with safety at 50 lbs. It is found to be a saving of fuel to work with high pressed steam for driving the engine, but for heating purposes it was at first found difficult to use; however, this is got over by reducing the pressure before it is allowed to go into the mill, and for this purpose an apparatus has been invented, and made by Mr. Auld, engineer, Glasgow, which does its work well. By using this apparatus, a considerable saving is made, and every manufacturer by power should have them, as the temperature of the dressing flat can be kept at the desired degree of heat by making it self-acting.

It is also important that the boilers be kept clean. The number of times the boilers should be cleaned during one year's working, will altogether depend upon the kind of water made use of; the best water is the purest, or that which contains the least amount of foreign matter, such as iron, magnesia, lime, &c., all of which are injurious to the boilers, by leaving a deposit, or incrustation upon the plates of the boilers, not only corroding and weakening them, but also prevents the perfect absorption of the caloric by the water. To remedy this defect, when pure water cannot be profitably obtained, various expedients have been resorted to, but perhaps the best method is to have a small cistern below the boiler and connected to it, with a blow-off cock, the frequent use of which will go far to keep the boilers clean; and, if thought proper, the water blown off can be made use of again after the objectionable matter is deposited at the bottom of the cistern.

To prevent the radiation of heat from the boilers and the steam pipes connected to them, they ought to be well covered over with some non-conducting substance, such as hair felt. Every boiler should have a water and steam gauge; they are ornamental to the boilers, besides very useful, as the engineman or any other person can see the state of the water and steam in the boilers at a glance. How to calculate for the weight to be put on the safety valve, to give a given pressure per square inch, will be seen in another place.

FURNACE—SMOKE-BURNING, &c.

To work engines economically, very much depends upon the construction and management of the furnaces. It would take up too much space to give even a mere outline of the different modes of furnaces that have been tried for the saving of fuel and the burning of smoke, and although no furnace does this to perfection, there are some that come very near it; and before giving a description of what is considered the best furnace, we will give an opinion of an eminent engineer upon prevention of smoke, to show the difficulties that have to be contended with.

He says, "I have approached this enquiry with considerable diffidence, and after repeated attempts at definite conclusions, have more than once been forced to abandon the investigation as inconclusive and unsatisfactory. These views do not arise from any defect in our acquaintance with the laws which govern perfect combustion, the economy of fuel, and the consumption of smoke. They chiefly arise from the constant change of temperature, the variable nature of the volatile products, the want of system, and the irregularity which attends the management of the furnace. Habits of economy and attention to a few simple and effective rules are either entirely neglected or not enforced. It must appear obvious to every observer, that much has yet to be done, and much may be accomplished, provided the necessary precautions are taken; first to establish, and next, to carry out a comprehensive and well organized system of operations. If this were accomplished, and the management of the furnace consigned to men of intelligence, properly trained to their respective duties, all these difficulties would vanish, and the public might not only look forward with confidence to a clear atmosphere in the manufacturing towns, but the proprietors of steam engines would be more than compensated by the saving of fuel, which an improved system of management and a sounder principle of operation would ensure. The attainment of these objects—the prevention of smoke, and the perfect combustion of fuel, are completely within the reach of all those who choose to adopt measures calculated for the suppression of the one and the improvement of the other."

It has been found from a series of experiments made with the furnace about to be explained, that besides consuming the smoke (as near perfection as any yet in use), a considerable amount of saving was made in fuel; and it has proved highly successful in numerous instances where it has been applied. The peculiar arrangement of the serrated bars, together with the movement imparted thereto, effectually prevents the formation of clinkers, and at the same time introduces a large volume of air, which becomes thoroughly heated before it reaches the gaseous matters evolved from the fresh fuel, which are thus flashed into flame, and the invisible vapour only passes off from the chimney.

Supposing this furnace be applied to a common boiler, the brick-work of it is arranged in the ordinary way. The furnace-mouth and dead-plate are of the usual kind; the back end of the ash pit is formed of a cast-iron plate; beneath the furnace bars on each side is a tubular shaft, which forms air passages; these shafts or air tubes are supported at the front end by curved brackets, from the dead-plate of the furnace. If found preferable, the front ends of the air-tubes may be supported on the inner side by a semi-circular pendent bracket, cast on the under side of the dead-plate, and outside by a corresponding moveable support bolted up to the dead-plate. The back end of each air-tube passes through and rests in the cast-iron plate, which forms the end of the furnace and back-bridge.

The fire-bars are arranged across the furnace at right angles to its length, and rest upon the air-tubes. On the inner portions of the peripheries of the air-tubes are cast the laterally projecting teeth, which act as cams to raise each alternate fire-bar, when the air-tube is turned partially round. The fire-bars are cast with laterally projecting teeth or serrations, the end teeth and one in the centre being made a little longer than the others, so that when arranged on the air-tubes, the bars are placed close together, these teeth serving to give steadiness to the bars, and, at the same time, leave a sufficient space between the intervening teeth. Each tooth of one bar enters the corresponding recess of the contiguous bar, but the elongated teeth at the ends and centres are the only ones which touch the neighbouring bar. The bars next the inner end of the dead-plate, and also the back-plate, are made with shorter teeth, but the edges of these plates might be serrated to correspond with the front and back bars. The other bars are put into their places, and arranged parallel, filling up the longitudinal extent of the furnace to the back-plate, which forms part of the back bridge. The cams on the air-tubes are made with recesses at the central part of each, and these are arranged at such a a distance asunder, that the lower part of each bar falls into one of these recesses on the one side, and at the other into the space between the cams. From this arrangement, it follows, that if the air-tubes are turned partly round, each alternate bar will be raised up at the end next the tube acted upon.

When the furnace is working, the stoker, from time to time, lifts the bars, by moving the air-tubes, the result of which breaks up the fuel, allows the ash to fall through, and prevents the formation of clinkers. The raising of the bars, from time to time, has also the effect of causing a large body of air to pass into the fuel, and it is thus kept in a state of intense combustion. The arrangement of this furnace, with its double back bridge and air-valve, along with the air-tubes, provides for the effectual combustion of the inflammable portion of the gaseous matter evolved, and this prevents the emission of visible smoke from the chimney. A description of this furnace, along with drawings of it, are given in the *Practical Mechanics' Journal*, for April, 1862.

STEAM ENGINE.

When the size of the factory will admit of it, it is better to drive the machinery with two engines than with one, as the motion will be more regular and steady. It is impossible to have a good working loom with an irregular drive. The advantage to be gained by using two engines, besides the regular motion, is, that less fuel is required to drive the machinery. The two engines are connected in such a manner, that when the one has no power the other will have its greatest power, and that the steam is made to enter the first cylinder at a high state of pressure. When the steam has done its work with the first engine, it enters the cylinder of the second; the cylinder of the second engine, having a capacity four times larger than the cylinder of the first, the steam is allowed to expand, consequently, the pressure will be only as one to four; but as this engine is connected to the condenser, it receives the advantage of the vacuum.

By using the steam for driving the engines, and connecting them as described above, very little of the steam is lost, and very little of the power is consumed driving a large fly wheel, which would be requisite to regulate the motion if only one engine was employed. Also, when two or three are working together, and they are properly arranged, very little expense will be required for the water used for condensing the steam. A great deal might be said concerning steam engines, but a few hints is all that is requisite for our purpose.

All the working parts in connection with the engine should be regularly cleaned and oiled. The large journals should have self-acting oil-cups, which will save both time and oil. A steam-gauge, also a vacuum one, should be fixed in some conspicuous place in the engine-house, to show the working state of the engine.

To give the manager or proprietor an opportunity of seeing the number of strokes the engines make in one hour, day, or week, an indicator, for that purpose, should be connected to the engines. This indicator should be one of those kinds that will show what day, and the hour of that day, the engines have been below or above their regular speed. If any accident happens which allows the engines to run far beyond their regular speed, there is a danger of something being broken, and, to prevent this, the governor should be so constructed that it will shut off the steam entirely. Few engines have this kind of governor, but it is better to prevent breakages than repair them, therefore, it is advisable for every engine proprietor to take the advantage of it.

GEARING.

Supposing the speed of the looms to be one hundred and fifty picks per minute, the shafts for driving them should make nearly that number of revolutions per minute, so that there may be very little difference between the diameter of the loom pulley and the drum that drives it; and it is advantageous to have the speed of the shafts brought up to the number of revolutions required, as near the engine as possible, if it is not convenient to have it done at the engine. By having the shafts running at a high speed, shafting of a much lighter description will answer the same purpose, which will be a saving in the first cost when erecting a new mill. Before giving the calculations for common gearing, we will give a description of driving looms without belting.

DRIVING LOOMS WITHOUT BELTING.

The outlay for gearing and belts amounts to a considerable sum for a new work, and the expense in keeping up the belts after the mill is started, has caused experiments to be made to ascertain how to do away with the present mode of driving looms. The most likely plan is to drive them with frictional gear, on the following system. Suppose the flat or shed to have twenty looms in one row, and six rows in the breadth of the flat, this will require three shafts (which we will name long shafts) the whole length of the mill, these shafts being driven by a cross shaft at the end of the flat. Each of the long shafts will drive forty looms. The looms are set in the usual way, all in a straight line. These long shafts are supported with brackets, which are bolted to the ends of the looms, so that the long shaft will be on a level with the top shafts of the looms. For each pair of looms there is a bevel pulley on the long shaft, made in all respects the same as a bevel wheel without teeth. On the end of the top shaft of each loom, there is a bevel pulley, made to correspond to the one on the long shaft. This pulley on the loom shaft is made, so as it can be shifted in, or out of gear with the pulley on the long shaft. The handle of the loom is of the common kind, and the lever that is made to shift the belt in the usual way of driving, is made to act upon the back of the pulley on the loom shaft. When the loom is to be put in motion, the handle is pulled into the notch in the same manner as for a loom driven with a belt, and a sufficient strength of spring is given to the handle, so as to press the pulley into contact with the other pulley, to drive the loom. It will be obvious, that the pulley on the loom shaft will require to be shifted a very small space, for the purpose of putting it in gear with the other, therefore, a very small movement of the lever, at the pulley, is required, which makes the loom driven in this way easier put on than when driven with a belt.

This plan of driving looms will necessitate the long shafts to be boxed in where they cross the passes. This is no objection, but rather an advantage to the weavers, if it is properly done, as they will have a place for holding their weft boxes and cloth. Another very important advantage in this mode of driving looms, is, that all danger of being caught with the belts is most effectually got quit of; in fact, it is at first cheaper, it is kept up with less expense, it is cleaner, because there is no teethed-gear to throw out dirty grease, and it looks much neater. There are some trifling things connected with putting the pulley in and out of gear, which have not been explained, but which will be apparent to any practical mechanic.

CALCULATION OF SPEEDS.

We propose to show briefly the method of calculating the speed of the different shafts and machines connected with a power-loom factory.

The first thing to be done is to find the speed of the engine, which is got by counting the number of strokes it makes during one minute; each stroke of the engine is equal to one revolution of the first shaft; and it may be remarked, that most of the old engines are driven far too slow to get the full advantage out of them. Although engineers are not agreed among themselves about the proper speed that an engine should be driven at, we may state what speed has been found in practice to answer very well. An engine, with a five or six feet stroke, may be driven at the rate of 350 feet per minute, without any apprehension of danger by breakages.

For illustration,—suppose the crank shaft of the engine makes thirty revolutions per minute; multiply the number of teeth which is in the wheel on the crank shaft by the number of revolutions, and divide the product by the number of teeth in the pinion, which gears into this wheel for driving the first shaft; and the answer will be the speed of the first shaft. The speed of the other shafts are found in the same manner, always multiplying the teeth in the driving wheel by the number of revolutions of the driving shaft, and dividing by the teeth in the driven pinion for the speed of the driven shaft; the driven shaft sometimes also becomes a driver, but this makes no difference in the mode of calculation. If the wheel on the crank shaft has 128 teeth, and the pinion on the first shaft 64 teeth, then the speed will be found as follows:—

EXAMPLE.

Number of teeth in driving wheel   128
Speed of engine per minute   30 strokes.

The number of teeth in pinion   64)3840(60 speed of the first shaft.
                                        384

But, as already stated, it is better to bring up the speed of the shafts as near the engine as possible; and for this purpose the pinion should have only 32 teeth, as in the following example:—

EXAMPLE.

Number of teeth in driving wheel   128
Speed of engine per minute   30 strokes.

The number of teeth in pinion   32)3840(120 speed of the first shaft.
                                       32
                                        64
                                        64

This wheel, with the 128 teeth, is made of sufficient weight so as no other fly-wheel is required for the engines. The first shaft passes from the engine-house to the weaving shed, and drives the long shaft, which we will call the second shaft; this second shaft being the one that drives the cross-shafts for the looms. On to the other end of the first shaft is fixed a bevel wheel with 56 teeth, which gears with one on the second shaft of 50 teeth, this will make the speed of the second shaft to be 134.4 revolutions per minute.

EXAMPLE.

The first shaft makes per minute 120 revolutions.
The number of teeth in driving wheel 56

```
                                             720
                                             600
                                             ———
Number of teeth in the driven wheel 50)6720(134.4 speed of 2d shaft.
                                             50
                                             ——
                                            172
                                            150
                                            ——
                                             220
                                             200
                                             ——
                                              200
                                              200
                                              ——
```

By putting on metre wheels on the second and cross-shafts, the speed of the cross-shafts will also be 134.4 revolutions per minute. On these cross shafts are hung the drums for driving the looms, and if the looms are to be driven at 150 picks per minute, and the driving pulleys of the looms be 11 inches in diameter, the diameter of the drum will be found by multiplying the speed of the loom by the diameter of the loom pulley, and dividing by the speed of the shaft.

EXAMPLE.

Speed of the loom per minute   150 picks.
Diameter of loom pulley   11 inches.

Speed of the shaft   134.4)1650.0(12.27
                            1344
                            3060
                            2688
                            3720
                            2688
                          10320
                           9408
                             912

This shows the diameter of the drum to be 12.27 inches, to give the loom 150 picks per minute; but, supposing the drum to be 14 inches in diameter, and the speed of the loom is required with a pulley 10 inches in diameter, multiply the speed of the shaft by the diameter of the drum in inches, and divide the product by the diameter of the loom pulley.

EXAMPLE.

```
Speed of shaft per minute      134.4
Diameter of Drum in inches      14
                              ─────
                               5376
                               1344
                              ─────
Diameter of loom pulley     10)18816(188.1   speed of loom.
                               10
                              ─────
                                88
                                80
                              ─────
                                81
                                80
                              ─────
                                16
                                10
                              ─────
                                 6
                              ─────
```

We do not require to give examples how to find the speed of the shafts for driving the winding, warping, and dressing machine, as the same principle of calculating speeds apply to all. But the young inquirer may wish to know the speed that these different machines should be driven at. This very much depends upon the kind of work these machines have got to perform, and the quality and fineness of yarn that is used in the factory. Therefore, we would advise those who have not got practical experience, to get the opinion of some party who is making the same kind of goods they intend to commence.

SAFETY VALVES

Are those valves that are placed upon the top of the steam boilers, or upon the steam chest, or dome, in connection with the boilers. For security, there should be more than one as they are liable to get out of order; but our object is to give a simple rule how to find the weight that should be put upon the lever, to produce a given pressure upon a square inch. Suppose the surface of the valve, where the steam acts upon, to be six inches in diameter, multiply the diameter of the valve, which is six inches, by 6, and the product by 7854, and, after taking off the four figures to the right hand, the remainder is the number of square inches contained in the valve, 6 × 6 is 36.

EXAMPLE.

.7854
36
―――
47124
23562
―――
28.2744

This shows 28 square inches to be in the valve after throwing off the fraction; and suppose that 30 lbs. to the square inch is required, then 28 × 30 is equal to

840 lbs., the weight required for a valve of six inches in diameter. When it can be conveniently done, it is safer not to use a lever; but if a lever is to be used it must be taken into calculation.

QUADRANT.

A Quadrant, as used by weavers, is an instrument for weighing yarn to find its size; they are made for 1 hank, 8 hanks, or 16 hanks. It is divided into a certain number of parts, and each part is numbered to show the size of the yarn. Every manufacturer should have one of them, or a small beam and scale, with proper weights, which are by some considered preferable.

NEW MODE OF PICKING.

After the description of Messrs. W. & J. Todd's patent loom was in type, Mr. Hunter, of Messrs. William Hunter & Co., their agents for Scotland, showed us a new arrangement of picking they had brought out, which can be readily applied to the ordinary loom. From what the writer saw of it, it appeared to be a very good method, and well-deserving of a trial. Drawings of this new mode of picking can be seen at Messrs. W. Hunter & Co.'s Office, 79 Glassford Street, Glasgow.

INDEX.

	Page.		Page.
Air pump pick	123	Chain	36
Allowance for waste	46	Charges	302
Arrangement of looms	104	Check and damask power-looms	153
Art of weaving	33		
Articles about a loom	147	Check loom for six shuttles	197
Average size of yarn	37		
		Check tape	294
Bags, weaving, for rice and sugar	279	Circumference of reel	34
		Cloth beam	148
Barrel, double	241	Cloth, double	272
Beam, yarn on	35	Cloth, plain	78
Beam, yarn	148	Cloth, three ply	284
Beam, cloth	149	Common power-loom	125
Beamers' tables	307	Connection rods	147
Beaming	66	Cope	36
Bed covers	280	Cords, weft	290
Bed tick	81	Costing goods	297
Belt, length of	105	Cotton, price of	27
Blanket, tweel	88	Covers, bed and toilet	280
Blue and white cross-over	50	Crank shaft	147
Board, hole	171	Cross-over	50
Breast beam	150	Crumb-cloths	284
Bullough's specification	127	Cylinder machine	73
Bundle	34		
		Damask power-loom	153
Calculation of speed	368	Damask tweels	89
Calculation of wefts	50	Dents	41
Calculations, tables, &c.	297	Description, Todd's	138
Calculation of warps	43-45	Diaper, three leaf	90-91
Cams or wypers	150	Diaper, four, five, and six leaf	92-95-263
Carpets	287		

	Page.
Diaper, seven and eight leaf	97-265
Diaper, ten leaf	100-267
Diapers, mounting for	234
Diaper and plain cloth	255
Diced work	271
Double barrel	241
Double cloth mounting	272
Double loom	119
Draughts and treading	77
Drawing	76
Dressing	68-71
Driving pulleys	147
Eight leaf diapers	98-99
Eight leaf tweel	86
Entering or drawing	76
Expenses for one year	303
Expenses, how to find the	305
Five leaf diaper	92
Five leaf tweel	84
Five leaf tweel for table covers	89
Float or scob preventer	141
Fly reed	126
Four leaf diaper	92
Four leaf tweel	82
Frames, sewing	227
Friction dressers	72
Gauze stripes	222
Gearing	152-366
Goods, costing	297
Grist of Yarn	33
Hanks	34
Hanks, short method to find the	46
Harness board	171
Harness pressure	185
Harness, to mount a	168
Harness, to prepare the	172
Harness twine	169
Heddles, three set of	272
Herring bone tweel	81

	Page.
Hindoo mode of weaving	10
Holland, Window	49
Introductory remarks	9
Jaconet, 12^{00}	50
Jacquard machine	181
Jane stripes	80
Lappet loom	207
Lappet weaving	205
Lappet wheel	208
Lay	149
Lay, Lappet	212
Leads	169
Linen yarn	37
Loom, Bullough's	125
Loom, check for six shuttle	197
Loom, double	119
Loom, common power	125
Loom, power	102
Loom, Todd's	137
Loom, vertical	120
Machine, cylinder	73
Machine, Tape-leg dressing	74
Mails	168
Manufacturers' tables	307
Manufacturers' rating tables	345
Motion, uptaking	151
Mounting a harness loom	168
Mounting for diapers	262
Mounting for ten and twelve leaf diapers	256
Mountings for tweels, diapers, &c.	234
Needles, lappet	211
Nine leaf tweel	87
New mode of picking	375
Old power-loom	115
Oncost or charges	302
Picking, new mode of	375

INDEX.

	Page.
Pick, air-pump	123
Picking arm	150
Picking stick	151
Pinion, to find the proper	112
Pins for lappets	211
Pirn winding	57
Pitch, to, the loom	107
Plain and diaper cloth	255
Plain and tweel stripes	255
Plain and tweel, four shots of	254
Plain and tweel with weft cords	290
Plain cloth	78
Porters	41
Power-looms	102-115
Pressure harness loom	185
Price of Cotton	27
Progress of weaving	25
Prospect of the cotton trade	29
Protector	109
Quadrant	375
Quantity of cloth woven	29
Rating tables for manufacturers	344
Rating for a blue and white check	300
Rating for a 12⁰⁰ tape check	299
Rating for a shirting	298
Rating, form of book for	301
Reed, English	41
Reed, fly	126
Reed, Scotch	39
Reel	33
Rice bags	279
Rocking Shaft	149
Rods, connection	147
Rollers, stenting	194
Safety valves	374
Scale of Reed	40
Scob preventer	141
Scotch ell	40
Set of Reed	40

	Page.
Seven leaf diaper	97
Seven leaf tweel	86
Sewing frames for looms	227
Shaft, crank	147
Shaft, rocking	149
Shaft, wyper	148
Shedding	196
Shirting	49
Shuttle changer	144
Six leaf tweel	85
Six leaf diaper	97
Sixteen leaf tweel	90
Sixteen leaf mounting	261
Sizing	68
Skein	34
Slabstock	170
Speed, calculations of	368
Spinning	36
Spyndle	34-38
Standers	172
Starching	69
Starting power-looms	102
Statement of expenses	303
Stenting rollers	194
Sugar bag weaving	279
Swords	149
Tables, manufacturers', warpers', and beamers',	307
Tape checks made with one shuttle	294
Tape-leg dressing machine	74
Ten leaf diaper	100
Three leaf diaper	91-263
Ticking	80
Todd's patent loom	137
Toilet covers	280
Top mounting for large tweels	259
Treading	77
Treadles	247
Tube weaving	275
Tweeling	79
Tweel and plain alternately	254
Tweel, blanket	88

	Page.
Tweels, damask, ten and twelve leaf	89
Tweel, four leaf	82-237
Tweel, five leaf	84-89-242
Tweel, six leaf	85-250
Tweel, sixteen leaf	90
Tweels, mounting for	234
Tweel, three leaf	80
Tweel, herring bone	81
Tweels, seven, eight and nine leaf	86-87-251
Twine, harness	169
Twist	36
Twisting	76
Two webs in one loom	120
Uptaking motion	116-151
Vertical loom	120
Warping	58
Warp in a web	43-45
Warping, striped work	61
Warpers' tables	307

	Page.
Weaving	54
Weaving broad cloth in a narrow loom	284
Weaving, diaper	90
Weaving, lappet	205
Weaving, tube	275
Web glass	40
Web, starting the	219
Wefts, calculation of	50
Weight of bundle	36
Wheel, lappet	208
Winding	55
Window, Holland	49
Wool yarn	39
Worsted yarn	39
Wypers or cams	150
Wyper shaft	148
Yards in a spyndle	39
Yarn	33
Yarn beam	148
Yarn in chain	35
Yarn on beam	35

www.ingramcontent.com/pod-product-compliance
Lightning Source LLC
Chambersburg PA
CBHW032024220426
43664CB00006B/358